THE MAKING OF
THE NATIONAL POET

Frontispiece. 'Garrick delivering the ode to Shakspeare at the Jubilee, surrounded by Shakspearean characters', 1784. Captioned with lines from the conclusion of Garrick's *Ode*—'Can British gratitude delay, | To him the glory of this Isle; | To give the festive day, | The song, the statue, the devoted pile? | To him, the first of Poets!—best of Men! | We ne'er shall look upon his like again!'—and dedicated to Elizabeth Montagu. *Robert Edge Pine (engraved by Charles Watson).* (Reproduced by courtesy of the Trustees of the British Museum.)

The Making of the National Poet

Shakespeare, Adaptation and Authorship, 1660–1769

MICHAEL DOBSON

CLARENDON PRESS · OXFORD

Oxford University Press, Walton Street, Oxford OX2 6DP

Oxford   New York   Toronto
Delhi   Bombay   Calcutta   Madras   Karachi
Kuala Lumpur   Singapore   Hong Kong   Tokyo
Nairobi   Dar es Salaam   Cape Town
Melbourne   Auckland   Madrid

and associated companies in
Berlin   Ibadan

Oxford is a trade mark of Oxford University Press

Published in the United States
by Oxford University Press Inc., New York

First published 1992
First published in Clarendon Paperback 1994

British Library Cataloguing in Publication Data
Data available

Library of Congress Cataloging in Publication Data
Dobson, Michael.
The making of the national poet: Shakespeare, adaptation and
authorship, 1660–1769/Michael Dobson.
Includes bibliographical references.
1. Shakespeare, William, 1564–1616—Criticism and interpretation—
History—18th century. 2. Shakespeare, William, 1564–1616—
Criticism and interpretation—History—17th century.
3. Shakespeare, William, 1564–1616—Appreciation—Great Britain.
4. Shakespeare, William, 1564–1616—Stage history—1625–1800.
5. National characteristics, English, in literature.
6. Shakespeare, William, 1564–1616—Adaptations. 7. Shakespeare,
William, 1564–1616—Authorship. 8. Theater—Great Britain—
History—18th century. 9. Theater—Great Britain—History—17th
century. I. Title.
PR2968.D6   1992   822.3'3—dc20   92–12096
ISBN 0–19–818323–2

Printed in Great Britain
on acid-free paper by
Biddles Ltd, Guildford and King's Lynn

To
Nicola Jane Watson

Acknowledgements

THIS book has been extremely fortunate in its sponsors at every stage of its conception and development, and at each of the various institutions at which they have been completed. In Oxford, Stanley Wells (Shakespeare Institute, University of Birmingham) oversaw the first stages of its research with infinite patience and expertise; valuable suggestions as to how an early draft might be revived with alterations were supplied by Stephen Wall (Keble College, Oxford) and Peter Holland (Trinity Hall, Cambridge); and my colleagues at Christ Church, Christopher Butler, Peter Conrad, and Richard Hamer, conspired between them to keep me from starving. At Harvard University, Marjorie Garber provided unfailing intellectual stimulation and support; Jean Newlin and her staff offered a warm welcome to the Harvard Theatre Collection; and the project was further aided and abetted by Kathleen Wilson (State University of New York, Stony Brook), Gwyn Blakemore Evans, and Kathy Rowe, as well as by the members of the Center for Literary and Cultural Studies Seminar on Eighteenth-Century Literature and Culture, particularly Susan Staves (Brandeis University). At Indiana University, further splendid research materials have been provided by the staff of the Lilly Library, and great indulgence has been shown by the excellent group of graduate students who enrolled for my seminar on Shakespeare and reception theory in the autumn of 1990. On leave at Northwestern University, I have profited immensely from the generosity of Joanna Lipking, and also that of Martin Mueller, who in addition to offering stringent readings of my work loaned the mighty camera with which I photographed Plate 3. Back home in England, my father Derek Dobson kindly loaned another such apparatus so that I could photograph Plate 2, and both pictures were expertly developed by Kevan Mayor. At Oxford University Press, Andrew Lockett has been a faithful and supportive editor throughout, and Connie Wilsack a scrupulous and diligent copy-editor.

I have been particularly lucky to have been working on Shakespeare's reception in the eighteenth century at a time when the subject has attracted the attention of a number of highly gifted viiiACKNOWLEDGEMENTS

and, furthermore, wonderfully helpful scholars. Stephen Orgel (Stanford), Margreta De Grazia (University of Pennsylvania), and Gary Taylor (Brandeis University) have offered invaluable advice and encouragement on reading sections of this study in draft, and have been extremely generous with unpublished materials, as has Laura Rosenthal (Florida State University). Jean Marsden (University of Connecticut) deserves particular thanks, having shared her work, minutely read and assisted my own, and instigated some extremely useful and interesting discussions on Shakespeare's reception in general, notably a memorable seminar at the 1988 MLA conference.

During the autumn of 1988 I was fortunate enough to be able to employ my formidable sister-in-law Lucy Watson as a research and secretarial assistant, a role she fulfilled with an incomparable energy and daring which have earned my lasting gratitude and respect. The limitlessly versatile Kevan Mayor took on the same role during the spring of 1989, more briefly, but no less stylishly or effectively.

I owe a special debt to all those people under whose roofs I have wrestled with different drafts of this book, a surprising number of whom are still talking to me. These include my parents, June and Derek Dobson, of Bournemouth, who have for years been tolerating my work to levels well beyond the call of duty, and my parents-in-law Peter and Elizabeth Watson, of Lymington, who are catching up fast.

My greatest and most pervasive debt, however, both intellectual and personal, is to Nicola Jane Watson, to whom this book, like its author, is affectionately dedicated.

Contents

List of Plates

Introduction

Then comes the 'resurrection'—on speculation. Betterton the player, and Rowe the writer, make a selection from a promiscuous heap of plays found in a garret, nameless as to authorship.... 'I want an author for this selection of plays!' said Rowe. 'I have it!' said Betterton; 'call them Shakespeare's!' And Rowe, the 'commentator,' commenced to puff them as 'the bard's', and to write a history of his hero in which there was scarcely a word that had the foundation of truth to rest upon.

This is about the sum and substance of the manner of setting up Shakespeare.[1]

THIS account of the collaboration between the playwright Nicholas Rowe and the veteran actor Thomas Betterton which in 1709 produced the first ever biographical preface to the Complete Plays has, understandably, attracted little serious attention among historians of Shakespeare's reception, however familiar the book from which it is drawn (Colonel Joseph Hart's *The Romance of Yachting*, 1848) has become among scholars of the interminable authorship controversy it helped to initiate. None the less, it is not without its share of inadvertent historical percipience. For Hart, 'Shakespeare' is a construction of the Restoration and eighteenth century, a ghost raised by the dubious powers of nascent capitalism ('"resurrection"—on speculation') and pressed into the national consciousness as the (literally) authoritarian father of a problematically wanton body of texts; and to this extent, as this study proposes to demonstrate, Hart is in many senses accurate. Certainly something happened during the century between the 1660s and the 1760s to engender the Bardolatry which Hart is here attempting so strenuously to debunk, something which indeed had the effect of 'authorizing' Shakespeare—both in the sense of promoting ('puffing') his plays to the status of canonical texts, and, concurrently, of canonizing Shakespeare himself as the paradigmatic figure of literary authority (making him into 'the bard', a 'hero').

In 1660, after all, at the start of Betterton's career in the theatre,

---

[1] Joseph C. Hart, *The Romance of Yachting* (New York, 1848), 210–12.

Shakespeare's plays had not been reprinted in a collected edition since the Second Folio appeared in 1632; very few living actors had any experience of performing them, and that experience dated from twenty years earlier, before the Civil Wars, at which time the number of Shakespeare plays still in the repertory had already dwindled to perhaps five—*Hamlet, Othello, Julius Caesar, The Merry Wives of Windsor*, and *1 Henry IV*.[2] By 1769, when almost every national newspaper and magazine reprinted Rowe's biography as part of their coverage of David Garrick's Stratford Jubilee, readers of Shakespeare might have consulted collected editions not only by Rowe but by an illustrious succession of prestigious writers including Alexander Pope, Sir Thomas Hanmer, and Samuel Johnson, and any actor in the employ of the Theatres Royal would have needed a working familiarity with at least twenty-four of Shakespeare's plays, revivals of which accounted for more than one in six of all dramatic performances given in London.[3]

Moreover, readers in the 1760s might also have consulted dictionaries of Shakespearean quotations, essays on Shakespeare, biographies of Shakespeare, poems on Shakespeare, even a Shakespearean novel (*Memoirs of the Shakespear's-Head in Covent-Garden. By the Ghost of Shakespear*, published anonymously, in two volumes, in 1755), and theatre-goers might have demonstrated their enthusiasm for the Bard not only by attending his own plays but by patronizing three popular entertainments about his genius: David Garrick's *Harlequin's Invasion* (first performed in 1759, and regularly revived for the next three decades); and two comedies depicting the first national Shakespearean festival— George Colman's *Man and Wife: or, The Shakespeare Jubilee*, and Garrick's own immensely successful *The Jubilee* (both premièred in 1769). This book aims to describe how this extraordinary change in Shakespeare's status came about, attempting in the process to replace Hart's conspiracy theory of the 'setting up' of Shakespeare (a type of explanation to which discussions of Shakespeare's canonicity are especially prone) with what I hope will be

---

[2] See the Master of the Revels's lists of plays acted at court in 1636 and 1638: Joseph Quincy Adams, *The Dramatic Records of Sir Henry Herbert, Master of the Revels, 1623–1673* (New Haven, Conn., 1917), 75–6.

[3] See Charles Beecher Hogan, *Shakespeare in the Theatre: 1701–1800* (2 vols.; Oxford, 1952–7), (hereafter Hogan), ii. 716–19.

a more persuasive account of how Shakespeare came to occupy the centre of English literary culture between the restoration of the monarchy and the Stratford Jubilee.

This process deserves close scrutiny, not least because so many of the conceptions of Shakespeare we inherit date not from the Renaissance but from the Enlightenment. It was this period, after all, which initiated many of the practices which modern spectators and readers of Shakespeare would generally regard as normal or even natural: the performance of his female roles by women instead of men (instigated at a revival of *Othello* in 1660); the reproduction of his works in scholarly editions, with critical apparatus (pioneered by Rowe's edition of 1709 and the volume of commentary appended to it by Charles Gildon the following year); the publication of critical monographs devoted entirely to the analysis of his texts (an industry founded by John Dennis's *An Essay upon the Writings and Genius of Shakespeare*, 1712); the promulgation of the plays in secondary education (the earliest known instance of which is the production of *Julius Caesar* mounted in 1728 'by the young Noblemen of the Westminster School'),[4] and in higher education (first carried out in the lectures on Shakespeare given by William Hawkins at Oxford in the early 1750s); the erection of monuments to Shakespeare in nationally symbolic public places (initiated by Peter Scheemakers' statue in Poets' Corner, Westminster Abbey, unveiled in 1741); and the promotion of Stratford-upon-Avon as a site of secular pilgrimage (ratified at Garrick's Jubilee in 1769). The fact that these ways of presenting and representing Shakespeare have endured for so long has tended to make their specifically Enlightenment origins and interests virtually invisible—to the extent that until comparatively recently, histories of Shakespeare's reception, especially his critical reception, have characteristically identified the eighteenth century as the period which simply 'rediscovered' Shakespeare and restored him to his natural pre-eminence in English culture.[5]

---

[4] *Daily Journal* (17 Feb. 1728).

[5] See e.g. Jacob Isaacs, 'Shakespearian Scholarship', in Harley Granville-Barker and G. B. Harrison, eds., *A Companion to Shakespeare Studies* (Cambridge, 1964), 305–24, esp. 311; also Michèle Willems, *La Genèse du mythe shakespearien* (Paris, 1979). The extent to which this particular evaluation of the period's treatment of Shakespeare is premissed on the continuing reproduction of the Enlightenment's own categories of thought has been expertly demonstrated by Margreta De Grazia in *Shakespeare Verbatim: The Reproduction of Authenticity and the 1790 Apparatus* (Oxford, 1991). On this point see esp. 1–13, 222–6.

I shall be touching on each of these now-familiar means of assimilating and reproducing Shakespeare in due course; however, the one with which I shall be most centrally concerned during this investigation of the rise of Bardolatry is a practice which has traditionally been held to signify not the naturalness of the Enlightenment's responses to Shakespeare but their irreducible otherness. For historians primarily interested in stage interpretations of Shakespeare, the period has been conspicuous for a very different series of innovations: to cite only a handful, the first conflation of two Shakespeare plays into one (*The Law Against Lovers*, created by Sir William Davenant from *Measure for Measure* and *Much Ado About Nothing* in 1662); the first *Troilus and Cressida* in which Cressida commits suicide to prove her innocence (John Dryden's *Troilus and Cressida, or, Truth Found Too Late*, first acted in 1679); the first *Henry V* in which the protagonist is pursued to France by his scorned ex-mistress Harriet, disguised as a page (Aaron Hill's *King Henry the Fifth, or, The Conquest of France by the English*, 1723); the first *As You Like It* to betroth Celia to Jaques and include *Pyramus and Thisbe* (Charles Johnson's *Love in a Forest*, performed in the same year); and the first *Cymbeline* to observe the unities of time and place (prepared by William Hawkins in 1759). To the embarrassment and perplexity of students of Shakespeare's reputation, precisely the same period which at some time saw the revival of every single play in the Shakespeare canon (excepting only *Love's Labour's Lost*) also saw the substantial rewriting of every single play in the Shakespeare canon (excepting only *Othello* and *1 Henry IV*), and although numbers of these adaptations never established themselves in the repertory, many of the plays upon which Shakespeare's reputation as the supreme dramatist of world literature is now most squarely based—including *Macbeth*, *The Tempest*, *King Lear*, *Coriolanus*, *Richard III*, *Romeo and Juliet*, and *The Winter's Tale*—were in practice only tolerated in the theatre in heavily revised versions, even while that very reputation was being established.[6]

This coexistence of full-scale canonization with wholesale

[6] For a comprehensive bibliography and anthology, see Michael Dobson (ed.), *Adaptations and Acting Versions, 1660–1980*, unit 22 of the *Bibliotheca Shakespeariana* microfiche collection, general ed. Philip Brockbank (Oxford, 1987; republished as *Shakespeariana*, Ann Arbor, Mich., 1990).

adaptation, of the urge to enshrine Shakespeare's texts as national treasures with the desire to alter their content, has long been regarded as a quaint paradox, the rewritten versions of the plays generally being dismissed as at best a bizarre cul-de-sac of literary history, inessential to the 'real' story of Shakespeare's reception. This view, I would argue, has seriously distorted our understanding of Shakespeare's changing roles in Augustan culture, and by implication—since the social and cultural forces which converged over that period to establish his supremacy have preserved it ever since—of his continuing presence in our own. I hope to show over the course of this study that adaptation and canonization, so far from being contradictory processes, were often mutually reinforcing ones: that the claiming of Shakespeare as an Enlightenment culture hero both profited from, and occasionally demanded, the substantial rewriting of his plays. In this light I shall be examining the adaptations produced during the crucial century from the 1660s to the 1760s alongside the prodigious numbers of other texts produced about Shakespeare during the same period ('legitimate' and otherwise) as complementary aspects of the extensive cultural work that went into the installation of Shakespeare as England's National Poet.

In choosing particular texts for close examination out of the enormous volume extant I have tried to select those pieces of evidence which make the underlying assumptions and mechanisms which inform this 'authorizing' of Shakespeare most visible. As a result, I shall be paying considerable attention to some of the period's hitherto neglected adaptations of Shakespeare's comedies and romances (plays which required especially drastic and thus especially revealing rewriting in order to be assimilated to the shifting values of Restoration and eighteenth-century society), as well as to a body of apparently minor or ephemeral writings which have much to say about the changing intellectual and social frameworks within which Shakespeare was being read and presented—prologues and epilogues, prefaces, occasional verse, advertisements, catchpenny playlets. (In treating such texts seriously I have been less inclined than some of my predecessors to identify commercial success with historical insignificance; the fact that many adaptations of Shakespeare were undoubtedly written quickly with the sole aim of catering lucratively to popular taste may, indeed, make them more useful indicators of contemporary beliefs and assumptions than some of the self-consciously 'higher' literary forms criticism has traditionally privileged.) Although I have chosen these materials for the clarity with which they highlight the specific and local needs fulfilled by Shakespeare in Augustan culture, needs obviously alien to our own, I should stress that in explicating such transparently interested assimilations of Shakespeare I do not mean to imply that they are ludicrously different in kind to the current uses of Shakespeare in which we ourselves participate (whether in the theatre, in academe, or in the culture at large)—I would certainly regard my own readings of the plays as every bit as historically contingent and socially invested as those I am chronicling, and, indeed, as profoundly affected by the Bardolatry they helped cumulatively to produce.

Although to use the term 'Bardolatry' at all may seem patronizing, I have no intention, either, of disparaging the Enlightenment's enthusiasm for Shakespeare; however flippantly the term may have been coined (by George Bernard Shaw),[7] its implication that the author-cult of Shakespeare has functioned, and continues to function, as a kind of religion is one which few cultural anthropologists would dispute.[8] It is with Bardolatry's rise to orthodoxy as a *national* religion that I shall be especially concerned here. Writing in the 1630s, Ben Jonson was careful to distinguish his own high regard for Shakespeare from profane adulation ('I lov'd the man, and doe honour his memory (on this side Idolatry) as much as any'),[9] but by the middle of the next century this distinction had all but vanished from many English writings on Shakespeare. At the climax of his Jubilee in 1769, David Garrick gesticulated towards a graven image of the Bard with the words, ''Tis he! 'tis he! | "The god of our idolatry!"',[10] (words which, characteristically, adapt and appropriate some of Shakespeare's

---

[7] See Jonathan Bate, *Shakespearean Constitutions: Politics, Theatre, Criticism, 1730–1830* (Oxford, 1989), 22 n. 1.

[8] On later 18th-cent. Bardolatry, see Robert Witbeck Babcock's pioneering (and still valuable) *The Genesis of Shakespeare Idolatry, 1766–1799* (Chapel Hill, NC, 1931); on its current form, see esp. Graham Holderness, 'Bardolatry: Or, The Cultural Materialist's Guide to Stratford-upon-Avon', in id. (ed.), *The Shakespeare Myth* (Manchester, 1988), 2–15.

[9] Ben Jonson, *Timber*, in *Workes: The Second Volume* (1641), 97.

[10] David Garrick, *An ode upon dedicating a building, and erecting a statue, to Shakespeare, at Stratford-upon-Avon* (London, 1769), 1. See Frontispiece.

own, from the balcony scene of *Romeo and Juliet*);[11] and even before this apogee of canonization Shakespeare had often been recognized as occupying a position in British life directly analogous to that of God the Father. In 1739 the playwright Thomas Cooke, in the epilogue to his play *The Mournful Nuptials*, identifies Shakespeare as one of the faiths of the ruling class, dividing Britain between 'They who are born to taste' and 'The tasteless vulgar', the former hailed as staunch believers in Shakespeare and the Church of England, the latter derided as schismatic followers of Harlequin and John Wesley.[12] Similarly, Arthur Murphy, in an essay addressed to the sceptical Voltaire in 1753, links Bardolatry with both Anglicanism and Little-Englandism, remarking that 'with us islanders *Shakespeare* is a kind of established religion in poetry'.[13]

From their time onwards, Shakespeare has been as normatively constitutive of British national identity as the drinking of afternoon tea, and it is now probably as hard for any educated Briton to imagine not enjoying the former as it would be to imagine forgoing the latter. This analogy may be less trivializing than it appears: the national habit of Shakespeare, after all, and the national habit of tea have their origins in exactly the same period of expanding trade abroad and vigorous nationalism at home— both rise from being novelties with Pepys in the 1660s to being addictions with Dr Johnson in the 1760s. That Shakespeare was declared to rule world literature at the same time that Britannia was declared to rule the waves may, indeed, be more than a coincidence. As Edward Capell points out, dedicating his edition

---

[11] Cf. *Romeo and Juliet*, II.i. 154–7:

> JULIET.   Do not swear at all,
> Or if thou wilt, swear by thy gracious self,
> Which is the god of my idolatry,
> And I'll believe thee.

Garrick's application of this particular phrase tellingly identifies Shakespeare not only as an object of worship but as an object of desire.

[12] Thomas Cooke, *The Mournful Nuptials* (London, 1739), 71–2.

[13] *Gray's Inn Journal*, 12 (15 Dec. 1753). It was the 18th cent. after all, which first decided that since Shakespeare was baptized on 26 April, he *must* have been born on 23 April, the feast day of England's patron saint, St George: by Murphy's time, indeed, Shakespeare's birthday had already become, for some, a more important cause for celebration. See e.g. the verses 'On the annual meeting of some Gentlemen to celebrate SHAKESPEAR'S BIRTHDAY', published in *London Magazine*, 24 (1755), 244.

of the Complete Plays to the Duke of Grafton just after the
colonial victories of the Seven Years War, to reproduce Shakespeare in the manner he deserves is to participate in an export
industry which has cornered all world markets, contributing thereby to the nation's cultural capital:

> The works of such great authors as this whom I now have the honour of
> presenting to your Grace, are part of the kingdom's riches: they are her
> estate in fame, that fame which letters confer upon her; the worth of and
> value of which or sinks or raises her in the opinion of foreign nations, and
> she takes her rank among them according to the esteem which these are
> held in: It is then an object of national concern, that they should be sent
> into the world with all the advantage which they are in their own nature
> capable of receiving; and who performs this office rightly, is in this a
> benefactor to his country, and somewhat entitl'd to her good will. The
> following great productions stand foremost in the list of these literary
> possessions; are talk'd of wherever the name of *Britain* is talk'd of, that is
> (thanks to some late counsels) wherever there are men.[14]

I shall be arguing over the course of this book that the transformation of Shakespeare's status from the comparative neglect of the
Restoration to the national, indeed global, pre-eminence celebrated
here constitutes one of the central cultural expressions of England's
own transition from the aristocratic regime of the Stuarts to the
commercial empire presided over by the Hanoverians.

With the exception of the important work on the subject published
by Christopher Spencer and Gunnar Sorelius in the 1960s,[15] and
the very recent contributions of Jean Marsden[16] and Laura

---

[14] Edward Capell (ed.), *Mr William Shakespeare, his Comedies, Histories, and
Tragedies* (10 vols.; London, 1768), i. a3^r–^{v}.

[15] See esp. Christopher Spencer (ed.), *Five Restoration Adaptations of Shake-
speare* (Urbana, Ill., 1965); Gunnar Sorelius, 'The Giant Race Before the Flood':
Pre-Restoration Drama on the Stage and in the Criticism of the Restoration
(Uppsala, 1966).

[16] See esp. Jean Marsden, 'The Re-Imagined Text: Shakespeare, Adaptation and
Theory in the Restoration and Eighteenth Century', Ph.D. thesis (Harvard, 1986),
which perspicaciously relates changes in the strategies of adaptation to a shift in
Shakespeare criticism from an approach centring on 'fable' and 'sentiments' (arguably preservable despite, or even by, adaptation) towards a view in which the value
of Shakespeare's plays resides in precise verbal details, the letter of the text: also
her anthology *The Appropriation of Shakespeare: Post-Renaissance Reconstructions of the Works and the Myth* (Hemel Hempstead, 1991).

Rosenthal,[17] the Restoration and eighteenth-century rewritings of Shakespeare's plays which illustrate this transition have attracted little sustained or sympathetic critical attention: in fact they have inspired such horror among Shakespeareans that to wish to look into them at all may seem perverse. George C. D. Odell, for example, writing in *Shakespeare from Betterton to Irving*, warns that: 'reading any one of them is like an attempt to see beloved features in a mist or in encircling gloom. Literally, Shakespeare is "smeared over" by the inferior stuff so proudly vaunted by the perpetrators. It is almost like a rouged corpse—a thing too ghastly to conceive of.'[18]

Likewise, his successor, Hazelton Spencer, describing the 1667 version of *The Tempest* produced by Sir William Davenant and John Dryden in what remains the best-known account of these texts, *Shakespeare Improved*, remarks in disgust that 'everything that the authors lay their hands on is defiled'.[19] The vehemence of these two influential accounts owes something to the historical situation of their authors—to Odell and Spencer, writing in the 1920s, the crusade against the use of 'adulterated' texts in the theatre still needed to be decisively won[20]—but the tone of much commentary on the adaptations remains one of straightforward denunciation; as recently as 1989, for example, Brian Vickers, distinguished editor of *Shakespeare: The Critical Heritage, 1623–1801*, wrote off the entire phenomenon as a symptom of the Restoration and eighteenth-century public's failure to achieve an educated standard of taste (in an article tellingly entitled 'Shakespearian Adaptations: The Tyranny of the Audience'),[21] and attacked Christopher Spencer as an 'apologist' in the process.

I do not share this particular attitude to the Enlightenment's adaptors of Shakespeare, but I do find its pervasiveness significant —not least because such commentators as Vickers are in effect

[17] See Laura Rosenthal, 'Shakespearean Adaptation and the Genealogy of Authorship', Ph.D. thesis (Northwestern University, 1990), which considers the practice of adaptation in relation to the emergence of copyright law.

[18] George C. D. Odell, *Shakespeare from Betterton to Irving* (2 vols.; New York, 1920–1), i. 79.

[19] Hazelton Spencer, *Shakespeare Improved: The Restoration Versions in Quarto and on the Stage* (Cambridge, Mass., 1927), 65.

[20] 'But not yet, though nearly three hundred years have passed, have we got wholly free of the Restoration attitude towards revision, or indeed of the Restoration versions themselves', laments Hazelton Spencer; ibid. 271.

[21] In Brian Vickers, *Returning to Shakespeare* (London, 1989), 212–33.

carrying on precisely where many eighteenth-century 'improvers' of Shakespeare's plays left off, simply reidentifying the corrupting enemy of Literature as the vulgarity of the Augustan theatre rather than the occasional vulgarity of Shakespeare's art itself. Furthermore, the impassioned, outraged rhetoric in which these adaptations are habitually repudiated—a vocabulary of 'mutilation', 'desecration', and 'perversion'—may point to their unacknowledged importance in the history of Shakespeare's authorial afterlife. It is abundantly clear from Odell's words above, for example (as, perusing the alterations of Tate or Cibber, he finds himself staring in horror at a 'rouged corpse'),[22] that what is at stake in preserving the Complete Works from adaptation is the integrity and indeed masculinity of Shakespeare himself. Inheriting the sometimes mixed metaphors deployed by Ben Jonson's elegy in the First Folio—in which Shakespeare's texts substitute both for his unbuilt London sepulchre and for his mortal body ('Thou art a Moniment, without a tombe, | And art aliue still while thy Booke doth live')[23]—Odell senses that to produce a different version of Shakespeare's book is to produce a different version of Shakespeare; to rewrite a play is to tamper not just with its text but with its father, the author. From Odell's post-Enlightenment perspective this activity is evidently heretical, constituting at once an emasculation and a violation of the 'true' Shakespeare; nevertheless, seen in the wider context of the Restoration and eighteenth century's other ways of defining and redefining both William Shakespeare and the Complete Shakespeare—whether through biography, editing, criticism, or statuary—adaptation may simply reveal itself as one of the various and contingent means by which that very idea of the 'true' Shakespeare was constructed.[24]

---

[22] This image inevitably calls to mind Edmund Malone's curious and mistaken insistence on the unbearable inauthenticity of the (make-up like) coloured paint on Shakespeare's Stratford monument, which in 1793 he succeeded in having returned to its 'original' stone colour (see De Grazia, *Shakespeare Verbatim*, 85); for Odell, adaptation likewise turns a dignified, classical image of the dead Shakespeare into something tackily pretending to be alive.

[23] Ben Jonson, 'To the memory of my beloued, The AUTHOR MR. WILLIAM SHAKESPEARE, AND what he hath left vs', *The First Folio of Shakespeare: The Norton Facsimile*, ed. Charlton Hinman (hereafter F1), 9 (Hinman's pagination).

[24] It is perhaps worth pointing out here that our own sense of adaptation as a literary activity of an altogether different order to more familiar ways of processing and interpreting Shakespeare's texts such as criticism or editing is in many senses anachronistic, the product of a separation of the stage from the study initiated but

If reluctant to endorse the older critical tradition on this subject, in considering the posthumous presence of Shakespeare in Augustan England (especially the participation of his plays in contemporary political culture), I have been greatly assisted by a growing body of more recent writing on Shakespeare's afterlife, whether dealing specifically with the later eighteenth century and Romantic period (notably the work of Margreta De Grazia and Jonathan Bate), covering a range of periods between the Renaissance and the present (studies by Gary Taylor and Marjorie Garber, and anthologies by Marianne Novy, Jean Howard and Marion O'Connor, and Jean Marsden), or dealing only with our own century (particularly the work of Terence Hawkes, Graham Holderness, and Hugh Grady).[25] Most of these treatments of the subject agree that the history of Shakespeare's changing significance for periods subsequent to his own is a history of different 'appropriations', but they diverge widely in their accounts of how the process of appropriation works.

To simplify and exaggerate the debate, these writers might be divided between three major schools. For some, Shakespeare's texts appropriate their readers—as in Garber's work, where Freud, Nietzsche, Delia Bacon, and others prove to be dutifully playing out the unconscious of the First Folio. For others, individual

not completed during this very period: many of Shakespeare's most important post-Restoration interpreters were, after all, practising playwrights. John Dryden produced some of the Restoration's most successful rewritings of Shakespeare as well as some of its most influential criticism. John Dennis and Charles Gildon, both dramatists before they were critics, wrote adaptations as well as essays. Nicholas Rowe, now best remembered as Shakespeare's first modern editor, was chosen as such because of his success in the theatre, and produced in his *Tragedy of Jane Shore* (1714) one of the period's most revealing comments on *Richard III*. Even Lewis Theobald, preserved in the amber of countless variorum editions as a tireless solver of textual cruces, offered a creatively refashioned version of *Richard II* (*The Tragedy of King Richard II . . . alter'd from Shakespeare*, 1720), as well as the more conservatively edited text of Shakespeare's play preserved in his 7-vol. *The Works of Shakespeare* (1733).

[25] De Grazia, *Shakespeare Verbatim*; Bate, *Shakespearean Constitutions*; Gary Taylor, *Reinventing Shakespeare: A Cultural History from the Restoration to the Present* (New York, 1989); Marjorie Garber, *Shakespeare's Ghost Writers: Literature as Uncanny Causality* (London, 1987); Marianne Novy (ed.), *Women's Re-Visions of Shakespeare* (Urbana, Ill., 1990); Jean F. Howard and Marion O'Connor (eds.), *Shakespeare Reproduced: The Text in History and Ideology* (New York, 1987); Marsden (ed.), *The Appropriation of Shakespeare*; Terence Hawkes, *That Shakespeherian Rag: Essays on a Critical Process* (London, 1986); Holderness (ed.), *The Shakespeare Myth*; Hugh Grady, *The Modernist Shakespeare: Critical Texts in a Material World* (Oxford, 1991).

readers either misappropriate Shakespeare's texts (if they are bad readers), or both appropriate them and are appropriated by them (if they are good readers)—as in Bate's work, which, conflating Gadamer's model of reception with the Oedipal machismo of Harold Bloom's account of influence, pictures Strong Readers such as Hazlitt arm-wrestling companionably with Strong Authors such as Shakespeare.[26] For others still, the hegemonic discourse of the ruling oligarchy appropriates both Shakespeare's texts and his readers, effortlessly co-opting all concerned in the interests of the state—as in the work of Hawkes, Holderness, and, to a lesser extent, Taylor.

Drawing to different extents on each of these models, this book is in outline the history of how Shakespeare's works were, by and large, successfully appropriated to fit what became the dominant, nationalist ideology of mid-eighteenth century England (as Holderness or Hawkes might put it), but it aims to show how that history was always one of multiplicity and contestation: it offers an account of how Shakespeare, or a series of alternative Shakespeares, came to dramatize, sometimes imperfectly, specific contemporary conflicts, rather than coming to embody a single, monolithic consensus. (The promotion of Shakespeare as national poet between the 1730s and 1760s, for example, was far more closely associated with excluded, radical pressure groups than with the Establishment, however successfully both that nationalism and its particular uses of Shakespeare have subsequently been assimilated within the state apparatus.) I am thus interested (like Bate) in exploring the range and variety of positions to which Shakespeare's works are assimilated over this period, and indeed in pointing out the extent to which Shakespeare's texts resisted certain readings and enabled others; but I am more inclined than Bate to emphasize the social and intellectual parameters which restrict the range of possible appropriations available within a particular society. (To use Stanley Fish's term, I am inclined to privilege the authority of the interpretive community as the most important factor in defining what Shakespeare's texts can mean at any given historical moment over that of either strong individual reader or strong author.)[27] If versions of Shakespeare readable as

[26] See esp. Bate, *Shakespearean Constitutions*, 210.

[27] See Stanley Fish, *Is There A Text In This Class? The Authority of Interpretive Communities* (Cambridge, Mass., 1980), esp. 'What Makes an Interpretation Acceptable?', 338–52.

'conservative' certainly did compete against versions readable as 'radical' at different points during the Restoration and eighteenth century, as I shall show, their areas of congruence, the assumptions about both Shakespeare and politics which they share and in which they may even collude, are often far more important than their differences. While I can thus accept Bate's surprisingly Burkean conclusion that 'Shakespeare is like the English Constitution',[28] it is only because I do not regard the English constitution as either limitlessly available for the representation of multiple viewpoints, or as possessed of any immutable, stable, and unchanging authority.

The ensuing pages chart, in essence, the emergence between the 1660s and the 1760s of a shared sense of the national importance of Shakespeare and a general agreement about the broader contours of his authorial image, if not about what specific local positions his plays endorse or in what adapted or re-edited forms they should be presented. I have divided the century over which this development takes place into four successive phases, corresponding broadly to four different sets of strategies by which both Shakespeare-as-author and the texts that make up the Shakespeare canon are rewritten and repositioned—loosely speaking, 1660–78, 1678–88, 1688–1735, and 1735–69.

During the first phase, the subject of Chapter 1, Shakespeare is imagined at worst as an artless rustic, at best as an archaic father-king: the rewritings which attempt to finish and update his works for a sceptical present (most successfully the William Davenant–John Dryden version of *The Tempest*, 1667) place their quasi-royal author at the mercy of contemporary politics, whether theatrical, governmental, or familial.

In the second phase, the subject of Chapter 2, which coincided with the constitutional crises of the 1670s and 1680s, Shakespeare's plays are rewritten sometimes to court such immediate topicality but more often to avoid it: their author is presented more than ever as a king (and is even brought onto the stage in the likeness of King Hamlet's ghost to introduce Dryden's version of *Troilus and Cressida* in 1679), but his dominion is now primarily over the private realm of the passions.

Revived in prologues as a disembodied author, Shakespeare, from the Glorious Revolution through the 1730s, is rewritten as

---

[28] Bate, *Shakespearean Constitutions*, 213.

such, his plays increasingly purged of their grosser, fleshlier comic details as he becomes a proper, and proprietary, Augustan author. From this period onwards, Shakespeare's texts are no longer simply modernized but are instead retrospectively and unobtrusively corrected, his antiquated style imitated by adaptors as they strive to polish his now venerable works into native classics. As Chapter 3 shows, adaptation and canonization become ever more mutual processes at this time, as biographers and panegyrists of Shakespeare attempt to construct an author worthy of the Complete Plays, and adaptors—and indeed editors—attempt in their turn to make the plays worthy of their author.

From the early eighteenth century forwards, adaptation diminishes in importance alongside other means of appropriating and promoting Shakespeare's authority, and I have thus dealt with the culminating phase of Shakespeare's canonization in two chapters, one dealing primarily with revisions, in various media, of his authorial image, and the other concentrating more extensively on contemporary treatments of his texts. Chapter 4 examines a series of conflicting attempts to embody Shakespeare's authorial persona between the 1730s and the 1760s, looking first at the different interests which converge on the project to erect a statue of Shakespeare in Westminster Abbey in the late 1730s—a political opposition group (the Patriots), a female pressure group (the Shakespeare Ladies' Club), and stage adaptors George Lillo and James Miller —and then at David Garrick's shrewd manipulation of the iconography it establishes in making his own highly successful claim to represent in himself the eighteenth century's definitive embodiment of Shakespeare, posing as the true son of Shakespeare's royal ghost. This revered authorial spirit is henceforward an acknowledged national forefather, and his texts are treated accordingly. Chapter 5 considers especially the covert rewriting of the national past in which Garrick's own adaptations participate, examining the mid-eighteenth century's preferred stage versions of, in particular, *The Winter's Tale*, *The Taming of the Shrew*, and *Cymbeline* in the context of a number of other contemporary texts—pamphlets, lectures, poems, prefaces—which despite virulent disagreements between themselves assimilate Shakespeare to a common agenda of domestic virtue at home and colonial warfare abroad. By this stage in the rise of Bardolatry, with Shakespeare enshrined as the transcendent personification of a national ideal,

even his unadapted texts seem virtually irrelevant to popular conceptions of his 'essential' British greatness, and it is thus appropriate that this final chapter should conclude by examining a
'Shakespeare' play which is not derived from any single Shakespearean original at all, namely Garrick's own dramatization of
the climax of Shakespeare's investiture as national poet, *The
Jubilee*.

Garrick's Stratford festivities, explicitly choosing Shakespeare to
be Britain's national deity, provide a fitting end to this account,
and a fitting point from which to review its implications for the
subsequent progress of his cult, on both sides of the Atlantic.
While I would not wish to argue that anything about Shakespeare
was settled once and for all by this extraordinary cultural event, it
may well be that even now, over two centuries later, what is most
striking about its traces is not their kitsch strangeness but their
unnerving familiarity. To a surprising degree, the Jubilee encoded
in itself the history to date of the Bardolatry it proclaims—'the
sum and substance of the manner of setting up Shakespeare', to
return to Colonel Hart's formulation—and it may furthermore
have substantially predicted the form in which, with however
many signs of strain, it still survives. If less avid for souvenir
cuttings of the mulberry tree allegedly planted by Shakespeare in
his garden at New Place than our eighteenth-century forebears,
in our continuing promotion of Shakespeare-dominated literary
studies as a nationally vital academic discipline able to subsume
law, theology, and even medicine, offering a stable antidote to all
mere intellectual fads, we are perhaps still voices in the chorus
Garrick's ballads led in 1769, enthusiastic participants in the same
triumphal procession:

With learning and knowledge the well-lettered birch
Supplies Law and Physic and grace for the Church.
But Law and the Gospel in Shakespeare we find,
And he gives the best physic for body and mind.
    All shall yield to the Mulberry Tree, *etc.*
    .   .   .   .

Then each take a relic of this hallowed tree,
From folly and fashion a charm let it be.
Fill, fill to the planter, the Cup to the brim,
To honour your country do honour to him.
    All shall yield to the Mulberry Tree,

> Bend to thee,
> Blest Mulberry,
> Matchless was he
> Who planted thee,
> And thou like him immortal be!

> *Drums, fifes, and bells ring.*
> *They all exit in a hurry, going to see the*
> *Pageant.*[29]

[29] David Garrick, *The Jubilee*, in *The Plays of David Garrick*, ed. Harry William Pedicord and Fredrick Lois Bergmann (6 vols.; Carbondale, Ill., 1981) ii, 114–15.

I

Romance and Revision

Up by 4 a-clock and walked to Greenwich, where called at Captain Cockes and to his chamber, he being in bed—where something put my last night's dream into my head, which I think is the best that ever was dreamed—which was, that I had my Lady Castlemayne in my armes and was admitted to use all the dalliance I desired with her, and then dreamed that this could not be awake but that it was only a dream. But that since it was a dream and that I took so much real pleasure in it, what a happy thing it would be, if when we are in our graves (as Shakespeere resembles it), we could dream, and dream such dreams as this—that then we should not need to be so fearful of death as we are this plague-time.[1]

SAMUEL PEPYS'S casual allusion, made as he reflects on his dream of a consummation devoutly to be wished with the king's mistress, Lady Castlemaine, at the height of the Black Death in 1665, may seem an inordinately trivial indicator of Shakespeare's position in the culture of the early Restoration, but it is none the less a telling one. It is an allusion, first of all, which invokes Shakespeare in a context of political and indeed theological wish-fulfilment, associating Hamlet's soliloquy both with Pepys's fantasy of supplanting Charles II in this life and his simultaneously poignant and blasphemous wishes for an eternity of posthumous gratification in the next; by this passing appeal to *Hamlet*, Pepys's euphoric dream of Oedipal usurpation is converted into a wistful glimpse of immortality. However fleetingly, Shakespeare here participates in both the sexual politics of the Stuart court and its philosophical insecurity, *Hamlet* clearly dramatizing something of both Pepys's secular hopes and his religious fears. Perhaps more typically, the perverse ingenuity of Pepys's implied reading of 'To be, or not to be'—apparently finding a promise of erotic consolation in the words 'To sleep, perchance to dream'—suggests something of the pliability of Shakespeare's texts for Restoration readers, their off-centred availability for appropriation. Although

[1] Samuel Pepys, *Diary*, ed. Robert Latham and William Matthews (11 vols.; Berkeley, Calif., 1970–6), 15 Aug. 1665.

positioning *Hamlet*'s author as in some measure an authority, '(as Shakespeere resembles it)', Pepys feels perfectly able to treat his work as amenable raw material, a stray passage coming to hand for use in addressing contemporary problems without any reference or regard to its original context: unlike later exponents of the wonderfully inappropriate Shakespearean allusion, Pepys is entirely unselfconscious, the sacrosanct canonical status of author and soliloquy alike as yet unestablished.[2]

In both of these respects, as will become clear, Pepys's remark is characteristic of attitudes to Shakespeare in the 1660s. During this first decade of public theatre after the twenty-year hiatus of the Interregnum, Shakespeare is imagined by detractors as an ignorant and archaic rustic and by admirers as a Divine Right monarch, but even the most admiring among his adaptors deliberately withhold his quasi-royal authority from his plays themselves, rewriting them in accordance with the particular scenarios of wish-fulfilment which became the stock-in-trade of the early Restoration theatre. Adapting his dramas for motives as much political as aesthetic (most frequently updating them as topical Fletcherian romances, committed to re-enacting the official account of the Restoration itself), playwrights simultaneously revere Shakespeare and deny him full rights in his own works, treating his texts much as Pepys treats *Hamlet* and usurping his authority much as Pepys dreams of usurping Charles's. This in every sense cavalier approach to Shakespeare's plays is pioneered in the work of Sir William Davenant, who initiated the practice of full-scale adaptation in 1662 with his hybrid of *Measure for Measure* and *Much Ado About Nothing*, *The Law Against Lovers*, and brought it to its fullest and most explicit development in the last and most enduringly popular of his adaptations, *The Tempest; or the Enchanted Island*, co-written with John Dryden in 1667. In the 1660s, Shakespeare's plays belonged to the theatre more significantly than they

---

[2] In fact Pepys later produced a Restoration adaptation in miniature of just this extract, commissioning the Italian composer Cesare Morelli to set the 'To be or not to be' soliloquy as a piece of operatic recitative. This text was published by Macdonald Emslie in *Shakespeare Quarterly*, 6: 2 (1955), 159–70, and has recently been analysed by Alan Levitan in his unpublished essay 'Some Metrical Implications of the Pepys–Morelli Setting of "To be, or not to be"'. I am grateful to Professor Levitan not only for his essay but for the performance of the piece with which he illustrated it at the Shakespeare Association of America conference in 1988.

belonged to Shakespeare, and it was first and foremost the situation of the reopened playhouses which dictated their form and their status.

Romance

The resumption of theatrical activity in London once the return of the Stuarts seemed inevitable (from late 1659 onwards) was quickly followed after Charles's return in the summer of 1660 by its being brought under the exclusive patronage and supervision of the Crown, when a monopoly on legitimate theatrical activity was granted to two courtiers, Sir Thomas Killigrew and Sir William Davenant, who became managers of the King's Company and the Duke of York's Company respectively.[3] This conspicuous royal involvement in the drama is only one of many indications of the close association between the political objectives of the restored monarchy and the activities of the reopened theatres, an association which Davenant himself was quick to underline in the prologue he contributed to the Restoration court's first dramatic command performance in 1660:

Greatest of *Monarchs*, welcome to this place
Which *Majesty* so oft was wont to grace
Before our Exile, to divert the Court,
And ballance weighty Cares with harmless sport.
This truth we can to our advantage say,

---

[3] This encroachment of court influence into the arts did not go unresented: independent companies, especially that led by George Jolly, campaigned bitterly against their suppression in favour of the patentees. See Leslie Hotson, *The Commonwealth and Restoration Stage* (Cambridge, Mass., 1928), 176–9, 201; John Freehafer, 'The Formation of the London Patent Companies in 1660', *Theatre Notebook*, 20 (1965), 6–30. As late as 1662 an anonymous verse letter is still treating both Davenant and Killigrew as dilettante intruders in a world best left to the old professionals:

Since you commande me to send you downe
The newes of all the Playes in Towne
Knowe they a Monopoly of them have made
And Courtiers have engross't the Trade
Nor shall we ever have good they suppose
Till every one medle with the trade that he knowes.

(BM Add. MS 34, 217 fo. 31b: quoted in Hotson,
The Commonwealth and Restoration Stage, 246–7)

They that would have no KING, would have no *Play*:
The *Laurel* and the *Crown* together went,
Had the same *Foes*, and the same *Banishment*.[4]

The immediate task of the royal theatre companies after the Restoration, as this prologue suggests, was a double and in some senses paradoxical one: by the renewal of their 'harmless sport' they were not only to celebrate the coronation of a new monarch and the establishment of a wholly new regime, but also to create the impression that the previous royal government had never really fallen, to return to the artistic forms popular 'Before our Exile' as though nothing had happened. Davenant, who as poet laureate immediately before the Interregnum had been employed to produce court entertainments designed, in essence, to convince Charles I that the English Revolution would not take place (most notably the last of the Caroline masques, *Salmacida Spolia*), now found himself, immediately after the Interregnum, employing the same scenic and theatrical techniques to produce entertainments designed, essentially, to convince both Charles II and his theatre-going subjects that the English Revolution had indeed not taken place.

The interconnections between this make-believe return to the 1630s, the early Duke's Company repertory, and royalist propaganda are well illustrated by a notable coup Davenant achieved in 1661. On 21 October his company revived his own play *Love and Honour*, originally premièred before Charles I in 1634, with the contemporary resonances of its high-flown assertions of divinely ordained social hierarchy emphatically underscored by its costuming—for Betterton, who played Prince Alvaro, Davenant had borrowed Charles II's coronation robes, and for Harris, who played Prince Prospero, he had obtained those of his brother and heir the Duke of York.[5] Ideally, the theatres could be used not only to provide, as here, the temporary, escapist illusion that the Civil Wars had never happened, but to supply harmlessly replayed

---

[4] [Sir William Davenant], *The Prologue to His Majesty at the First Play Presented at the Cock-pit in Whitehall; Being Part of That Noble Entertainment Which Their Majesties Received Novemb. 19. from His Grace the Duke of Albermarle* (London, 1660).

[5] See John Downes, *Roscius Anglicanus* [1708], ed. Judith Milhous and Robert Hume (London, 1987), 52; Emett L. Avery, *et al.*, *The London Stage, 1600–1800* (5 pts. in 11 vols.; Carbondale, Ill., 1960–8), (hereafter *The London Stage*), 1: 41.

versions of the Interregnum itself, plays depicting tyrannous usurpations reassuringly concluded by the providential restorations of legitimate heirs.[6] In fact these two objectives could be achieved simultaneously by the revival and imitation of a single pre-Civil War genre, namely Fletcherian romance.

As Lois Potter has pointed out in *Secret Rites and Secret Writing: Royalist Literature, 1641–1660*, romantic tragicomedy had been established even before the Civil Wars as the royalist literary genre *par excellence*,[7] and it is surely no mere accident of aesthetics that the early Restoration repertory depended heavily on productions of *A King And No King*, *Philaster*, and *The Loyal Subject*,[8] or that the tradition of Restoration heroic drama begins with plays obviously derived from these models. As Potter observes:

The two Charleses acted out virtually every role available to a ruler in romance or drama: the disguised lover, the husband parted from his wife/kingdom, the loving father of his country, the sacrificial victim, the wandering prince. The domination of this period by tragicomedies, both high and low in style, can thus be seen not as an escape from reality but as a reflection of it.[9]

Evoking tragic responses from improbable situations, only to dispel them by the provision of still less probable happy endings, the Fletcherian tragicomic formula was perfectly fitted to the royalist view of the Interregnum, and equally dependent on an unusually willing suspension of disbelief. Even if everyone knew that the trial and execution of Charles I and the military successes of the New Model Army had disproved the idea that God protected all

[6] On the royalist politics of early Restoration drama, see Susan Staves, *Players' Scepters: Fictions of Authority in the Restoration* (Lincoln, Nebr., 1979), 43–73; Laura Brown, *English Dramatic Form, 1660–1760: An Essay in Generic History* (New Haven, Conn., 1981), 3–65; Nicholas José, *Ideas of the Restoration in English Literature, 1660–1671* (Cambridge, Mass., 1984), ch. 7: 'Theatrical Restoration', 120–41.

[7] See Lois Potter, *Secret Rites and Secret Writing: Royalist Literature, 1641–1660* (Cambridge, 1989), ch. 3: 'Genre as Code: Romance and Tragicomedy', 72–112.

[8] See Arthur Colby Sprague, *Beaumont and Fletcher on the Restoration Stage* (Cambridge, Mass., 1926), 6–24.

[9] Potter, *Secret Rites*, 107. 'The psychological need to interpret the Restoration as the comic ending to a tragic sequence might even be one of the factors in the period's notorious inability to write tragedy' (ibid. 111). Cf. the publication by 'a Person of Quality' of *Cromwell's Conspiracy. A Tragy-Comedy, Relating to our latter Times. Beginning at the Death of King Charles the First, And ending with the happy Restauration of King Charles the Second* (London, 1660).

legitimate kings and would personally curse usurpers, it was necessary to pretend in 1660 not only that Divine Right was still a viable political principle but that the sordid, contingent negotiations which had permitted Charles II's return had conclusively proved it. The new generation of playwrights who shadowed the events of the Commonwealth and the Restoration were thus naturally drawn to a genre in which, as Eric Rothstein and Frances Kavenik describe it:

a conclusion often does not follow more than broadly from the episodes that precede it. Fletcher's own plays often have predictable, broadly moral conclusions; but the moral ending, as for example in *A King And No King*, may run counter to the apparent thrust of the plot and the 'truth' of the characters.[10]

The Restoration was itself, from a royalist perspective, a thoroughly Fletcherian event, a half-providential, half-arbitrary awakening from the tragedy of the Interregnum into the implausible (if not downright unbelievable) poetic justice of the Act of Indemnity and Oblivion. The point is eloquently made by a document dating from the early days of the reopened theatres, which celebrates the cessation of military raids on theatrical performances by casting the entire Commonwealth and Restoration as a Fletcherian comedy, a domestic rebellion (and, with its farcical chase sequences between soldiers and playgoers, a harmlessly theatrical one) now concluded, indeed miraculously inverted, by a sudden 'prospr'ous change'. The actor who pronounced '*A Prologue to a Comedy call'd* The Tamer Tam'd, June 25. 1660' entered studying the playbill in consternation, to exclaim:

The *Tamer Tam'd*, what do the Players mean?
Shall we have *Rump* and *Rebel* in the scene?
Juncto's of safety with the righteous rabble

[10] Eric Rothstein and Frances M. Kavenik, *The Designs of Carolean Comedy* (Carbondale, Ill., 1988), 45. Rothstein and Kavenik's useful discussion of the predominance of Fletcherian romance in the early 1660s (pp. 41–52), surprisingly, does not relate this aspect of the repertory to the political circumstances of the time. On the formal patterns of Fletcherian tragicomedy, see also Eugene M. Waith, *The Pattern of Tragicomedy in Beaumont and Fletcher*, Yale Studies in English, 120 (New Haven, Conn., 1952), 36–40; Philip Edwards, 'The Danger not the Death: The Art of John Fletcher', in John Russell Brown and Bernard Harris (eds.), *Jacobean Theatre*, Stratford-upon-Avon Studies, 1 (London, 1960), 159–77. On its influence see John Harold Wilson, *The Influence of Beaumont and Fletcher on Restoration Drama* (Columbus, Oh., 1928).

Of *Apron-Peers*, knights of Sir *Arthurs* Table?
Shall *Baxter, Hewson, Scot* and *Fox* be nam'd?
These were our Tamers, but I hope they'r tam'd . . .
.   .   .   .

This Play, *The Tamer tamd*, is *Fletcher's* wit,
A man that pleas'd all pallats; therefore sit
And see the last scene out: pray do not run
Into confusion, till the Play be done . . .
.   .   .   .

Pray keep your seats, you do not sit in fear,
As in the dangerous dayes of *Oliver;*
It is not now (in good time be it spoke)
'*Enter* the Red-coats', '*Exit* Hat and Cloak';
But such a prosp'rous change doth now attend ye,
That those who did affront ye shall defend ye.[11]

Fletcher thus provided one principal dramatic mode for the newly restored theatres: such was his centrality in the theatre of the 1660s, indeed, that *The Tamer Tamed*, a mere sequel to *The Taming of the Shrew*, took precedence over its source; when Shakespeare's comedy was revived by the King's Company, perhaps as much as seven years later, it was rewritten by the comic actor John Lacy in ways largely designed to make it a better companion piece for Fletcher's spin-off.[12] Of the other two pre-war playwrights preserved in folio it was Jonson, not Shakespeare, who most regularly supplemented Fletcher's example.[13] As far as

---

[11] Printed in Thomas Jordan, *A Nursery of Novelties or Variety of Poetry* (1660): reprinted in *Shakespeare Society Papers*, 4 (1848), 140–42; quoted in Sprague, *Beaumont and Fletcher*, 8–9. See also *The London Stage*, 1: 11.

[12] Lacy's adaptation, which transfers the action of Shakespeare's Italian comedy to London to match Fletcher's Anglicized sequel, was probably written specifically to precede revivals of *The Tamer Tamed*; see Petruchio's concluding couplet: 'I've *Tam'd the Shrew*, but will not be asham'd | If next you see the very *Tamer Tam'd*.' John Lacy, *Sauny the Scott: or, The Taming of the Shrew* (London, 1698), 48. See Sprague, *Beaumont and Fletcher*, 46; Hazelton Spencer, *Shakespeare Improved*, 280. On Lacy's adaptation and its relation both to Fletcher and to Restoration domestic ideology, see Staves, *Players' Scepters*, 133–4. The earliest recorded performance took place in 1667 (see Pepys, *Diary*, 9 Apr. 1667), but since the Master of the Revels proposed to collect a fee for checking the 'Revived Play Taminge the Shrew' in November 1663 (in an entry which also refers to Davenant's *Macbeth* in similar terms), the adaptation may have been produced considerably earlier: see Adams, *Dramatic Records of Sir Henry Herbert*, 138.

[13] Cf. Robert D. Hume, *The Development of English Drama in the Late Seventeenth Century* [1976] (Oxford, 1990), 235: 'The early Carolean dramatists seem to have felt pulled between the genteel Fletcher tradition and the city comedy tradition headed by Ben Jonson.'

the task of therapeutically trivializing and dismissing the Interregnum was concerned, two of his comedies, *The Alchemist* and
Bartholomew Fair, were already conveniently laced with anti-
Puritan satire,[14] and before 1666 alone there are records of seven
performances of each play, along with nine performances of
Epicoene, or the Silent Woman (making it the second most popular pre-Civil War comedy, beaten only by Fletcher's *The Humorous Lieutenant*: its nearest Shakespearean competitor, *The Merry
Wives of Windsor*, achieved four) and three of *Volpone*.[15] Just as
Fletcher's most popular plays could be imitated to produce heroic
romances implicitly depicting the Restoration as a providential
return to legitimacy and order, so Jonson's could be mined to
produce comedies explicitly depicting the Commonwealth as a
temporary ascendancy of humours-infested religious hypocrites
and disreputable cozeners—comedies which moreover represent
human character as reassuringly stable despite the violent shifts of
ideological allegiance which the Restoration audience had been
compelled to experience. The task of rewriting recent history to
blame regicide, sequestration, and republicanism on a caricatured
minority of Jonsonian humourists, all invariably gulled by right-
thinking Cavaliers over the course of the action, is enthusiastically
taken up by the new generation of Restoration comic dramatists.
The best-known successful comedies of the period include, of
course, Abraham Cowley's *Cutter of Coleman Street*, 1661 (which
features a disguise-prone 'sharking fellow' called Worm, who is
essentially, as his name suggests, Jonson's Brainworm without the
brains);[16] Sir Robert Howard's *The Committee*, 1662 (whose

---

[14] The political 'use' of Jonson in this respect is helpfully glossed by Pepys: in
1668, another viewing of *Bartholomew Fair*, his favourite Jonson play, served
principally to elicit the diarist's growing scepticism about the Restoration settlement in general: 'saw no sights, my wife having a mind to see the play, *Bartholomew
Fayre* with puppets; which we did, and it is an excellent play; the more I see it, the
more I love the wit of it; only, the business of abusing the Puritans begins to grow
stale, and of no use, they being the people that at last will be found the wisest'
(Pepys, *Diary*, 4 Sept. 1668).

[15] See Rothstein and Kavenik, 'Appendix 2: The Carolean Comic Repertory',
268–69; *The London Stage*, 1: 3–89. Dryden, of course, attempts to prove that
the English excel at comedy at least as thoroughly as do the French by appealing
primarily to Jonson, providing an '*Examen of the Silent Woman*' ('the pattern of a
perfect Play') as his conclusive example. See John Dryden, *Of Dramatic Poesie, an
Essay* (London, 1668), 50, 47.

[16] Abraham Cowley, *Cutter of Coleman Street* (1661), ed. Darlene Johnson
Gravett (New York, 1987), 'THE PERSONS', 43. According to Downes, *Every Man*

eponymous Puritan sequesterers are evidently close relations of
Zeal-of-the-land Busy and Tribulation Wholesome), and Sir George
Etherege's immensely popular first play *The Comical Revenge; or,
Love in a Tub*, 1664 (which features a Commonwealth Sir Politick
Would-Be as its chief gull in the person of 'SIR NICHOLAS CULLY,
knighted by Oliver').[17] With the sole exception of *The Committee*,
these plays, significantly, include not only these Jonsonian elements but Fletcherian love-plots, whose honour-steeped Cavaliers
speak either in blank verse or in heroic couplets proper: the comic
drama for which the period is most often remembered thus emerges
from a politically appropriate hybridization of Jonson and Fletcher.
Its sole important debt to Shakespeare is transmitted, as I shall
show, via one of Davenant's similarly hybrid adaptations.

Shakespeare's fortunes in this repertory were mixed, to say the
least. Some of the earliest and most successful Shakespeare revivals, in keeping with the Restoration theatre's general fidelity to
the court culture of the 1630s (a fidelity at first inevitable, given
the dearth of new playwrights after the twenty-year hiatus of the
Interregnum), were of plays which had been popular in royal
circles when the Caroline theatres closed in 1640. *Othello* among
the tragedies, *1 Henry IV* among the histories (significantly, a play
about the successful suppression of a rebellion), and *The Merry
Wives of Windsor* among the comedies (Shakespeare at his most
Jonsonian) soon established themselves as mainstays of the King's
Company repertory;[18] *Hamlet*, the sole 'stock' Shakespeare play
of the pre-war years conceded to Davenant, became a similar
fixture for the Duke's Company. (The other Caroline favourite,
Julius Caesar, dramatizing with a considerable degree of sympathy

In His Humour was among the King's Company's 'Old Stock Plays' in the early
Restoration years, along with *Every Man Out Of His Humour* and *The Devil Is
An Ass*; see Downes, *Roscius Anglicanus*, 24–5. The pressure towards complete
political conformity in the early Restoration theatre is well illustrated by the case
of Cowley's play, which was severely criticized for depicting a Cavalier in a less
than wholly admirable light.

[17] Sir George Etherege, *The Comical Revenge*, in *The Plays of Sir George
Etherege*, ed. Michael Cordner (Cambridge, 1982), 'DRAMATIS PERSONAE', 6. On
these early Restoration comedies, 'trampling on the remains of the Commonwealth', see Hume, *Development of English Drama*, 238–40.

[18] These three plays were already being performed by the company known as
the 'Old Actors' (who became the core of the King's Company) at the Red Bull inn
before the establishment of the Killigrew–Davenant monopoly: see Adams,
Dramatic Records of Sir Henry Herbert, 82.

an assassination easily read as regicide, was tactfully withheld until later in the decade.)[19] While these four plays acquired the status of reliable classics, attempts to extend this proven 'core' Shakespeare repertoire without resort to adaptation were in general less successful. The only other Shakespeare play to achieve any degree of commercial success in unadapted form during the early years of the Restoration, tellingly, was the most uncomplicatedly providential of the romances, *Pericles*, briefly revived at around the time of the Restoration itself but laid aside thereafter.[20] Of the other romances, *The Tempest* was felt to require extensive reworking before its appearance in 1667, and the Shakespeare–Fletcher *Two Noble Kinsmen* was rewritten by Davenant in 1664 as *The Rivals*, a version which instinctively cuts all the passages now believed to have been written by Shakespeare and out-Fletchers Fletcher by providing an unambiguously happy ending, keeping its Arcite alive to marry Emilia and pairing off the Gaoler's Daughter with Palamon.[21]

Richard III was performed at some time in the early 1660s, presented by a pious prologue as one more tragicomedy about the Commonwealth and its inescapable downfall:

This day we Act a Tyrant, ere you go
I fear that to your cost you'll find it so.
What early hast you have made to pass a Fine,
To purchase Fetters, how you croud to joyne
With an Usurper, be advis'd by me
Ne're serve Usurpers, fix to Loyalty . . .

  . . . .

Tyrants (like childrens bubbles in the Air)
Puft up with pride, still vanish in despair.

[19] For the Caroline court repertory, see the lists of 'Playes acted before the Kinge and Queene this present yeare of the lord. 1636', and 'before the king & queene this yeare of our lord 1638', ibid. 75–6. On the whole (vexed) question of the division of the pre-Civil Wars canon between Davenant and Killigrew, see Gunnar Sorelius, 'The Rights of the Restoration Theatre Companies in the Older Drama', *Studia Neophilologica*, 37 (1965), 174–89: also Hume, *Development of English Drama*, 19–23, as well as his essay 'Securing a Repertory: Plays on the London Stage, 1660–5', in Antony Coleman and Antony Hammond (eds.), *Poetry and Drama, 1500–1700: Essays in Honour of Harold F. Brooks* (London, 1981), 156–72.

[20] On this production and its immediate topicality, see Gary Taylor, *Reinventing Shakespeare*, 21–3.

[21] See Pepys, *Diary*, 10 Sept. 1664; Downes, *Roscius Anglicanus*, 55; Sprague, *Beaumont and Fletcher*, 129; Mongi Raddadi, *Davenant's Adaptations of Shakespeare* (Uppsala, 1979), 15, 124–5.

But lawful Monarchs are preserv'd by Heaven,
And 'tis from thence that their Commissions given.
Though giddy Fortune, for a time may frown,
And seem to eclipse the lustre of a Crown.
Yet a King can with one Majesticke Ray,
Dispearse those Clouds and make a glorious day.
This blessed truth we to our joy have found,
Since our great master happily was Crown'd.
So from the rage of *Richards* tyranny,
Richmond himself will come and set you free.[22]

Even presented as such a triumphantly orthodox parable, how-ever, the play does not seem to have become a particular favourite until Colley Cibber's adaptation of 1699; apart from *1 Henry IV*, the only history to be received with favour in the 1660s was the already part-Fletcherian *Henry VIII*, first staged by Davenant with much spectacular royal pageantry, rather along the lines of his own revived *Love and Honour*, in 1663.[23]

Among the tragedies, a revival of *Romeo and Juliet* in March 1662 did little for the play's reputation (Pepys noted, 'It is the play of itself the worst that ever I heard in my life'; *Diary*, 1 Mar. 1662), and it was subsequently transformed into a timely parable of the healing of civil broils by heroic love: 'This Tragedy of *Romeo and Juliet*, was made some time after into a Tragi-comedy, by Mr. *James Howard*, he preserving *Romeo* and *Juliet* alive.'[24]

A 1664 production of *King Lear* seems to have provided no hint of the play's later popularity in Nahum Tate's similarly cheering version;[25] meanwhile, experiments with unaltered Shakespearean comedy proved even less successful. *A Midsummer Night's Dream*, revived in 1662, perhaps on the strength of the underground pop-ularity it seems to have enjoyed during the Commonwealth in the form of the droll *The Merry conceited Humors of Bottom the*

[22] '*Prologue to* Richard *the third*', preserved in A.B. (comp.), *Covent Garden Drollery* [1672], ed. Montague Summers (London, 1927), 11.

[23] See Downes, *Roscius Anglicanus*, ed. Milhous and Hume, 55–6; *The London Stage*, 1: 72–5. Such was the generally low profile of Shakespeare's histories in the 1660s that neither Roger Boyle's heroic play *Henry the Fifth* (produced in 1664) nor John Caryll's *The English Princes, or the Death of Richard III* (produced in 1667) betray any knowledge of the existence of Shakespeare's plays on the same subjects.

[24] Downes, *Roscius Anglicanus*, ed. Milhous and Hume, 52–53. Howard's adaptation, sadly, does not survive.

[25] Ibid. 59 n. 167.

Weaver,[26] signally failed to impress Pepys ('The most insipid ridiculous play that ever I saw in my life'; *Diary*, 29 Sept. 1662), and it disappeared from the repertory thereafter. *Twelfth Night*, revived in 1661 and 1663, received a similar response ('but a silly play'; 6 Jan. 1663); and only one other performance of the play in its original form is recorded before the mid-eighteenth century, in 1669—a revival which still failed to convince Pepys, who now termed it 'one of the weakest plays that ever I saw on the stage' (20 Jan. 1669). On the early Restoration stage, Shakespeare's plays, among the oldest in the repertory, seemed anomalous, even the most popular appearing to some observers outmoded: 'I saw *Hamlet* Pr: of Denmark played,' noted John Evelyn in 1661, 'but now the old playe began to disgust this refined age; since his Majestie being so long abroad.'[27]

Evelyn's remark is all the more interesting, given that the version of *Hamlet* he saw performed was almost certainly the revised text published in 1676, extensively cut and with its diction frequently modernized and simplified.[28] Even one of the most highly regarded of Shakespeare's plays needed its language clarified for this new generation of playgoers, apparently, and even with such assistance the tragedy might still seem out of date, incongruous in a theatrical repertory whose chief business was to nurture the particular romantic fictions that were among the premises of Charles II's court.

Revision

Critical perceptions of Shakespeare in the early Restoration, however admiring, frequently collude with the pragmatic recognition

---

[26] *The Merry conceited Humors of Bottom the Weaver* (London, 1661), republished in Francis Kirkman, *The Wits, or Sport upon Sport* (2 parts; London, 1672–3). Two of this latter collection's other short interludes of the Commonwealth years derive from Shakespeare, 'The Bouncing Knight' (a 'Falstaff sketch', abbreviated from *1 Henry IV*) and 'The Grave-makers' (from *Hamlet*): tellingly, no fewer than 14 others are drawn from the Beaumont and Fletcher canon.

[27] *The Diary of John Evelyn*, ed. E. S. de Beer (6 vols.; Oxford, 1955), 3, 304 (26 Nov. 1661).

[28] *The tragedy of Hamlet, Prince of Denmark: as it is now acted at his Highness the Duke of York's Theatre* (London, 1676). The modifications were probably carried out by Davenant: on this text of the play, see esp. Gary Taylor, *Reinventing Shakespeare*, 46–51.

of theatrical practitioners such as Lacy, Davenant, and Howard that his plays might profitably be rewritten. This is partly because mid-seventeenth-century ideas of the English theatrical tradition in general are shaped so decisively by the three great single-volume collections of pre-Civil War drama (the Jonson, Shakespeare, and Beaumont and Fletcher folios) and their respective introductory materials. Here again, as in the theatrical repertory, Shakespeare is placed in context by the often more sharply focused literary *personae* of Jonson and Fletcher. The introductory pages of the Shakespeare folio of 1623 (including Heminge and Condell's dedicatory letters, and the commendatory verses supplied by Jonson, Digges, and others) are concerned above all to constitute Shakespeare as the literary exemplar (in both style and subject) of 'Nature', setting him in opposition to the Jonson presented as the master of Art by his own earlier folio of 1616. This opposition is reaffirmed and supplemented by Humphrey Moseley's 1647 folio edition of the Beaumont and Fletcher canon, which repeats the contrast between artful Jonson and natural Shakespeare but goes on to assert that Fletcher combines both. 'By casting the 1647 collection in relation to its 1616 and 1623 predecessors,' as Margreta De Grazia points out, 'Moseley territorialized the native dramatic domain into Art, Nature, and Art plus Nature (sometimes termed "Wit").'[29] This conceptual division of the Renaissance theatrical heritage is most fully developed in Sir John Denham's dedicatory poem (addressed to Fletcher) in the Beaumont and Fletcher folio itself, in which the writer looks nostalgically back to a Jacobean golden age,

When JOHNSON, SHAKESPEARE, and thy selfe did sit,
And sway'd in the Triumvirate of wit—
Yet what from JOHNSONS oyle and sweat did flow,
Or what more easie nature did bestow
On SHAKESPEARES gentler Muse, in thee full growne
Their Graces both appeare.[30]

---

[29] De Grazia, *Shakespeare Verbatim*, 47. On the relations between these three folios, and especially on the 1623 preliminaries' importance in establishing the 'Poet of Nature' view of Shakespeare, see ibid. 33–48. It is perhaps worth noting here that the Restoration's own edition of the Shakespeare folio, the Third (1663–4), gives unusual prominence to these prefatory materials, reprinting them, with the expanded collection of commendatory poems from the Second, in large type so that they fill more pages than in either the Second (1632) or the Fourth (1685).

[30] John Denham, 'On Mr. JOHN FLETCHER's VVorkes', in Francis Beaumont and John Fletcher, *Comedies and Tragedies* (London, 1647), b1ᵛ.

Denham's characterization of the playwrights of the pre-war years
as a mutually defining trio—Jonson standing for Art, Shakespeare
representing Nature, and the university-educated Fletcher refining
the one by the other to embody Wit—proved remarkably durable,
and it is reiterated in most discussions of the English dramatic
tradition published over the whole Commonwealth and Restoration period. Francis Kirkman boasts in 1652 that 'no Nation ever
could glory in such Playes, as the most learned and incomparable
Johnson, the copious *Shakespeare*, or the ingenuous *Fletcher* com-
pos'd':[31] similarly in 1664 Richard Flecknoe writes that 'to compare our English Dramatick Poets together (without taxing them)
Shakespear excelled in a natural Vein, *Fletcher* in Wit, and *Jonson*
in Gravity and ponderousness of Style'.[32] In 1687 William Winstanley is still referring to 'the happy *Triumvirate* . . . of the chief
Dramatick Poets of our Nation, in the last foregoing age', although
he places Shakespeare last among the three.[33] As well he might;
defined as the playwright of neither Art nor Wit, the 'natural,'
copious Shakespeare, with small Latin and less Greek, is put into
the position of a naïve, perhaps even vulgar, provincial. In keeping
with this construction, the most enthusiastic and sympathetic
account of his work published during the Restoration—a letter
written by Margaret Cavendish, Duchess of Newcastle in 1662—
is prompted by the need to defend Shakespeare against an often-
repeated charge that his plays are 'made up onely with Clowns,
Fools, Watchmen, and the like',[34] and even a prologue written ex-
pressly in his praise for an early revival of *Julius Caesar* (*c.*1669)
equates him squarely with his own more rustic characters, at first
Jaquenetta or Audrey and then, most tellingly, the Warwickshire
yokel Christopher Sly:

[31] Francis Kirkman (tr.), *The Loves and Adventures of Clerio & Lozia. A
Romance* (London, 1652), 'Dedication'.

[32] Flecknoe is in complete agreement with Denham on the mutually defining
qualities of the three writers: 'Comparing [Jonson] with *Shakespeare*, you shall see
the difference betwixt Nature and Art; and with *Fletcher*, the difference betwixt
Wit and Judgement . . .'; Richard Flecknoe, *A Short Discourse of the English Stage*,
published with *Love's Kingdom* (1664), sig. G5^r: quoted in Brian Vickers (ed.),
Shakespeare: The Critical Heritage, 1623–1800 (6 vols.; London, 1974–81), i. 46.

[33] See William Winstanley, *The Lives of the most Famous English Poets, or the
Honour of Parnassus* (London, 1687), 123–33.

[34] Margaret Cavendish, *CCXI Sociable Letters, written by the Thrice Noble,
Illustrious, and Excellent Princess, The Lady Marchioness of Newcastle* (London,
1664), 244.

IN Country Beauties as we often see,
Something that takes in their simplicity.
Yet while they charm, they know not they are fair,
And take without their spreading of the snare;
Such Artless beauty lies in *Shakespears* wit,
'Twas well in spight of him what ere he writ.
His Excellencies came and were not sought.
His words like casual Atoms made a thought:
Drew up themselves in Rank and File, and writ,
He wondring how the Devil it were such wit.
Thus like the drunken Tinker, in his Play,
He grew a Prince, and never knew which way.[35]

In a cultural context established by the learned Jonson and the suave Fletcher, Shakespeare might appear even to his admirers as a peasant only just sustaining the role of a Prince, or a 'Country Beauty' needing instruction in the ways of the world. This status certainly endeared him to some readers, notably Aphra Behn, who by the same gendered logic visible in this prologue (which goes on, inevitably, to play off natural Shakespeare against artful Jonson) is able to claim him as an ally, an honorary woman writer. 'Plays have no great room for that which is men's great advantage over women, that is Learning; We all well know that the immortal Shakespeare's Plays (who was not guilty of much more of this than often falls to women's share) have better pleas'd the world than Johnson's works.'[36] To many, however, it was simply clear that his plays, whether valorized as natural or denigrated as ignorant, needed cultivation: 'as another [said], of *Shakespeare*'s writings', Flecknoe relates, ''twas a fine Garden, but it wanted weeding'.[37]

In this critical climate, the willingness of theatrical professionals to alter Shakespeare's plays for performance seems less surprising;[38] indeed, the widespread view of Shakespeare's plays as virtually

---

[35] *Covent Garden Drollery*, 7. This prologue has sometimes been attributed to Dryden; see Vickers, *Critical Heritage*, i. 141.

[36] Aphra Behn, 'Preface to *The Dutch Lover*', in *Works*, ed. Montague Summers [1915], (6 vols.; rpt. New York, 1967), i. 224. See Marianne Novy, 'Preface' in id. (ed.), *Women's Re-Visions of Shakespeare*, esp. 2–3.

[37] Flecknoe, *A Short Discourse*. On Restoration criticism of the 'Triumvirate', see esp. Sorelius, *Giant Race*, 77–144.

[38] The patents granted to Killigrew and Davenant, after all, paid at least lip-service to the idea that the two managers should in one respect alter not just Shakespeare but the entire pre-war repertory: see, e.g. the King's grant of 21 Aug.

unmediated expressions of Nature, different in kind to the more finished performances of Jonson and Fletcher, could not only mandate their rewriting but license their wholesale repossession. While Davenant might have been able, had he so wished, to claim a feudal, hereditary right to Shakespeare's plays (given that he used to hint that he was Shakespeare's illegitimate son),[39] his attitude to the proprietorship of Shakespeare's texts, once his company had secured performing rights from the Crown, appears in practice to have anticipated John Locke's more progressive theory of ownership, according to which whatever someone 'removes out of the state that Nature hath provided, and left it in, he hath mixed his *Labour* with, and joyned to something that is his own, and thereby makes it his *Property*'.[40] This is most signally visible in the case of the first of all Restoration rewritings of Shakespeare, *The Law Against Lovers*, performed in February 1662, which, as one anonymous contemporary points out, treats Shakespeare merely as a source of natural raw materials, a larder of ingredients:

Then came the Knight agen with his Lawe
Against Lovers the worst that ever you sawe
In dressing of which he playnely did shew it
Hee was a far better Cooke then a Poet
And only he the Art of it had
Of two good Playes to make one bad.[41]

1660: 'And we doe further Hereby authorize and Command them the said Thomas Killegrew and Sir William Davenant, to peruse all playes that haue been formerly written, and to expunge all Prophaneness and Scurrility from the same, before they be represented or Acted'; Adams, *Dramatic Records of Sir Henry Herbert*, 88. It is unlikely, however, that the often-quoted preamble to Davenant's warrant of 12 Dec. 1660 (LC 5/137, 343) granting him performing rights to a share of the pre-war drama, which states that it is issued in response to his 'proposition of reformeinge some of the most ancient Playes that were playd at Blackfriers and of makeinge them, fitt for the Company of Actors appointed vnder his direction and Comand', legally required adaptation on any larger scale than this sort of incidental censorship. For a different interpretation, however, see Freehafer, 'London Patent Companies'; Hume, *Development of English Drama*.

[39] See Samuel Schoenbaum, *William Shakespeare: A Documentary Life* (Oxford, 1975), 164–6.

[40] John Locke, 'The Second Treatise of Government', in *Two Treatises of Government*, ed. Peter Laslett (2nd edn., Cambridge, 1967), 306.

[41] BM Add. MS 34, 217 fo. 31b: quoted in Hotson, *The Commonwealth and Restoration Stage*, 246–7.

The two good plays in question are *Measure for Measure* and *Much Ado about Nothing*, but this commentator seems to have been alone in recognizing them: four other witnesses to the play's performances (Pepys, who thought it 'a good play and well performed', two Dutch visitors, who record that it was considered the Duke's Company's 'best play', and John Evelyn)[42] make no reference to Shakespeare, and neither does the play's printed text, published in Davenant's posthumous folio of 1673. Davenant's work apparently removes *Measure for Measure* and *Much Ado* from the state of Nature in which Shakespeare left them, transferring the result into the category of his own Works.[43] Such a view of the adaptor as proto-Lockean appropriator is indeed made explicit by a subsequent reviser, Thomas Shadwell, whose 1678 alteration of *Timon of Athens* explains the adaptor's right to have his name on the title page instead of Shakespeare's by prefacing it with a description of the crucial work he has carried out on the text in question: 'Made into a PLAY. By THO. SHADWELL'.[44] To Davenant, Shakespeare's plays as they stand are not quite works, and Shakespeare is thus treated as not quite an author, his texts available for recycling much as the old *Leir*, *The Famous Victories of Henry V*, or the ur-*Hamlet* had been in Shakespeare's own time.

The Law Against Lovers, in its willingness silently to appropriate two separate plays, is one of the most thoroughgoing of all the period's adaptations, and an inspection of Davenant's use of the materials he chooses suggests something of the tremendous pressure towards political orthodoxy under which the re-authoring of Shakespeare's plays in the early 1660s was carried out. The play combines and modifies its Shakespearean ingredients in order to conform doubly to the dramatic requirements of the early Restoration, simultaneously reviving two favourite dramatic charac-

[42] Pepys, *Diary*, 18 Feb. 1662; Ethel Seaton, *Literary Relations of England and Scandinavia in the Seventeenth Century* (Oxford, 1935), 335; Evelyn, *Diary*, iii. 347 (18 Dec. 1662).

[43] Cf. Dryden's preface to the Davenant–Dryden *The Tempest; or the Enchanted Island*, quoted below, according to which Davenant's additions to Shakespeare's play have completed what was a hitherto unfinished design by putting 'the last hand to it'.

[44] Thomas Shadwell, *The History of Timon of Athens, the Man-Hater* (London, 1678). Cf. 'The Epistle Dedicatory': 'it has the inimitable hand of *Shakespear* in it, which never made more Masterly strokes than in this. Yet I can truly say, I have made it into a Play.'

ters of the pre-war court (whose names Charles I had penned in his copy of the Second Folio as 'Benedik and Betrice')[45] and setting them into a Fletcherian variation on the plot of *Measure for Measure* which obviously parallels the history of the Commonwealth but which painstakingly defuses its every detail.[46] At the opening of Davenant's play, a legitimate prince (the Duke) prepares to leave his country not under compulsion as the result of defeat but voluntarily and as the result of victory: unlike his hasty and cryptic Shakespearean original, Davenant's Duke even uses Charles II's own famous euphemism for his exile, 'my travels', innocuously transformed into the result of a premeditated whim; 'Victory gives me now free leisure to | Pursue my old design of travelling' (Davenant, *Works*, 273). In fact, of course, the Duke in this story does not go into exile at all, safely overseeing the Puritan regime which succeeds him while disguised as a member of the established Church. Being the Duke's deputy, Angelo, the leader of this temporary Puritan government (Turin being referred to as a 'Commonwealth' throughout Angelo's stewardship), is not even technically a usurper, and the ultimate crime of his regime—not irrelevantly, a judicial murder by beheading, that of Claudio—never actually takes place. Angelo, however, is permitted to believe that it does, and thus has ample opportunity, when at last facing punishment by the Duke (part of which, in an excess of poetic justice, is to be the sequestration of his estates), to voice repentance and expiation (324–5).

Not only is the Puritan government gratifyingly and conclusively overturned at the close of the play, but it encounters throughout its existence spirited resistance from a group of dashing Cavaliers (not a collaborator among them) who at last prompt the Duke's self-restoration to power by staging a successful coup, in which they storm the prison where their comrade Claudio is incarcerated.

[45] J. O. Halliwell-Phillipps, *Memoranda*, 59; quoted in H. H. Furness (ed.), *Much Ado About Nothing*, New Variorum edn. (Philadelphia, 1899), 6.

[46] On the form if not the politics of this adaptation, see Raddadi, *Davenant's Adaptations*, 97: 'In my opinion . . . *The Law Against Lovers* does in fact show strong indebtedness to the pattern commonly called Fletcherian tragicomedy.' See also Sorelius, *Giant Race*, 150–2. Davenant explicitly acknowledges the formal pattern to which his play conforms in the last scene, where Benedick observes of the now fully married Julietta that 'She has been advis'd by a bauld Dramatick Poet | Of the next Cloister, to end her Tragy-Comedy | With Hymen the old way'. Sir William Davenant, *The Law Against Lovers*, in *The Works of Sr. William D'Avenant Kt* (London, 1673), 326.

This resistance movement is characterized by an absolute loyalty both to the Duke and to Caroline literary styles—Claudio and Julietta, more thoroughly betrothed than their originals, speak in rhyming couplets (very much in the style of, for example, Beaufort, Graciana, Bruce, and Aurelia in the royalist sub-plot of Etherege's *The Comical Revenge*), and each offers heroically to remain in prison as the price of the other's liberty; their friends Lucio and Benedick pose as gallant libertines in the matter of love, but are as passionately devoted to honour as Claudio, Benedick single-handedly defeating not only all the prison·guards but a detachment of his brother Angelo's soldiers during the coup. Civil warfare in this play is entirely heroic, and the honourable Cavaliers win against all the odds.[47]

The Duke's self-restoration at the close of this uprising erases the crimes, discomforts, and civil strife of Angelo's regime as thoroughly as Davenant's royalist drama wishes to erase those of the Commonwealth. All the story's various threats to life and property prove to have been mere Fletcherian dramatic hypotheses all along. The supposedly Puritan Angelo has been, at heart, a Cavalier throughout: relapsing into rhyming couplets towards the end of the play, he explains that the enforcement of the chastity laws and sentencing of Claudio were only pretexts to bring Isabella, whom he already loved, out of the convent, and that his attempts on her honour were purely theoretical, experiments designed to prove her chastity rather than destroy it (315). Mariana having been left out of Davenant's adaptation (replaced in the cast list by a new female character, Beatrice's musical but not yet marriageable younger sister Viola),[48] and the Duke offering a quite miraculously chaste and paternal version of Charles II, this penitent Angelo (guilty in the play's terms only of a breach of the love-and-honour code in not placing sufficient faith in the virtue

---

[47] Ibid. 321. Angelo's guards are not even native supporters of his government, but 'Zwits'—foreign mercenaries. The wish-fulfilment civil skirmish in *The Law Against Lovers* apparently does not even kill anyone—'The fury of the last encounter has | Not lost me any of my Subjects lives,' announces the Duke (327), perhaps leaving one wondering, however, about the fate of the hapless Zwits.

[48] Viola, the first role played by Mary 'Moll' Davis, in her sexual naïveté and curiosity, forms a 'missing link' in Davenant's drama between the young man who has never seen a woman, Gridonel, in *The Platonick Lovers* (1635) and the similarly inexperienced 'hermaphrodite' Hippolito in *The Tempest, or the Enchanted Island* (1667), probably also played by Davis; see below.

of his beloved) can finally achieve his objective after all, one more
beneficiary of the Duke's spectacular concluding act of indemnity
and oblivion:

[DUKE.]   But now I come
  To count'nance the Reclaim'd. I can relate
  Your latter story, *Angelo*; and am
  Not ignorant, *Benedick*, of yours; but in
  Remembrance of your former merits I
  Forget your late attempts...
          .   .   .   .

  Remember, *Bernardine*, your Vows to Heaven;
  And so behave yourself in future life,
  That I shall ne'er repent my mercy...
          .   .   .   .

  Your slanders, *Lucio*, cannot do me harm.
  Be sorrowful, and be forgiven...
          .   .   .   .

                          ...Lend me,
  Chast *Isabella*, your fair hand; which with
  Your heart I dedicate to *Angelo*;
  He now sufficiently that virtue knows,
  Which he too much, too curiously has tried...
          .   .   .   .

  Provost, open your Prison Gates, and make
  Your Pris'ners free. The story of this day,
  When 'tis to future Ages told, will seem
  A moral drawn from a poetick Dream.
                    FINIS.

                         (327–9)

The plot of *Measure for Measure* is indeed rewritten in *The
Law Against Lovers* as a 'poetick Dream', perhaps the most dis-
ingenuously harmless of all the early Restoration theatre's drama-
tizations of the official perspective on the preceding twenty years.
Although of enormous importance to the development of English
drama through its inception, via the transplanting of Beatrice and
Benedick, of the 'gay couple' tradition which became a hallmark
of contemporary comedy,[49] *The Law Against Lovers* remained in

---

[49] Dryden's *The Wild Gallant* (1663) has traditionally been credited with establishing this convention: see esp. John Harrington Smith, *The Gay Couple in
Restoration Comedy* (Cambridge, Mass., 1948), 47–8. The only critic who, fleetingly, gives *The Law Against Lovers* its due in this respect is Alfred Harbage, in

the repertory for less than a year, in this respect perhaps a victim of its own impeccable royalist politics. The far greater long-term success of Davenant's next adaptation, his much better known operatic treatment of *Macbeth* (1663–4), may be in part attributable to its failure to reduce Shakespeare's tragedy to anything like the same degree of optimistic conformity. Although evidently designed (like the prologue to *Richard III* quoted above) to turn Shakespeare's play into one more reassuring tragicomedy about the fall of a usurping tyrant (having Fleance, for example, ancestor of the Stuarts, return to Scotland in time for the final battle from an exile spent, pointedly, in France),[50] Davenant's adaptation, as Lois Potter has shown, dramatizes not only the Restoration audience's supposed moral certainties about the Interregnum but its actual experience of ambiguity and compromise.[51] The very structure of Shakespeare's original play resists the transformation of Macbeth into an entirely unsympathetic figure for Cromwell, and Davenant's expansion of the roles of the Macduffs to provide a virtuous counterpoint to the Macbeths gives rise to a notable scene, set just after Macbeth's coronation, in which they debate the awkward political choices posed by their situation; Lady Macduff argues against her husband for a passive acceptance of Macbeth's rule, trusting to Providence to dethrone him in its own good time.[52] However incidental a feature of Davenant's symmetrical design this scene may appear, it must in 1663 have seemed, as Potter suggests, 'agonisingly relevant... For that majority of Davenant's audience who had been quiescent under Cromwell, this argument externalises an inner conflict which badly needed ventilating.'[53] While the piously rosy *Law Against Lovers* disappeared after December 1662, this more ambiguous adaptation remained in the repertory throughout the Restoration period and

---

Cavalier Drama: An Historical and Critical Supplement to the Study of the Elizabethan and Restoration Stage (New York, 1936), 86.

[50] [Sir William Davenant], *Macbeth, a Tragedy: With all the alterations, amendments, additions, and new songs* (London, 1674), 60.

[51] Potter, *Secret Rites*, 202–7. On the provenance and dating of this adaptation, see Christopher Spencer (ed.), *Davenant's Macbeth from the Yale Manuscript* (New Haven, Conn., 1961), 1–16. For other readings of the play, see Raddadi, *Davenant's Adaptations*, 99–118; Christopher Spencer (ed.), *Five Restoration Adaptations*, 14–16; Hazelton Spencer, *Shakespeare Improved*, 152–74.

[52] [Davenant], *Macbeth*, 30–1.

[53] Potter, *Secret Rites*, 206.

beyond,[54] its more complex presentation of political conflict enabling it to outlive the specific anxieties it originally dramatized.

Family Romance

The more extensively Shakespeare's plays were thus conscripted to address the issues of the 1660s, the more thoroughly they were wrested away from their original author and across the cultural gap separating the reigns of Elizabeth and James from the Restoration. This process is nowhere more self-consciously apparent than in Davenant's equally timely last play, *The Tempest; or the Enchanted Island*, produced in collaboration with Dryden in 1667. No other Restoration adaptation of Shakespeare makes such extensive or inventive use of the restored theatre's most conspicuous innovation, the professional actress, and this particular marker of Davenant and Dryden's distance from Shakespeare's own theatre helps both to motivate and to determine the strategies by which their adaptation simultaneously promotes and evades Shakespeare's authority.

Dryden's prologue to this remarkable play opens by at once making Shakespeare an honorary Stuart and placing him firmly in the past:

As when a Tree's cut down the secret root
Lives under ground, and thence new Branches shoot;
So, from old *Shakespear*'s honour'd dust, this day
Springs up and buds a new reviving Play.[55]

'Old' Shakespeare is here identified with the restored monarchy, likened to the oak tree which first protected and later came to symbolize Charles II, but at the same time he is identified with the irretrievably dead Charles I—like the Globe, a victim of the axe during the Interregnum. In common with the monarchy itself, Shakespeare is indeed reviving, but with (officially unacknowl-

[54] Davenant's adaptation was replaced as the principal acting text of *Macbeth* by a version prepared by David Garrick in 1744; this version, however, retains many of Davenant's elaborations to the witches' scenes, which continued to be performed well into the 19th cent.

[55] [John Dryden], 'Prologue to the *Tempest, or the Enchanted Island*', ll. 1–4. [Sir William Davenant and John Dryden], *The Tempest, or the Enchanted Island* (London, 1670), (hereafter *The Enchanted Island*).

edged) alterations:[56] if he is venerable, he is also to some degree
outdated. Amplifying this casting of Shakespeare as a king from
the good old days, Dryden sets out a by-now familiar view of the
'triumvirate of wit', once more treating Shakespeare's plays as
Nature, anterior to the fully processed works of art produced by
his junior colleagues, and the trope as ever risks highlighting the
extent to which Art and Wit have outgrown Nature:

Shakespear, who taught by none did first impart
To *Fletcher* Wit, to labouring *Johnson* Art.
He Monarch-like gave those his subjects law,
And is that Nature which they paint and draw.
Fletcher reach'd that which on his heights did grow,
Whilst *Johnson* crept and gather'd all below.
This did his Love, and this his Mirth digest:
One imitates him most, the other best.
If they have since out-writ all other Men,
'Tis with the drops which fell from *Shakespear's* Pen.
The Storm which vanish'd on the neighb'ring shore,
Was taught by *Shakespear's* Tempest first to roar.
That Innocence and Beauty which did smile
In *Fletcher*, grew on this *Enchanted Isle*.

(ll. 9–18)

To assert Shakespeare's royal greatness by pointing out that he
provided the raw materials for the two writers who have since
'out-writ all other Men' (including Shakespeare himself?) is praise
of a mixed kind, and it says much about Shakespeare's relation to
Fletcher in the repertory of the 1660s that this first Restoration
appearance of *The Tempest* is both preceded by a revival of
Fletcher's *The Sea-Voyage* (albeit an unsuccessful one—'The Storm
which vanish'd on the neighb'ring shore') and recommended to
the public's notice as Fletcher's source play. Apparently subsumed
by Fletcher and Jonson, Shakespeare is a king who has for the
time being been rendered largely obsolete by his own subjects.
These sneaking reservations about Shakespeare's royal power become more evident as Dryden, implicitly connecting Shakespeare
with Prospero, moves on to describe Shakespeare's presentation of

---

[56] Pepys, an enthusiastic admirer of this play, shows no sign of having gathered
that it was an adaptation at all, referring to it simply as 'an old play of Shakespeare's' (*Diary*, 7 Nov. 1667).

the supernatural as the sole feature of his work not perfected in
the more modern plays of his fellow triumvirs:

But *Shakespear*'s Magick could not copy'd be,
Within that Circle none durst walk but he.
I must confess 'twas bold, nor would you now,
That liberty to vulgar Wits allow,
Which works by Magick supernatural things:
But *Shakespear*'s pow'r is sacred as a King's.
Those Legends from old Priest-hood were receiv'd,
And he then writ, as people then believ'd.
                    (ll. 19–26)

The juxtaposition of Dryden's assertion that 'Shakespear's pow'r
is sacred as a King's' to his dismissal of 'old Priest-hood' and the
superstitions it fostered is a dangerous one: a prologue which
permits Shakespeare to dabble in the discredited realm of the
supernatural on the grounds that he is like a monarch (while
pointedly reminding its audience that they no longer believe in
magic) cannot help but imply a certain enlightened scepticism
about the sanctity of kingship itself.[57] Master of a form of magic
no longer tenable, Shakespeare, in being nostalgically promoted to
the rank of archaic, Divine Right monarch, is in effect being
kicked upstairs, leaving room for his latterday subjects Davenant
and Dryden to get on with rewriting his play.

If hailed with qualified enthusiasm as a father-king, Shakespeare
is none the less presented with considerable awe in this prologue
as a father *per se*, depicted as being capable even posthumously of
fertilizing new reviving trees and declared, in effect, to be the
genetic father of the works of Jonson and Fletcher, their plays
produced by artificial insemination 'with the drops which fell
from Shakespear's pen'. As in his presentation of Shakespeare as
Nature, Dryden is here completely in accordance with the Folio
preliminaries: in fact the language of biological paternity employed by Heminge, Condell, and Jonson, in which Shakespeare's
plays are 'his issue' (F1, 10), can be seen to condition not only
Dryden's explicit representation of Shakespeare as author but the

---

[57] Cf. Gary Taylor, *Reinventing Shakespeare*, 30: '"Shakespear's pow'r is
sacred as a King's"; but in England even the king was not above the law. Like
others, Dryden conspicuously proclaimed the king's supremacy, while in practice
confining it within the limits set by the national rational consensus.'

reauthoring of Shakespeare carried out in the adaptation itself. Defined by Dryden's prologue in terms of the patriarchal family, Shakespeare is rewritten in the same terms in the play that follows. Much as Davenant produces *The Law Against Lovers* by establishing kinship relations between *Much Ado* and *Measure for Measure* (making Angelo into Benedick's brother, making Beatrice cousin to Julietta, and so on), so he and Dryden supplement and qualify Shakespeare's fatherhood of *The Tempest* by extending Prospero's family. In their version, the Duke of Milan acquires two entirely new dependants, a dangerously naïve younger daughter, Dorinda, and an equally troublesome ward, Hippolito.

Just as the addition of Dorinda and Hippolito calls into question Shakespeare's paternal authority over *The Tempest*, so these Restoration contributions to its cast create new problems for Prospero, but the crisis of authority which the play dramatizes has generally been examined simply in terms of the restored monarchy, rather than of the wider family ideology on which that monarchy depended. To Katharine Maus, for example, the adaptation is 'determinedly a play about government',[58] and her own analysis centres on the severe modifications the adaptors impose on Prospero's ducal power. Maus's reading of the play, with which I am in substantial accord, emphasizes its presentation of a qualified version of Stuart patriarchal kingship. The Restoration Prospero, she points out, is more repressive than Shakespeare's (confining Miranda and her new sister Dorinda in one cave and the equally naïve Hippolito in another, and actively resisting their comic attempts to become mutually acquainted), and considerably more vindictive (persecuting an already penitent Alonzo and Antonio and willing to sentence Ferdinand to death after his inadvertent manslaughter of Hippolito). He is also less powerful (unable to prevent the meetings and misunderstandings which lead to this near-tragic incident), and he is further reduced in stature by the expanded antics of the sailors, who, cheerfully ignorant of his

---

[58] Katharine Eisaman Maus, 'Arcadia Lost: Politics and Revision in the Restoration *Tempest*', *Renaissance Drama*, NS 13 (1982), 201. On the more immediate political content of this adaptation, see George R. Guffey, 'Politics, Weather and the Contemporary Reception of the Dryden–Davenant *Tempest*', *Restoration*, 8 (1984), 1–9; James Winn, *John Dryden and his World* (New Haven, Conn., 1987), 187–9.

existence until the end of the fifth act, experiment with alternative forms of government. These comic scenes, while crudely parodying the new contractual theories of popular sovereignty developed during the Interregnum, cannot help but acknowledge their currency and appeal.[59] In the late 1660s, Maus observes, the figure of the father-king was already becoming anachronistic; it is thus not surprising that the revised Prospero seems 'so threatened by change, so willing to resort to repressive tactics in order to maintain his shaky authority' (202). Despite this potentially hostile or satiric view of its senior protagonist, the play remains a conservative one: Prospero is in the end triumphantly restored to his throne without renouncing his magic, and without even having to learn anything, largely thanks to the loyalty and initiative of one particular subject. 'When D'Avenant and Dryden separate Prospero's kingly authority from any special innovative genius, they do not so much repudiate the possibility of political creativity as relocate it,' argues Maus, suggesting that the real hero of the adaptation, the character who despite Prospero's intransigence 'learns to exploit repressive circumstances in creative ways' (206), is Ariel, who by providing a supernatural cure for the catatonic Hippolito enables the play to conclude happily.[60] She thus accounts for the appeal of both the play of 1667 and its operatic expansion of 1674 (the designs for which, she notes, include the royal arms mounted on the centre of the proscenium arch, further stressing the entertainment's engagement with issues of monarchist philosophy) by emphasizing its dramatization of the Restoration's vitiated and anxious loyalty to the Stuart dynasty:

In an era when the Stuart mythology seemed increasingly inappropriate, as well as indispensable, the average Restoration playgoer must have been keenly—even painfully—sensitive to the various claims of competing

---

[59] See especially the first dialogue between Mustacho, Stephano, and Ventoso:

VENT. This Isle's our own, that's our comfort, for the Duke, the Prince, and all their train are perished.
MUST. Our Ship is sunk, and we can never get home agen: we must e'en turn Salvages, and the next that catches his fellow may eat him.
VENT. No, no, let us have a Government . . .

(*The Enchanted Island*, 19)

[60] Given the analogy drawn in Dryden's prologue between Shakespeare and Prospero, this better-informed Ariel, successfully completing (and modifying) Prospero's plans by arts of which his master is ignorant, could easily be read as a figure for the play's adaptors.

ideologies. A play which acknowledged such difficulties, but which also transmuted them into gorgeous and apparently escapist spectacle, must have been extraordinarily compelling. If the Restoration audience greeted the revised *Tempest* with unparalleled enthusiasm, it is probably because Dryden and D'Avenant, and the operatic producers after them, managed to address the hopes and fears of large numbers of their contemporaries.[61]

Persuasive as it is, this account of *The Enchanted Island*'s impact does not seem in itself adequate to explain the popularity Dryden and Davenant's revisions continued to enjoy well into the nineteenth century, more than a hundred years after the patriarchal rationale for monarchical government for which the play's depiction of Prospero offers its limited support had, according to Maus, received its 'death blow' from Locke.[62] I would argue that while the play's initial success, like that of Davenant's *Macbeth*, can certainly be accounted for in part by its successful and ambiguous dramatization of Restoration political conflicts, *The Enchanted Island* owes its lasting appeal to its representation not only of patriarchal monarchy but of the patriarchal family which both provided its basis and served (as it arguably still does) as the last refuge of its ideology. It is not just the authority of father-kings but the authority of fathers *tout court* which is most centrally at stake in *The Enchanted Island* (from the moment Davenant and Dryden begin to alter Shakespeare's 'issue', *The Tempest*), and here again the play is profoundly engaged with the competing claims of Divine Right royalism and contractualism, albeit through its depiction of the familial underpinnings of both.

The only section of Dryden's preface to the play which has anything specific to say about its modifications to Shakespeare's *Tempest*, significantly, draws attention not to Prospero's beleaguered royal vengeance but to his new responsibilities as a parent, Dorinda and Hippolito:

---

[61] Maus, 'Arcadia Lost', 208–9. For other readings of this play, see esp. Don Sheldon Casanave, 'Shakespeare's *The Tempest* in a Restoration Context: A Study of Dryden's *The Enchanted Island*', Ph.D. thesis (University of Michigan, 1972), esp. 39–158; Rothstein and Kavenik, *Carolean Comedy*, 85–107: Rosenthal, 'Shakespearean Adaptation'; Matthew Wikander, '"The Duke My Father's Wrack": The Innocence of the Restoration *Tempest*', *Shakespeare Survey*, 43 (1991), 91–8.

[62] Maus, 'Arcadia Lost', 202. On the later history of this adaptation, see Michael Dobson, '"Remember | First to Possess his Books": The Appropriation of *The Tempest*, 1700–1800', *Shakespeare Survey*, 43 (1991), 99–108.

Sir William Davenant, as he was a man of quick and piercing imagination, soon found that somewhat might be added to the Design of
Shakespear ... and therefore to put the last hand to it, he design'd the
Counterpart to *Shakespear*'s Plot, namely that of a Man who had never
seen a Woman; that by this means those two Characters of Innocence and
Love might the more illustrate and commend each other. This excellent
contrivance he was pleas'd to communicate to me, and to desire my
assistance in it. I confess that from the very first moment it so pleas'd me,
that I never writ any thing with more delight.

('Preface', The Enchanted Island, A2^v)

Few commentators have felt that this 'excellent contrivance' offered
Dryden anything more than the opportunity for what Hazelton
Spencer terms 'genteel smut',[63] but it is at very least striking that
the events which transpire between Miranda, Dorinda, Hippolito,
and Ferdinand on Prospero's desert island supply, however comically, a crucial missing term in the arguments of each of the
conflicting political philosophies identified by Maus as the play's
principal subtexts. Neither patriarchalists like Filmer (who, following James I, argued that the authority of kings in the state
found its ultimate foundation in the 'natural' authority of fathers
within the family) nor contractual theorists such as Hobbes (who
claimed that sovereignty originated in arrangements negotiated in
the state of nature between men for their mutual self-preservation)
provided any account of the 'natural' emergence of the male-
dominated monogamy on which their respective models of civil
society are premised. If patriarchalists were prepared to deny that
this constituted a problem, resorting to the authority of Scripture
('God at the creation gave sovereignty to the man over the woman,'
declared Filmer[64]), contractualists were prepared at least to give
the issue passing attention, and the Restoration's need for (and
failure to provide) an adequate account of the origins of male
sovereignty is accordingly most visible in the work of Hobbes and
Locke. Finding the first origins of power not in divine prescription
but in human parenthood, Hobbes is forced to concede that 'in
the state of nature, every woman that bears children becomes both

---

[63] Hazelton Spencer, *Shakespeare Improved*, 203. See also ibid. 201: 'One aim
and one aim alone animated its authors: to pander.'

[64] Sir Robert Filmer, 'Observations concerning the original of Government'
[1652], in *Patriarcha and Other Political Works*, ed. Peter Laslett (Oxford, 1949),
59.

a *mother* and a *lord* ... in the state of nature it cannot be known who is the *father*, but by testimony of the *mother*; the child therefore is his whose the mother will have it, and therefore her's'.[65] Hobbes's model never explains, however, quite how or why this naturally ordained matriarchy is replaced; but replaced it is, for when Hobbes comes to describe civil society it proves to have been constituted only by 'men ... in the mutual fear they had of each other', and its women are virtually excluded even from the family, which Hobbes defines as either 'a father with sons and servants, grown into a civil person by virtue of his paternal juris-diction' or a 'civil government' of husband over wife where 'the children are the father's' (Hobbes, vi. 121). Locke's *Second Treatise of Government* performs the same elision, abandoning the sexual egalitarianism of the *First Treatise* (which rebuked Filmer for leaving mothers out of the Fifth Commandment) in favour of a view of the origins of government based solely on private prop-erty,[66] which Locke defines as an exclusively male preserve, the product of male labour: in the end he too, for all his scepticism, is forced to resort to scriptural prescription in the form of Adam's condemnation to work after the Fall in order to explain why his anti-patriarchalist model of government remains essentially patri-archal. Whether absolutist or contractual, Restoration political ideology simply failed to account for the subordination of women, and women thus disappear from Hobbes's and Locke's texts at crucial moments, the reasonable transactions by which they have come to be subjected to fathers and husbands never described.[67] Given this lacuna, it seems less strange that *The Enchanted Island*, redesigning the main plot of *The Tempest* to shore up an outmoded belief in Stuart paternalism and altering its comic subplot to flirt heavily with Hobbes, should add the story of how a man and

---

[65] Thomas Hobbes, *The English Works of Thomas Hobbes of Malmesbury*, ed. Sir William Molesworth (11 vols.; 1839–45; Aalen, Germany, 1962): *Philoso-phical Rudiments concerning Government and Society*, ii, 116–17.

[66] 'The greatest and *chief end* therefore of Mens uniting into Commonwealths, and putting themselves under Government, ... is the *Preservation of their Prop-erty*'; Locke, 'Second Treatise of Government', 368–9.

[67] See esp. Carole Pateman's excellent *The Sexual Contract* (Stanford, 1988), 46–9, 52–3, 83–5, 91–4; Hilda L. Smith, *Reason's Disciples: Seventeenth Cen-tury English Feminists* (Urbana, Ill., 1982), ch. 2; Staves, *Players' Scepters*, 136, 140, 142–4. For a contemporary critique of Hobbes on this issue, see Ruth Perry, *The Celebrated Mary Astell* (Chicago, 1986), esp. 201.

woman in a state of nature (or at least a state of total ignorance) come to deduce the 'naturalness' of patriarchal monogamy. The adaptation seems compelled to compensate for the liberties it takes with Shakespeare's paternal rights in *The Tempest* by mounting an insistent defence, in contemporary terms, of fatherly authority itself: its new love plots thereby supply, however playfully, an imaginary solution to a genuine problem in contemporary ideology.

This may sound like a high-flown claim to make for a piece of popular entertainment, and before turning to the text itself it may be worth pointing to a precisely contemporary instance of a similar and rather better-known plot being used to explore just these issues. In the same year that *The Tempest, or the Enchanted Island* had its first performances, a friend and colleague of Davenant and Dryden published his own justification of paternal authority, centring on another account of what happens when a woman who has never seen a man meets a man who has never seen a woman:

> Return fair *Eve*,
> Whom fli'st thou? whom thou fli'st, of him thou art,
> His flesh, his bone; to give thee being I lent
> Out of my side to thee, nearest my heart
> Substantial Life, to have thee by my side
> Henceforth an individual solace dear;
> Part of my Soul I seek thee, and thee claim
> My other half: with that thy gentle hand
> Seiz'd mine, I yielded, and from that time see
> How beauty is excelld by manly grace
> And wisdom, which alone is truly fair.[68]

Like *The Enchanted Island*, *Paradise Lost* explains and naturalizes the social relations between the sexes by appealing to the test case of what happens between a man and woman (uninstructed by custom) in a state of nature: fittingly, Dryden, having co-adapted the one with such 'delight', sought and ultimately received permission to dramatize the other (as *The State of Innocence, and Fall of Man*, 1677). In this passage Milton deals with exactly the problems raised by Hobbes and Locke in the passages cited above,

---

[68] John Milton, *Paradise Lost*, iv. 481–91, in *The Complete Poems*, ed. B. A. Wright and Gordon Campbell (London, 1980).

exactly the issues Dryden tackles in his favourite sections of *The Enchanted Island*. Adam claims authority over Eve not only by God-given superiority (which in itself she does not recognize, turning back from Adam to resume the contemplation of her own reflection in the pool as the passage quoted begins: her acknowledgement of Adam's intellectual pre-eminence, when it comes, follows so closely on her account of his seizure of her wrist that it almost seems to be exacted under threat of force), but, effectively, by the natural right of maternity. The biblical story of Eve's creation from Adam's rib enables Milton to base the subordination of women on precisely that which in Hobbes's description of the state of nature grants them dominion, maternity: Adam, the father of mankind, is also the mother of womankind. Davenant and Dryden's innocent young couples, however, have to be seen to consent to their audience's social norms outside the realm of myth and without divine assistance: in *The Enchanted Island*, empiricism can be seen in the process of supplanting the Great Chain of Being, its love scenes resembling a hybrid between a court masque and a carefully rigged Royal Society experiment.[69]

This 'empirical' display of the natural structure of the family is prompted and enabled by the availability to the Restoration stage of real female bodies: determined to display and exploit to the full the un-Shakespearean novelty of the professional actress, Davenant and Dryden, adding Dorinda to *The Tempest*'s dramatis personae and rewriting Miranda for titillating performance by a woman, simultaneously provide and prescribe female roles. The principal function served by their first dialogue, apart from confirming their complete ignorance of civil society (on which the value of the whole 'experiment' depends), is to demonstrate that even before encountering their respective future mates the sisters, instinctively heterosexual, share an innate enthusiasm for being at the disposal of husbands who will assume their father's authority.

[69] On empiricism and gender in *The Enchanted Island*, see also Catherine Belsey, *The Subject of Tragedy: Identity and Difference in Renaissance Drama* (London, 1985), 81–6. That contemporaries similarly recognized the play as a quasi-scientific inquiry into sexuality and its socialization is suggested by a predominantly gynaecological text from the 1690s, *The Ladies Dictionary*, which refers to Miranda and Hippolito while considering the question 'Suppose a Man and Woman were shut up in a room together, who had never seen nor heard of the difference of Sexes before, how d'ye think they'd behave themselves?—wou'd they ———— ?' N.H., *The Ladies Dictionary; being a general entertainment for the fair-sex* (London, 1694), 95–6.

[MIR.] ... And shortly we may chance to see that thing
  Which you have heard my Father call, a Man.
DOR. But what is that? for yet he never told me.
MIR. I know no more than you: but I have heard
  My Father say we Women were made for him.
DOR. What, that he should eat us, Sister?
MIR. No sure, you see my Father is a man, and yet
  He does us good. I would he were not old.
DOR. Methinks indeed it would be finer, if we two
  Had two young Fathers.
                    (*The Enchanted Island*, 13)

Just as significantly, they display an equally spontaneous predis-
position towards child-rearing:

DOR. How did he come to be our Father too?
MIR. I think he found us when we both were little, and grew within the
  ground.
DOR. Why could he not find more of us? pray sister let you and I look up
  and down one day, to find some little ones for us to play with.
MIR. Agreed ...
                                   (Ibid.)

With an odd insistence readily explicable in terms of the anxieties
about maternity (latent in *The Tempest* itself)[70] voiced by Hobbes
and Milton, Dryden goes on to have Miranda unwittingly agree to
undergo labour pains as the price of her interest in a 'young
Father'. Having been warned by Prospero in her next scene that
she and Dorinda should stay away from Hippolito on the grounds
that 'no woman can come | Neer [men] but she feels a pain full
nine Months' (27), she concludes a particularly Miltonic exchange
with her sister with an explicit if unconscious acceptance of the
penalty of Eve:

MIR. But how shall we hereafter shun him, if we do not Know him first?
DOR. Nay I confess I would fain see him too. I find it in my Nature,
  because my Father has forbidden me ...
MIR. And if I can but scape with life, I had rather be in pain nine Months,
  as my Father threatn'd, than lose my longing.
              [*Exeunt.*]
                         (28)[71]

---

[70] On this now frequently observed aspect of Shakespeare's play, see especially
Stephen Orgel, 'Prospero's Wife', in Margaret Ferguson, Maureen Quilligan, and
Nancy Vickers (eds.), *Rewriting the Renaissance* (Chicago, 1986), 50–64.
[71] There is a curious submerged pun at work here: Miranda's willingness to

After these demonstrations of women's natural aptness for precisely the roles to which seventeenth-century society consigned them (and of their natural contrariness, the pretext for the male authority to which they are subjected), Dryden can move on to justify the ways of marriage to men. The ensuing encounters between the sisters and the two 'young Fathers' are largely dedicated to displaying the reasonableness of matrimony from a perspective simultaneously Hobbesian—as a necessary agreement made between men in the mutual fear they have of each other—and Lockean—as a civil government designed with the chief end of preserving male property. After his first forbidden meeting with Dorinda has come to Prospero's attention, Hippolito seems unproblematically to embrace monogamy as the condition of possession:

PROSP. What would you do to make that Woman yours?
HIP. I'd quit the rest o'th' world that I might live alone with
    Her, she never should be from me. . . .

(47)

It transpires, however, that this unprompted willingness to forsake all others is premissed on his ignorance that any others exist. Condemned after his first interview with Miranda to sharing a cave with Hippolito (a punishment easily as wearisome as the log-shifting it replaces), it is Ferdinand who dispels this ignorance—with drastic results. It soon becomes clear that outside civil society the male of the species is anything but chaste:

HIP. I will have all of that kind, if there be a hundred of 'em.

FERD. But noble youth, you know not what you say.
HIP. Sir, they are things I love, I cannot be without 'em:
    O, how I rejoyce! more women!
FERD. Sir, if you love you must be ty'd to one.
HIP. Ty'd! how ty'd to her?
FERD. To love none but her.
HIP. But, Sir, I find it is against my Nature. . . .

(49–50)

undergo 'labour' as the price of having Ferdinand takes the place of Ferdinand's Adamic labour (his enforced log-carrying, cut by the adaptors) as the price of having Miranda.

Faced with a rival completely ignorant of the claims of civil law, Ferdinand has to resort to more primitive means of securing his rights of possession in Miranda:

[HIP.]   ... I'le have as many as I can,
   That are so good, and Angel-like, as she I love.
   And will have yours.
FERD. Pretty youth, you cannot.
HIP. I can do any thing for that I love.
FERD. I may, perhaps, by force restrain you from it.
HIP. Why, do so if you can. But either promise me
   To love no Woman, or you must try your force.
                                        (50)

Hippolito intuits, true Hobbesian that he is, that for men the 'state of nature' is a state of 'war of all against all' for dominion over women. Startlingly prefiguring Freud's account of the origins of the taboos against incest and endogamy, he even identifies his surrogate father as a combatant: 'I now perceive that *Prospero* was cunning; | For when he frighted me from woman-kind, | Those precious things he for himself design'd' (51).[72] Finding himself inextricably caught up in this primal struggle, Ferdinand is in effect reduced to the same state of nature as that of the naïve islanders, and in the following scene he comes to believe, after Miranda has artlessly tried to persuade him to 'love' Hippolito for her sake, that natural women are as sexually anarchic as the natural man he has just met. In keeping with the whole tenor of the play's rationalistic interest in providing empirical, natural origins for gender roles, Ferdinand's aside supplies a quasi-scientific explanation for Miranda's apparent wantonness:

It is too plain: like most of her frail Sex, she's false,
But has not learnt the art to hide it;
Nature has done her part, she loves variety:
Why did I think that any Woman could be innocent,
Because she's young? No, no, their Nurses teach them
Change, when with two Nipples they divide their
Liking.
                                        (54)

---

[72] Cf. Sigmund Freud, *Totem and Taboo: Resemblances Between the Psychic Lives of Savages and Neurotics*, tr. A. A. Brill; (London, 1919), 1–30.

The perception of the state of nature as a sexual free-for-all is further elaborated in the scene immediately following this revelation, where Trincalo (Shakespeare's Trinculo), having paired off with Caliban's new sister Sycorax to claim the island by matrimonial alliance, finds himself at odds first with Caliban:

TRINC. Why then I'le tell thee, I found her an hour ago under an Elder-tree, upon a sweet Bed of Nettles, singing Tory, Rory, and Ranthum, Scanthum, with her own natural Brother.
STEPH. O Jew! make love in her own Tribe?

(63)

and then, in what becomes a full-scale (English) Civil War involving the entire cast of the sub-plot, with Stephano:

VENT. Who took up Arms first, the Prince or the People?
TRINC. This false Traytor has corrupted the Wife of my Bosom.

(64)

Once the next scene has shown Ferdinand, sufficiently desperate to lay aside his scruples about Hippolito's complete ignorance of swordplay, killing the right heir of the dukedom of Mantua in a duel (incidentally confirming the justice of Prospero's parental edict against premature dating), the adaptors feel they have gone far enough in demonstrating the disadvantages of sexuality without civil government, and the play promptly sets about resolving itself by hurriedly constructing the institution of marriage from scratch. Hippolito, recovering from his wound after being magically revived by Ariel, is nursed by Miranda, while Dorinda begs Prospero to spare Ferdinand's life. As a result, all four young lovers rapidly find themselves entangled in jealousies and misunderstandings which, on purely mathematical grounds, can be resolved without further bloodshed only by the adoption of conjugal fidelity on all sides:

FERD. We all accuse each other, and each one denys their guilt,
  I should be glad it were a mutual errour.
  And therefore first to clear myself from fault,
  Madam, I beg your pardon, while I say I only love
  Your Sister.   [To Dorinda.
MIR. O blest word!

I'm sure I love no man but *Ferdinand*.
DOR. Nor I, Heav'n knows, but my *Hippolito*.
HIP. I never knew I lov'd so much, before I fear'd
    Dorinda's constancy; but now I am convinc'd that
    I lov'd none but her, because none else can
    Recompence her loss.

(78)[73]

In the end, the fear of other men and the jealous desire to preserve his property convince even Hippolito of the empirical necessity for marriage: the hereditary princes and princesses prove to be better versed in social contract theory than the mutinous Commonwealth-men of the sub-plot. At this fortunate moment, legitimate paternal authority arrives on the stage in the persons of Prospero and Alonzo, and the former, ratifying the arrangement, goes on further to underline the dividing and ruling of women by men which it entails:

[PROSP.] I give you my *Dorinda* for your Wife, she shall
    Be yours for ever, when the Priest has made you one ...
   ·   ·   ·   ·   ·   ·   ·   ·   ·   ·
... *to his daughter*.] My *Ariel* told me, when last night you quarrel'd

You said you would for ever part your beds,
But what you threaten'd in your anger, Heaven
Has turn'd to Prophecy;
For you, *Miranda*, must with *Ferdinand*,
And you, *Dorinda*, with *Hippolito* lye in
One Bed hereafter.

(79–80)

Preoccupied to the last with displaying the natural subordination of motherhood to fatherhood, the final words Dryden has Miranda

---

[73] That Dryden and Davenant's conservative solution to the problem of a sexuality perceived as inherently lawless depends on their careful provision of equal numbers of eligible women and eligible men is suggested by another contemporary text interested in the same issues in which the mathematics work out very differently, Henry Neville's *The Isle of Pines, or, A Late Discovery of a forth Island near Terra Australis, Incognita* (1668). Its narrator, an Englishman who with one Negress and four Englishwomen has populated a hitherto unoccupied island with 47 second-generation inhabitants, concludes that monogamy is a mere arbitrary social convention, he and his colleagues having ceased to feel guilt soon after their arrival; 'custom taking away the shame, there being none but us, we did it more openly, as our lust gave us liberty'. Philip Henderson (ed.), *Shorter Novels: Seventeenth Century* (New York, 1930), 233.

and Dorinda utter in the entire play reinforce yet again their untaught eagerness to supply their governors with heirs:

ALONZ. And Heaven make those Beds still fruitful in
  Producing Children to bless their Parents
  Youth, and Grandsires age.
MIR. TO DOR. If Children come by lying in a Bed, I wonder you
  And I had none between us.
DOR. Sister it was our fault, we meant like fools
  To look 'em in the fields, and they it seems
  Are only found in Beds.

(80)

Having thus emphatically confirmed the sisters' perfect readiness for normal married life, it remains only for Dryden and Davenant to discipline the mutinous sailors (who, driven on to the stage by Ariel, yield perfunctorily to legitimate authority and bid a relieved farewell to Sycorax and Caliban) and have Prospero free Ariel before bidding a fond adieu to the Enchanted Island; the audience can then be sent home both entertained and reassured. Whether inclined to support the explicitly patriarchal ideology of the Stuart monarchy or the implicitly patriarchal ideology of the contractualism which would ultimately come to replace it, no spectator, monarch or commoner, needed to feel antagonized by this ingenious defence of domestic patriarchy itself. 'The house mighty full; the King and Court there,' summed up Pepys after the première, 'and the most innocent play that ever I saw ... no great wit; but yet good, above ordinary plays. Thence home with W. Penn, and there all mightily pleased with the play' (*Diary*, 7 Nov. 1667).

While in this way *The Enchanted Island* seems to offer a comfortably unambiguous view of fatherhood and nature alike, there is one important respect in which it none the less encodes a troubling counter-story about gender both more subversive (and, as things turned out, more finally royalist) than this interpretation alone would suggest. If the staged female body, however its advent may mandate the violation of Shakespeare's authority through rewriting, is in the persons of Miranda and Dorinda suitably and willingly subjected to paternal authority, it is deployed elsewhere in *The Enchanted Island* in ways which threaten to overbalance the play's account of the family altogether. To return once more

to Dryden's prologue, in being introduced to the play's central
concerns the audience are alerted neither to the adaptation's modifications to the role of Prospero nor to its elaboration of Shakespeare's original love plot, but instead have their attention directed
to another metamorphosis entirely:

> But, if for *Shakespear* we your grace implore,
> We for our Theatre shall want it more:
> Who by our dearth of Youths are forc'd t'employ
> One of our Women to present a Boy.
> And that's a transformation you will say
> Exceeding all the Magick in the Play.
> Let none expect in the last Act to find,
> Her Sex transform'd from man to Woman-kind.
> What e're she was before the Play began,
> All you shall see of her is perfect man.
>
> (ll. 27–36)

Exceeding all the magic in the play, the actress's body is in this
instance in dangerous excess, too, of the supposedly normative
male role it inhabits. Accepting one widespread hypothesis as to
which Duke's Company actress in particular presented a boy on
this occasion, Mary ('Moll') Davis can be accorded a major place
in English theatrical history as the first ever Principal Boy, creating
the role of the 'Pritty youth' Hippolito and thereby adding dimen-
sions to the performance which both blur and threaten the play's
ostensible meaning.[74] Dryden's explanation to his auditors that
they are not to confuse the boyish Hippolito's role in the narrative
with the supposedly extraneous fact that it is being played by a
woman invites scrutiny of the very detail it seems to be requesting
them to overlook, and the play itself, apart from profiting visually
throughout from the display of Davis's famous legs in close-fitting
breeches, regularly derives comic capital from its audience's aware-
ness of what else those breeches do and do not conceal. Hippolito's
first dialogue with Ferdinand provides a typical example:

---

[74] Although the *London Stage* speculates that Jane Long may have played
Hippolito (1: 123), see John Harold Wilson, *All the King's Ladies: Actresses of the
Restoration* (Chicago, 1958), 83; Jocelyn Powell, *Restoration Theatre Production*
(London, 1984), 72; Wikander, 'The Duke My Father's Wrack', 96. I am grateful
to Laura Rosenthal for a draft copy of her unpublished essay on the Restoration
actress, 'Counterfeit Scrubbado' (1991), which is similarly interested in the role of
Hippolito.

[FERD.] So give me leave to ask you, what you are.
HIP. Do not you know?
FERD. How should I?
HIP. I well hop'd I was a man, but by your ignorance
   Of what I am, I fear it is not so:
   Well, *Prospero*! this is now the second time
   You have deceiv'd me.

                                                        (48)

Here specifically opposed to the version of the truth about gender
offered by the legitimate patriarch within the play, the audience's
knowledge of the 'real' sex of Hippolito suggests a perspective on
the relations between maternity and paternity diametrically opposite to the one on which the play otherwise appears to insist. The
casting of Davis as a boy draws an equation between youth and
femaleness that, contradicting Milton's biblical story of how
women originate from men, highlights the anxious truth (briefly
acknowledged by Hobbes) that men develop from women.[75] The
play comically underlines this point; Hippolito's initial disability
in competing with Ferdinand, after all, derives from the fact that
he has not yet acquired a sword (a 'lack' perhaps punningly
suggested by the prologue's 'dearth of Youths'), and this *risqué*
pun is made explicit later in the play during his jealousy-provoking
therapeutic encounter with Miranda.

   [*Enter* Miranda . . . *with* Hippolito's *Sword wrapt up* . . .]
MIR. I am come to ease you. [*She unwraps the Sword.*
HIP. Alas! I feel the cold air come to me,
   My wound shoots worse than ever.
                        [*She wipes and anoints the Sword.*
MIR. Does it still grieve you?
HIP. Now methinks there's something laid just upon it.
MIR. Do you find no ease?
HIP. Yes, yes, upon the sudden all the pain
   Is leaving me, sweet Heaven how I am eas'd!

                                                    (76−7)[76]

The text of the play may claim that the differences between men
and women are naturally ordained givens, but this troubling

---

[75] Cf. the classical, Galenic account of sexual difference, in which the male
sexual organs are simply the 'perfected' form of the female: on this model, see esp.
Thomas Laqueur, *Making Sex: Body and Gender from the Greeks to Freud*
(Cambridge, Mass., 1990), 25−62.
[76] On the staging of this scene, see Powell, *Restoration Theatre Production*, 74.

anomaly in its realization, pointed up by the script without ever being explained away in the plot, seems instead to dramatize the fact that sexual roles are just that—roles; and alarmingly dependent on mere props at that. Even more potentially disturbing than the Elizabethan stage practice it inverts (which persists in the sub-plot, Sycorax—in the adaptation not Caliban's dam but his Dame—being played by a man), Mary Davis's performance seems to suggest that the masculine may be a mere constructed sub-set of the feminine, capable of being assumed for the entirety of *The Tempest* so successfully that at its conclusion Prospero appears to sanction the sexual union of two women.[77] If Shakespeare's *Tempest* obsessively expels the matriarchal and polices the female,[78] this aspect of its Restoration variant stages their revenge.

The prologue, however, has anticipated this dangerous reading, and its concluding couplet does all it can to claim the transvestite prince in advance for patriarchally authorized, empirically determinable gender categories:

> Or if your fancy will be farther led,
> To find her Woman, it must be abed.
>
> (ll. 37–8)

Hippolito/Davis's 'real' gender can, finally, be proven (in every sense), but not in the theatre, nor in any legitimate sphere of social relations at all, but only as a by-product of the sexual services she may perform to supplement her theatrical income. This tantalizing joke-cum-invitation, which can promise real 'knowledge' of Hippolito/Davis's sex only to someone willing to act as her keeper, was in fact taken up within a month of *The Enchanted Island*'s première—by Charles Stuart, king of England.[79] For the rest of the audience, Hippolito's problematic gender remained just another

---

[77] Davis/Hippolito's performance had been anticipated in this respect by the all-women production of Killigrew's *The Parson's Wedding* in October 1664, which would be revived, alongside all-women productions of Beaumont and Fletcher's *Philaster* and Dryden's *Secret Love; or, the Maiden Queen*, at Lincoln's Inn Fields in June 1672. See the prologues and epilogues preserved in *Covent Garden Drollery*, 1–4, 14–16, esp. the prologue and epilogue to *Secret Love*, ascribed to Dryden (1–3), which make explicit many of the sexual undercurrents of the Hippolito scenes in *The Enchanted Island*.

[78] See Orgel, 'Prospero's Wife'.

[79] On Davis's liaison with the king, see Downes, *Roscius Anglicanus*, 55; Pepys, *Diary*, 11 Jan. 1668; Philip H. Highfill, Kalman A. Burnim, and Edward A. Larghams, *A Biographical Dictionary of Actors, Actresses, Musicians, Dancers,*

matter on which, for the time being, they would have to accept royal authority.

Both the rigorously orthodox and the potentially subversive perspectives on fatherhood (royal, domestic, and authorial) presented by this adaptation are helpfully glossed by the most detailed contemporary commentary which survives, Thomas Duffett's *The Mock-Tempest*, a meticulous travesty of the Duke's Company's slightly expanded, operatic *Enchanted Island* (prepared by Thomas Shadwell in 1674),[80] first performed by the rival King's Company in November of 1674. Attesting to the popularity and familiarity of *The Enchanted Island* by its very existence, Duffett's skit, like many other contemporary exercises in travesty and burlesque, veers between inverting and traducing its original and simply replicating it in slightly recast terms, and many of its scenes seem rather to explicate than to satirize the play it parodies. This becomes clear even in Duffett's 'Introduction', which glosses Dryden's parting joke about the sexual availability of Dorset Garden's Hippolito/Moll Davis with an extended piece of mock blackmail offered on the play's behalf by Drury Lane's more democratic hermaphrodite, Betty Mackarel, a notoriously promiscuous orange-seller promoted on this occasion to the onstage role of Ariel:

[MR. HAINS] Think of thy high calling *Betty*, now th'art here,
   They gaze and wish, but cannot reach thy Sphere,
   Though ev'ry one could squeeze thy Orange there.
   .   .   .   .
   Examin[e] your Consciences Gentlemen!
   When urg'd with heat of love, and hotter Wine,

Managers, and Other Stage Personnel in London, 1660–1800 (10 vols. to date; Carbondale, Ill., 1973–), (hereafter *BDA*), iv. 222–6: on the status of such liaisons see Katharine Eisaman Maus, 'Playhouse Flesh and Blood: Sexual Ideology and the Restoration Actress', *English Literary History*, 46 (1979), 595–617. Both the convergence of Charles's royal and sexual authority and this final definition of Hippolito/Davis's gender purely by male sexual knowledge are usefully glossed by Rochester: 'His sceptre and his prick are of a length' (*A Satyr on Charles II*, l. 11, in *The Complete Poems of John Wilmot, Earl of Rochester*, ed. David M. Vieth (New Haven, Conn., 1968), 60), and 'Where'er it pierced, a cunt it found or made' (*The Imperfect Enjoyment*, l. 43, ibid. 39).

[80] See Downes, *Roscius Anglicanus*, 73–4; for the text, see Sir William Davenant and John Dryden [and Thomas Shadwell], *The Tempest, or the Enchanted Island* (London, 1674).

How have you begg'd, to gain your lewd design:
Betty, dear, dear, dear *Betty*,
I'le spend five Guinnyes on thee, if thou'lst go:
And then they shake their (d'ee conceive me) *Betty* is't not so, their
    yellow Boyes?
BET. Fie Mr. *Hains*, y'are very rude (d'ee conceive me).
HA. Then speak your self.
BET. Gentlemen! you know what I know.
  If y'are severe, all shall out by this light:
  But if you will be kind, I'le still be right.[81]

The royal dimension of Dryden's reference to the sexual favours
of actresses is alluded to later in Duffett's play, when a sly *double
entendre* has the performer playing Dorinda hint that she has been
subjected to the same monarchical scrutiny as Moll Davis:

MIR. Are you not breeding Teeth Sister?
DOR. Zooks, if I am, the King shall know't.
      (Duffett, *Mock-Tempest*, 92–3)

Like these two jokes, the main plot of *The Mock-Tempest* generally
takes up and amplifies points made in Dryden and Davenant's text
without structurally modifying them. Duffett's travesty supports a
reading of its original as a play centrally concerned with the
defence of the contemporary patriarchal family, a concern which
the travesty, transferring the story's location from a desert island
to low-life Restoration London, can make still more explicit: in
Duffett's play, Prospero, demoted from ducal status, is the keeper
of the Bridewell prison for prostitutes, the state's official punisher
of unruly women.[82] The only important difference between the
love plots of the original and their revision in the travesty lies in
Duffett's replacement of the 'innocence' of Dryden's 'genteel smut'
with an inverted and openly cynical view of matrimony: Duffett's
Miranda and Dorinda are ignorant not of men (far from it, as the
above quotation suggests) but simply of husbands:

---

[81] Thomas Duffett, *The Mock-Tempest: or the Enchanted Castle*, in *Three
Burlesque Plays of Thomas Duffett*, ed. R. E. DiLorenzo (Iowa City, 1972), 59–
60. Cf. the opening of Miranda's epilogue: 'Gentlemen look'ee now, pray, my
Father sayes that I and my Sister must have ye all i'fads'. ibid. 111.

[82] The concerns of *The Enchanted Island* are further glossed a decade later by
Thomas Durfey's closely imitative semi-opera adaptation of, ironically, *The Sea-
Voyage*, the Fletcher play cited in Dryden's prologue as already a derivative of *The
Tempest*: Durfey's imitation is entitled *A Commonwealth of Women* (London,
1686).

DOR. Husband, what's that?

MIR. Why that's a thing like a man (for ought I know) with a great pair of Hornes upon his head, and my father said 'twas made for Women, look ye.

DOR. What, must we ride to water upon't Sister?

MIR. No, no, it must be our Slave, and give us Golden Cloaths Pray, that other men may lye with us in a Civil way, and then it must Father our Children and keep them.

DOR. And when we are so Old and Ugly, that no body else will lye with us, must it lye with us it self?

MIR. Ay that it must Sister.

(73)

The reduction of the original's crucial terms 'civil' and 'father' to their weakest senses (as here, where 'civility' is reduced to a style and 'fathering' to a social fiction) is one of the travesty's favourite running jokes: meanwhile the structure of the plot remains the same—the two girls, already gleefully predisposed to the roles of Restoration wives as defined by Prospero, learn to acquire appropriate husbands, Duffett's reversal of Dryden's prescriptions for marriage (his presentation of docile husbands as the convenient properties of naturally promiscuous wives) underlining the original's insistence on the contrary perspective. *The Mock-Tempest*, like *The Enchanted Island*, is open to readings which regard it as a vindication of the subordination of women to patriarchal control (its sub-plot, duplicating the original's equations between sexual and political government, translates the republican mutineers into a team of whores undergoing due punishment in Prospero's jail), and equally to readings which instead view the play as complicit with all of its disorderly women, from the ludicrously cross-dressed Betty Mackarel onwards. Whichever reading one adopts, it is clear that Duffett's play registers the fact that *The Tempest, or the Enchanted Island* owed at least part of its overwhelming appeal for Restoration playgoers to its spectacular contribution, elaborated from its own unease about the paternal Shakespeare it both underwrites and undermines, to the continuing debates about the family and its relation to contemporary politics.

The immense success of *The Enchanted Island*—which became the most frequently revived play of the entire Restoration period —had an enormous influence on the theatrical treatment of Shakespeare's plays over the next two decades. Its placing of either added or supplemented domestic female roles at the centre of its revisions to Shakespeare's subject-matter is followed closely, for example, in each of the next two adaptations to be produced, Dryden's own *All for Love*, 1678 (the climax of which, in many ways, is the personal confrontation it adds to *Antony and Cleopatra* between Cleopatra and Octavia) and Shadwell's *The History of Timon of Athens, the Man-Hater*, 1678 (which elaborates on Shakespeare's opposition between false friends and faithful servants to complicate Timon's personal life with a mercenary fiancée, Melissa, and a loyal mistress, Evandra), and is developed still more importantly in the wave of adaptations produced over the following four years. But however influentially *The Enchanted Island* thus helped to modify Shakespeare's authorial profile, it is its oddly scant acknowledgement of his original authorship which is perhaps the most striking feature, to modern readers, of this *Tempest*, as of all the adaptations of the 1660s. The 1674 quarto of Davenant's *Macbeth* mentions neither Shakespeare nor Davenant, recording only that the edition offers the text 'with all the alterations, amendments, additions and new songs. As it is now Acted at the Dukes Theatre', just as the quarto of Davenant's 1664 *Two Noble Kinsmen* mentions neither Davenant, Shakespeare, nor Fletcher (giving the play simply as *The Rivals: a comedy: acted by His Highnes the Duke of York's servants*). Similarly, the printed text of Lacy's version of *The Taming of the Shrew* credits only its adaptor (*Sauny the Scott: or, the Taming of the Shrew: A Comedy. As it is now ACTED at the THEATRE-ROYAL. Written by J. LACEY, Servant to His MAJESTY. And Never before Printed*); and, as we have seen, *The Law Against Lovers* is quietly published in 1673 as entirely Davenant's. Duffett's *Mock-Tempest*, so far from attempting to vindicate the usurped author of the original *Tempest*, never mentions the Swan of Avon at all, and, furthermore, clearly finds the Shakespearean passages retained by the adaptors among the more obviously ludicrous aspects of the play. *The Mock-Tempest*'s version of 'Full fathom five', for example, includes the lines 'Youth of mortal race, give ear, | Thy Daddies dead, thy Daddies dead. . . . His feet Stockfish, his ears Pilchards, his flesh | Thornback . . .' (88), and its rendition of Prospero's first dialogue with Miranda provides further evidence of Duffett's sense of the fustiness of the surviving Shakespearean passages:

PROS. Thy Mother was all Mettle.—As true as Steel, as right's my Legg, and she said thou wert my Daughter; canst thou remember when thou wert Born, sure thou canst not, for then thou wert but three days old.

MIR. I'fads, I do remember it Father, as well as 'twere but yesterday.

PROS. Then scratch thy tenacious Poll, and tell me what thou findest backward in the misty back and bottomless Pit of time.

(71)

In fact without resort to the Shakespeare Folio, Duffett, even had he cared, would have had no way of knowing precisely which parts of the adaptation derived directly from Shakespeare and which did not: Dryden's paean to Shakespeare's Magic never explicitly points out that it has been drastically altered in the play which is to follow, and his preface to the printed edition (not published until 1670) gives the impression that he and Davenant have altered *The Tempest* only by adding the Hippolito/Dorinda scenes and some of '*The Comical parts of the Saylors*'.[83] The title pages of this edition and of all the many subsequent editions of Shadwell's operatic expansion which succeed it after 1674 mention no writer at all, describing the play only as 'a Comedy; as it is now acted at His Highness the Duke of York's theatre'. In the 1660s, Shakespeare is not quite the author of his own texts: his plays belong in part to the theatres, and in part to anyone prepared to undertake the work required to make them worth performing there. However strenuously *The Tempest* is mobilized by Dryden and Davenant in the cause of patriarchy, Shakespeare's plays themselves remain just outside the account of authoritative paternity their adaptation offers, treated by the playwrights of the 1660s as orphaned and available portions of 'Nature' not yet fully identified as the property of the fertile authorial body hymned by Dryden's prologue. It is the construction of this crucial missing link between William Shakespeare's body and the Shakespearean corpus, the retrospective invention of Shakespeare as himself a Lockean economic individualist, which conclusively establishes the Bard as the author of his own works, a process delayed until the early eighteenth century. From the 1670s through the 1700s, as my next chapter will show, the most crucial determinant both of Shakespeare's authorial persona and of the shape of his texts remains the political situation of the playhouses.

---

[83] 'Preface', *The Enchanted Island*, A2^v ff.

2

Politics and Pity

THE Fletcherian version of romance towards which Davenant manipulated *Measure for Measure*, *Macbeth*, and *The Tempest* in the 1660s had lost its ascendancy in the theatrical repertory by the end of the next decade. In the late 1670s and early 1680s a completely new wave of Shakespeare adaptations appeared (nine between October 1678 and June 1682 alone), chiefly of tragedies and histories, which, while sharing the interest in female roles of their early Restoration precursors, ransack their Shakespearean originals in search of quite different generic patterns. These new adaptations pursue modes either unknown since before the Civil Wars or completely unprecedented—less reassuring forms of tragicomedy, variations on the chronicle play and, in particular, affective tragedy. Generically different from their predecessors, these plays are also different in their orientation towards Shakespeare. While of all the 1660s' adaptations only *The Enchanted Island* boasts a prologue discussing the author of its source play, of the nine alterations produced during the Exclusion Crisis only three do not explicitly and extensively advertise themselves as derived from Shakespearean originals. The accession of Shakespeare to full authorial status gathers fresh momentum here; and it owes a great deal to the specific and extraordinary circumstances of these four theatrical seasons.[1]

Although extensively revived and panegyrized at this time, Shakespeare proved neither infallibly profitable nor safely uncontroversial. Of the nine adaptations produced, five, it is true, would remain in the repertory for over forty years—Edward Ravenscroft's *Titus Andronicus, or, The Rape of Lavinia* (1678), John Dryden's *Troilus and Cressida; or, Truth Found Too Late* (1679), Thomas Otway's *The History and Fall of Caius Marius* (based on

---

[1] For a general survey of developments in the theatrical repertory over this crucial period, see Hume, *Development of English Drama*, 340–60; *The London Stage*, 1: 271–312. See also John Loftis, *The Politics of Drama in Augustan England* (Oxford, 1963), 15–21.

Romeo and Juliet; 1679), Nahum Tate's celebrated *The History of King Lear* (1681), and Thomas Durfey's *The Injured Princess* (from *Cymbeline*, 1682)—and these plays would furthermore be closely imitated by subsequent adaptors: but of the other four, two disappeared without trace (John Crowne's *The Misery of Civil-War*, from *3 Henry VI*, and Nahum Tate's *The Ingratitude of a Common-Wealth: Or, the Fall of Caius Martius Coriolanus*), and two were actively suppressed by the Lord Chamberlain, namely Nahum Tate's *The History of King Richard the Second* (1680) and John Crowne's *Henry the Sixth, The First Part* (1681).[2] Despite a tradition (dating back to the mid-eighteenth century) of reading these adaptations simply as object lessons in the follies of neo-classicism,[3] these two acts of state censorship provide the most accurate indication of the reasons behind this sudden renewal of interest in Shakespeare. Between 1678 and 1682, both the state and the stage were suffering the consequences of Titus Oates's terrifying allegations that an imminent 'Popish Plot' was about to decimate the Anglican establishment and force Britain to return to the Catholic fold:[4] these consequences included not only bills in Parliament to exclude Charles's Catholic brother James from the throne, a spate of executions for treason, and the largest street processions seen in London since the Civil Wars, but also, I shall argue, the revival of *Titus Andronicus*, *Troilus and Cressida*, *Romeo and Juliet*, *King Lear*, and *Cymbeline* in versions which participate in and enact the ideological turmoil of this extraordinary passage of constitutional history. The Exclusion Crisis, with its multiple paranoias about aristocratic Catholic conspiracies to destroy the Church of England and Dissenting schemes to restart the English Revolution, generated a theatrical climate in which every play produced was potentially controversial, certain to be scrupulously interrogated by censors and audiences alike for

---

[2] See *The London Stage*, 1: xxix, lxiii, cxlviii, 293–4.

[3] See e.g. William Guthrie, *An Essay upon English Tragedy. With Remarks upon the Abbe de Blanc's Observations on the English Stage* (London, 1747), 10, where the additions of this period are stigmatized as 'the tinsel ornaments of the French academy' (quoted below, ch. 5): cf. Odell, *Shakespeare from Betterton to Irving*, i. 79.

[4] See Titus Oates, *A True Narrative of the Horrid Plot and Conspiracy of the Popish Party Against the Life of His Sacred Majesty, The Government and the Protestant Religion* (London, 1679). On the whole crisis, see esp. J. P. Kenyon, *The Popish Plot* [1972], (Harmondsworth, 1984).

covert or explicit propagandist intentions, secret plots or dangerous sympathies, and this flurry of adaptations demands to be read
not as an anthology of inept Shakespeare criticism but as a series
of often astute experiments in politicizing and depoliticizing the
contemporary stage.[5] Recognizing two advantages possessed by
unpolished Shakespeare over the more courtly Jonson and Fletcher
—his mastery of pathos, and his creation of a body of plays
specifically concerned with British history—these adaptations,
furthermore, promote a simultaneously domestic and national
Shakespeare, susceptible of being praised for his timeless ability to
move the heart even as his plays are being rewritten for immediate
polemical ends.

Politics and Genre

A ludicrous fiction with fatal consequences, a matter for carnival
processions and public executions, the Popish Plot almost inevitably inspired a polemical literature of profound generic uncertainty, an uncertainty which decisively infects the adaptations
composed at this time. Even outside the theatre, indeed, the confusions and contradictions of these four anxious years are pervasively registered in dramatic terms. Summing up after the accession
of James II, an anonymous poem celebrated Oates's ultimate flog-
ging for perjury as *The Tragick-Comedy of Titus Oates* (1685);[6]
this sense of the whole affair as a breach of normal categories of
experience was already widespread during the climax of Plot fever
in 1678–9, when even writers utterly convinced of the gravity and
literal truth of Oates's narrative found themselves unsure as to
what mode of composition could best vilify the Catholics, simultaneously imagined in terms of comic folly and of tragic villainy.
For example, a flippant pamphlet describing an anti-Catholic
demonstration in Wales, *The Pope's Down-fall at Abergaveny*,

---

[5] On the politics of this spate of Shakespeare adaptations, see esp. Matthew H.
Wikander, 'The Spitted Infant: Scenic Emblem and Exclusionist Politics in Restoration Adaptations of Shakespeare', *Shakespeare Quarterly*, 37 (1986), 340–58. See
also Sorelius, *Giant Race*, 187–95.

[6] Oates himself sought to reappropriate this dramatic metaphor in less ambiguous terms a decade later, when he attempted a comeback (with new allegations,
this time about a plot to kill William of Orange) in a pamphlet entitled *A tragedy,
called the Popish plot, reviv'd* (London, 1696).

anxiously corrects its apparent light-heartedness by assuring its readers that 'this Comical Act that afforded so much pleasure and contentment to the Spectators, ended with a Tragical Epilogue',[7] appending a thoroughly apocryphal story of how one local Catholic proselyte, enraged by his Anglican father's merry description of the proceedings over supper, committed parricide with the carving knife (6). Reversing this order of incompatible genres, each issue of Henry Care's savage *The Weekly Pacquet of Advice from Rome* (1678–83) is supplied with a supplement, *The Popish Courant, or, Some occasional Jaco-serious Reflections on Romish Fopperies* (a collection of trivial jests at the expense of saints and nunneries), the first issue of which, in equally theatrical manner, likens the Irish priests allegedly preparing for an invasion of England to Falstaff's regiment in *1 Henry IV*.[8] Care repeats this format for his subsequent *New Anti-Roman Pacquet, or, The Memoirs of Popes and Popery since the Tenth Century* (1680), published with the appendix *The Popes Harbinger, By way of Diversion*, which demotes Catholicism to an even lower form of diversion:

Our *Church of Rome* is wont to compare herself to the *Sun* in the Meridian, to a *City* on a hill, to a *Ship* at Sea, and to I know not what besides; but let me never be a *Cardinal*, if I can meet with anything that more exactly resembles her than *Bartholdom Fair*.[9]

In fact by the time this issue of *The Popes Harbinger* appeared, both of these tropes—the degradation of Catholicism to tragicomic theatre and its banishment to Bartholomew Fair—had already been literally enacted, in some of the first texts to register the impact of the crisis on the drama itself. William J. Burling, discussing the cessation of summer productions at the patent houses between 1678 and 1681, speculates about a 'declining interest in

---

[7] *The Pope's Down-fall at Abergaveny* (London, 1679), 5.

[8] Henry Care, *The Popish Courant, or, Some occasional Jaco-serious Reflections on Romish Fopperies* (London, 1678–83), 8. This ploy of likening Catholics to something from Shakespearean comedy would be echoed by John Crowne, whose dedication to *Henry the Sixth, The First Part* remarks that 'What serves here to make the Comical part of a Play, does in the Popish Countries compose the gravest part of their Devotion.' John Crowne, *Henry the Sixth, The First Part. With the Murder of Humphrey Duke of Gloucester* (London, 1681), 'Epistle Dedicatory', A2.

[9] Henry Care, *The Popes Harbinger, By Way of Diversion* (London, 1680), 63.

the theatre due to political events, such as the Popish Plot',[10] but (laying aside the fascination with theatre as metaphor illustrated above) if such a decline is discernible in the takings of the two legitimate theatres, no such decline affected the illegitimate ones. The Plot panic led to an insatiable demand for topical drama of all kinds, at no matter what venue: indeed, the largest public demonstrations it inspired took the form of street theatre, in the shape of elaborate annual processions to burn effigies of the pope and his alleged agents at Temple Bar on the anniversary of Queen Elizabeth's accession, 17 November, which in 1679 and 1680 were designed and scripted by the Whig playwright Elkanah Settle.[11] At Bartholomew and Southwark fairs, theatrical booths thrived, to the scorn and dismay of reputable playwrights such as Dryden, whose prologue to Tate's *The Loyal General* in 1679 contemptuously urges the less refined section of his audience to 'Go back to your dear dancing on the rope, | Or see what's worse, the Devil and the Pope.'[12] The earliest of these fairground plays to survive from the plot period is, to quote the whole of its title page:

The Coronation of Queen Elizabeth, With The Restauration of the Protestant Religion: or, The Downfal of the Pope. Being a most Excellent Play, As it was Acted, both at Bartholomew and Southwark Fairs, This present Year 1680. With great Applause, and Approved of, and highly Commended by all the Protestant Nobility, Gentry and Commonalty of England, who came to be Spectators of the same.

[10] William J. Burling, 'Summer Theatre in London, 1661–1694', *Theatre Notebook*, 47 (1988), 19.

[11] An anonymous engraving, *The Solemn Mock Procession of the Pope Cardinalls Jesuits Fryars &c: through the Citty of London November the 17th, 1680* (London, 1680), commemorates Settle's second, most developed work in this genre: at the close of the event, after the Pope's effigy had been burnt in front of a statue of Elizabeth 'adorn'd with a Crown of Laurel, and a Shield, on which was inscrib'd Protestant Religion and *Magna Charta*', the 'Protestant' represented undergoing the tortures of the Inquisition on the ninth and final pageant-wagon broke free and addressed a poem to Elizabeth I, in effect an epilogue; see Frank C. Brown, *Elkanah Settle: His Life and Works* (Chicago, 1910), 61–4. On these processions, which remained an important annual event in popular political culture well into the 18th cent., see Tim Harris, *London Crowds in the Reign of Charles II: Propaganda and Politics from the Restoration until the Exclusion Crisis* (Cambridge, 1987), 120–8.

[12] Nahum Tate, *The Loyal General* (London, 1679), 'Prologue, by Mr. Dryden'. On such anti-Catholic drolls, see also the poem 'Bartholomew-Fayr' in *A Choice Compendium; or an Exact Collection of the Newest, and most Delightful Songs* (1681), which refers to '*The Whore of Babylon, the Devil and the Pope*': cited in *The London Stage*, 1: 288.

Like Care's schizophrenic journal, this play, closely related to Settle's pageant of the same year, is unsure of how lightly to wear its Protestant zeal, and like many of the more respectable dramas of the Plot, including some of its Shakespeare adaptations, it suffers as a result from a curious uncertainty of tone. In its main plot, Elizabeth is crowned and banishes the Vatican's ambassadors; news of this is greeted with horror in Rome, whence a clumsy assassination attempt is launched, identical to that described by Oates. This attempt is foiled by the loyal Protestant plebeians; meanwhile, egged on by 'the Devil in the habit of a Jesuit',[13] the Pope seduces a nun, Dulcimenta, who is stabbed by her outraged father, Cardinal Moriscena, who is in turn stabbed by the Pope. So far the Roman scenes have been dealt with in an earnest pastiche of the heroic style, and kept safely removed from the comic relief offered by the English mob (whom 'J.D.' the author, avoiding the charge of all-out populism, carefully depicts as amazingly stupid), but from this point onwards high tragedy and low comedy are intermingled with wild abandon. The Devil conveys the Pope to England, where he is treated to a morally instructive scenic effect characteristic of Plot drama: '[*The Scene suddenly draws off, and discovers Hell full of Devils, Popes and Cardinals, with the ghosts of* Moriscena *and* Dulcementa *wounded....*]' (19).

There follows a harrowing musical number, copied, intriguingly, straight from the 'Masque of Devils' with which Ariel torments the consciences of Alonzo and Antonio in the 1674 operatic *The Enchanted Island*. In J.D.'s play, the devils who rise from *The Enchanted Island*'s stage to sing '*Where does the black Fiend Ambition reside ...?*'[14] are replaced by two singers who, assisted by these various deceased Catholics, perform:

VOICE. Where, where's the Pope?
ANSWER. Come to die in a Rope:
   Or his Breath expire, by the flames of hot fire.
   To meet the just Plagues that his sins do require.
VOICE. Pray what is his Crime?

[13] J.D., *The Coronation of Queen Elizabeth, With the Restauration of the Protestant Religion: or, The Downfal of the Pope* (London, 1680), 13.
[14] Davenant–Dryden [and Shadwell], *The Tempest, or, The Enchanted Island*, 27–8.

[ANSWER.] For coming to popedom before 'twas his time;
  For Murther and Whoredom, for Poison and Rape,
  For killing the Father and making escape,
  From the Chair of St. *Peter* to a Heretick City;
  Mid'st the Rabble, to suffer without any pity.
  A round, a round, round, inclose the Pope round;
  Push him and toss him on Prongs; all yet quicker,
  Till he cryes there's no hope, for bloody, bloody Pope,
  And a cheating old fool of a Vicar.

(J.D., 19)

The Dryden/Davenant/Shadwell masque, with its references to the evils of overweening kings ('Who are the leaders of the damned Host? | Proud Monarchs, who tyrannize most', *The Enchanted Island*, 28), is here claimed for the popular opposition, J.D.'s substitution of a wicked Pope for the wicked kings lashed in the original reinforcing the Whig equation between Popery and Stuart absolutism. After this show-stopper the hapless pontiff is left at the mercy of the English, represented by 'Tim, Brush, Honeysuckle, *and others of the Rabble*' (20), and the play now collapses into a style closer to that of *The Mock-Tempest* than that of *The Enchanted Island*:

TIM. Pray Sir, if a Man may be so bold to ask, what are you Sir?
[*A dismal Voice from above.*

VOICE. He's a Pope-
TIM. Ha,—hark ye there Neighbours, there's something says he is a Pope.
ALL. O law!
TIM. Pray, Sir, are you a Pope?
POPE. No.
TIM. Why then you might have told a body so at first.
VOICE. He lies.
TIM. Ha, there's something says he lies, but I don't know what it is, yet 'tis no matter, let it be what it will, we are bound to believe it; for it can't lie so long as it speaks against the Pope. [*Goes to him*] Pray Sir what Pope are you?
VOICE. He's the Pope of *Rome*.
TIM, Ha,—hark you there Neighbours;—nay, if he be the Pope of *Rome*, he shall quickly know his doom.

(Ibid.)

At this, they go to Elizabeth and obtain permission to burn the Pope at Temple Bar to celebrate victory over the Armada. Responding with all the theatrical resources it can muster to the perceived Catholic threat to Britain, a threat simultaneously imagined in terms of high villainy and low comedy, the play faithfully dramatizes the Plot crisis as a wild farrago of heroic tragedy, semi-opera, travesty, horror, and farce.[15]

This illicit play, obscure and glibly exploitative as it is, adumbrates in miniature the problematic instability of genre experienced by even the most politically unambiguous plays mounted in the legitimate theatres. Settle's *The Female Prelate*, for example, an unremittingly Protestant account of the downfall of Pope Joan (dedicated to the Whig leader Shaftesbury), veers constantly between horrific tragedy and bathetic comedy, concluding incoherently, after much genuine anguish, with the old joke about the Vatican avoiding making the same mistake again by checking the sex of all subsequent popes through a hole in the seat of the pontifical throne.[16] In fact for most serious dramatists working during the Plot, existing Restoration genres were not only inadequate to the task of producing cogent topical plays, but could be positively dangerous. As public meeting-places of citizens and courtiers, operating under the direct patronage of the king and the Duke of York respectively, the licensed theatres were in themselves highly charged political venues, and as such regularly became sites of open factional conflict: at the Duke's Company's Dorset Garden theatre there was even a full-scale sword skirmish in June 1679 between the defence witnesses from a recent treason trial

[15] The same uneasy form of tragicomedy—part gory tragedy of state, part low comic romp—is found in another illicit anti-Catholic play, *Rome's Follies: or, The Amorous Fryers* (London, 1681), dedicated to the Whig leader Shaftesbury and performed at 'A Person of Quality's House' at around the time of his acquittal on treason charges in late 1681. The farcical excesses of the Fryers in question (a pair of libidinous Jesuits), which occupy much of the play, conclude in a solemn procession of phantom popes uttering terrible warnings in heroic verse about the ultimate destination of Catholic souls: again, the Popish Plot's simultaneous fore-grounding of both the traditional anti-Catholic joke and the traditional serious anti-Catholic conspiracy theory proves inimical to earlier Restoration standards of dramatic decorum.

[16] Elkanah Settle, *The Female Prelate: being the history of the life and death of Pope Joan* (London, 1680), 42. On this play see Hume, *Development of English Drama*, 346. Appropriately, one enraged Papist—Charles's Catholic mistress Louise de Kerouaille, the Duchess of Portsmouth—attempted to minimize Settle's profits by taking the entire court to the rival theatre on Settle's third night, where the Duke's Company were reviving a more politically and generically orthodox play, Davenant's *Macbeth*. See *The London Stage*, 1: 287.

and a mob of zealous Protestants led by the chief prosecution witness, the awful William Bedloe.[17] Even without the provocation of partisan drama, performances were in constant danger of interruption by spontaneous demonstrations, such as those described in a letter from the dowager Countess of Sunderland in January 1680:

> You must needs hear of the abominable disorders amongst us, calling all the women whores and the men rogues in the playhouses—throwing candles and links—calling my Lord Sunderland trator, but in good company; the Duke, rascal; and all ended in 'God bless his Highness, the Duke of Monmouth. We will be for him against the world.'[18]

In this atmosphere, every play was in danger of attack, either from Tories accusing it of treason against the monarchy, or from Whigs accusing it of nurturing Catholic sympathies; as an epilogue of 1681 puts it:

> Our Popes and Fryers on one side offend,
> And yet alas the City's not our Friend.[19]

Plays that were considered too anti-Catholic or anti-Royal might be banned—as were Nahum Tate's tactless adaptation of *Richard II* (despite his portrayal of Bolingbroke as a proto-Whiggish demagogue and Richard as a martyr), Nathaniel Lee's republican *Lucius Junius Brutus* (after which Charles threatened to cancel the Duke's Company's patent), and John Crowne's *Henry the Sixth, The First Part* (a version of 2 *Henry VI* which gave offence to James thanks to Crowne's J.D.-style additions, described by his prologue as '*A little Vineger against the* Pope').[20] On the other side of the question, plays considered implicitly pro-Catholic might simply be booed off the stage. Crowne's prologue to his version of 3 *Henry VI*, rechristened *The Misery of Civil-War*, pleads with this more vocal faction of his audience:

---

[17] On both this incident and Bedloe's perjuries (which resulted in the executions of several innocent people), see Kenyon, *The Popish Plot*, 186–9. It says much about the market for topical drama during the crisis that one mediocre rhymed tragedy was spuriously and misleadingly published as *The Excommunicated Prince, or, The False Relique: Being the Popish Plot in a Play. As it was Acted by His Holiness's Servants. By Capt. Bedloe* (London, 1679).

[18] Henry Sidney, *Diary of the Times of Charles the Second by the Honourable Henry Sidney* (2 vols.; London, 1843), i. 237.

[19] Thomas Shadwell, *The Lancashire Witches* (London, 1681), 76.

[20] Crowne, *Henry the Sixth, The First Part*, 'Prologue'; see Hume, *Development of English Drama*, 345–6.

Good Heaven! Sirs! are there no other ways
To damn the Pope, but damning all our Plays?[21]

Caught thus in the crossfire of the emerging two-party system, playwrights found the composition of both tragedies and comedies fraught with risks. Heroic tragedy, already close to ideological obsolescence by this time,[22] depended on a set of assumptions about the absolute prerogatives of legitimate monarchs which the case of the current heir, the Duke of York, undeniably legitimate and unashamedly Catholic, called alarmingly into question. As the possibility of a rebellion on behalf of Charles's illegitimate but Protestant son the Duke of Monmouth became ever more threatening, the issues of loyalty and insurrection around which the Restoration heroic play had traditionally been constructed became too hot to handle, as Dryden and Lee found when *The Duke of Guise*, originally blatantly entitled *The Parallel*, was banned at the personal request of Monmouth in July 1682.[23]

Meanwhile Restoration comedy, nothing if not topical, had become similarly risky. The conflict between courtiers and citizens, its favourite standing joke, was now being played out in deadly earnest. Shadwell, perceiving very clearly that this was no time to risk full-scale satire, told his audience:

Of your gross follies if you will not hear,
With inoffensive Nonsense you must bear.[24]

This he duly provided in his predominantly slapstick *The Lancashire Witches* in 1681, which apart from the incidental satire provided by the corrupt Anglican clergyman Smirk and his infinitely more corrupt Irish Catholic counterpart Teague O'Dively is in essence a kind of Restoration *Ghostbusters*. Shadwell's prefatory apology for this play describes very clearly the problems faced by comic playwrights during the Exclusion Crisis:

Fops and Knaves are the fittest Characters for Comedy, and this Town was wont to abound with variety of Vanities and Knaveries till this unhappy division. But all run now into Politicks, and you must needs, if you touch upon any humour of this time, offend one of the Parties. The Bounds being then so narrow, I saw there was no scope for the writing of

[21] John Crowne, *The Misery of Civil-War* (London, 1680), 'Prologue'.
[22] As Susan Staves has argued in *Players' Scepters*, ch. 4.
[23] See *The London Stage*, 1: xxix, lxiii, 310.
[24] Shadwell, *Lancashire Witches*, 76.

an entire Comedy (wherein the Poet must have a relish of the present time), and therefore I resolved to make as good an entertainment as I could, without tying myself up to the strict rules of a Comedy; which was the reason of my introducing of Witches.

(A2)

Under these conditions, left with a choice between possible bannings or barrackings, or resorting to sheer farce, it is perhaps less surprising that so many writers took refuge in the rewriting of Shakespeare.

Politics and Shakespeare

Today the Poet does not fear your Rage,
Shakespeare by him reviv'd now treads the stage:
Under his sacred Lawrels he sits down,
Safe, from the blast of any Criticks Frown.[25]

Thus did Edward Ravenscroft, with audible relief, introduce the first of the Popish Plot's wave of Shakespeare adaptations, *Titus Andronicus, or, The Rape of Lavinia*, during the hysteria of autumn 1678. Publishing the play after the accession of James, after Oates had been publicly whipped as a perjuror and Shaftesbury had died in exile, Ravenscroft finally comes clean about the political purport of this adaptation: abandoning his claim simply to be paying due respect to Shakespeare's genius, he announces that he chose to resurrect *Titus* as a satire on Oates and the Whigs,

since it shew'd the Treachery of Villains, and the Mischiefs carry'd on by Perjury and False Evidence; and how Rogues may frame a Plot that shall deceive and destroy both the Honest and the Wise; which were the reasons why I did forward it at so unlucky a conjuncture, being content rather to lose the Profit, then not expose to the world the Picture of such Knaves and Rascals as then Reign'd in the opinion of the Foolish and Malicious part of the Nation . . . For when Ill Manners and Ill Principles

---

[25] Quoted in Gerard Langbaine, *An Account of the English Dramatick Poets* (Oxford, 1691), 465. Ravenscroft himself seems deliberately to have omitted this prologue from the printed text of his adaptation (not published until 1687); see below.

Reign in a State, it is the business of the Stage, as well as Pulpits, to declaim and Instruct: That was my design when I writ.[26]

Ravenscroft is undoubtedly benefiting from considerable hindsight here (this 1687 printed text of his play omits the professedly apolitical prologue about Shakespeare's laurels, for example, presumably lest it should qualify the preface's retrospective claim that Ravenscroft qualifies as an outspoken royalist martyr for having dared to produce the play in 1678 at all), but it is certain that his adaptation's general atmosphere of horror and treachery made it seem topical enough to survive during an otherwise extremely thin season, with Ravenscroft securely sheltered from any accusation of propagandist intentions by Shakespeare's 'Sacred Lawrels'. The original *Titus Andronicus* here provides both a vehicle for topical comment and a useful cover-story, Ravenscroft deploying canonization—the promotion of Shakespeare as an author supposedly above and beyond contemporary politics—as a way of creating a space of sanctuary around his own adaptation. Ravenscroft's prologue thus carefully points out that he has merely 'purified' an existing Shakespeare play, instead of presenting *Titus* as his own work:

Like other Poets, he'll not proudly scorn
To own, that he but winnow'd *Shakespear*'s Corn...
    (Ravenscroft, prologue to *Titus Andronicus*, in Langbaine, 465)

Shakespeare's works, a superabundant (if unrefined) harvest of wheat, are here once again represented as expressions of Nature, a trope which during the Plot years not only implies the appropriateness of adapting them but (misleadingly) claims a status of political neutrality for the adapted texts themselves. This ploy of presenting a highly topical adaptation under the flag of convenience provided by Shakespeare's sacred laurels is developed most fully by Dryden, who in his prologue to *Troilus and Cressida, or, Truth Found Too Late* (1679) resurrects Shakespeare as a Trojan horse by which to smuggle a guarded royalist polemic onto the stage of the Duke's Theatre. Expanding on his earlier prologue to *The Enchanted Island*, Dryden again presents Shakespeare as a king, a figure on to which contemporary anxieties about royal suc-

[26] Edward Ravenscroft, *Titus Andronicus, or, The Rape of Lavinia* (London, 1687), 'Preface', A2^r–^{v}.

cession can be neatly displaced in the form of a highly Bloomian discussion of its poetic equivalent. From being identified as a distant, archaic Prospero, Shakespeare has metamorphosed into a contemporary Old Hamlet, a royal ghost (capable of curing the poetic King's Evil with one touch of his laurels) impatient with the feeble efforts of his heirs:

The Prologue Spoken by Mr. Betterton,
Representing the Ghost of Shakespear.

SEE, my lov'd *Britons*, see your *Shakespeare* rise,
An awfull ghost confess'd to human eyes!
Unnam'd, methinks, distinguish'd I had been
From other shades, by this eternal green,
About whose wreaths the vulgar Poets strive,
And with a touch, their wither'd Bays revive.
Untaught, unpractis'd, in a barbarous Age,
I found not, but created first the Stage.
And, if I drained no *Greek* or *Latin* store,
'Twas, that my own abundance gave me more.
On foreign trade I needed not rely
Like fruitfull *Britain*, rich without supply.
In this my rough-drawn Play, you shall behold
Some Master-strokes, so manly and so bold
That he, who meant to alter, found 'em such
He shook; and thought it Sacrilege to touch.
Now, where are the Successours to my name?
What bring they out to fill a Poets fame?
Weak, short-liv'd issues of a feeble Age;
Scarce living to be Christen'd on the Stage!
        .   .   .   .

Sit silent then, that my pleas'd Soul may see
A Judging Audience once, and worthy me:
My faithfull Scene from true Records shall tell
How *Trojan* valour did the *Greek* excell;
Your great forefathers shall their fame regain,
And *Homers* angry Ghost repine in vain.
                    (Dryden, *Troilus*, b4ʳ)

This is the first of Shakespeare's many posthumous personal appearances on the stage, the first of many occasions on which he is deduced from his own *œuvre* as a dramatic character in order to authorize the revival of one of his plays, and it is important to note how politically motivated this influential instance is. Magni-

fying Shakespeare to enable him to stand not only as a type of the
current troubled dynasty but as a figure for 'fruitfull *Britain*' itself
(anticipating in this regard the broader nationalist appropriation
of Shakespeare developed more fully in the decades after Dryden's
death), this prologue dramatizes the adaptor's Oedipal relation to
this 'awfull ghost' in a manner which carefully distracts attention
from the political content of the adaptation which is to follow.
Indeed Dryden deliberately gives the misleading impression that
his anxiety of influence has prevented him from altering Shakespeare's play at all ('He shook; and thought it Sacrilege to touch'),
and closes by a further displacement of the audience's attention
from Dryden's negotiations with Shakespeare's ghost to Shakespeare's relation to Homer's. In the process, however, Shakespeare's ghost does point very tactfully towards the pertinence of
the play which follows, incidentally reminding the audience that in
listening to his account of 'How Trojan valour did the Greek
excell' they will be restoring the fame of their own forefathers: by
this passing allusion to the Brut legend, *Troilus and Cressida*
becomes, implicitly, an honorary British history play.[27] In fact, the
Troilus which ensues has been carefully modified for its occasion,
laced with incidental jibes about priests to clear it of any imputed
Popish sympathies and enlisted in unambiguous support of Ulysses'
views on social discipline. It is Ulysses, indeed, who pronounces
Dryden's less than subtle last couplet:

Then, since from homebred Factions ruine springs,
Let Subjects learn obedience to their Kings.[28]

(Dryden, *Troilus*, 69)

What is perhaps most significant, however, about this didactic
version of *Troilus and Cressida* and Ravenscroft's sensationalist
Titus alike is the way in which both adaptations tend to blur the

---

[27] This distracting prologue enacts in miniature the similar strategy pursued by
the printed edition of the play, published in the same year, which prefaces the play
not only with this prologue but with Dryden's dissertation on 'The Grounds of
Criticism in Tragedy', an extensive discussion of Shakespeare's art from every
perspective *except* that of the monarchist politics this adaptation sponsors. On this
famous essay, see esp. Robert D. Hume, *Dryden's Criticism* (Ithaca, NY, 1970),
117–23.
[28] On the politics of this play, see Lewis D. Moore, 'For King and Country:
John Dryden's *Troilus and Cressida*', *College Language Association Journal*, 26
(1982), 98–111: see also Hume, *Development of English Drama*, 325.

political issues of the plays they adapt by further distracting attention from the issues of loyalty and kingship onto the sheer
pathos offered by the spectacle of their suffering heroines (in
Dryden's version Cressida is completely innocent, only feigning to
flirt with Diomed in a bid to escape to Troy, and she finally stabs
herself to convince Troilus of her unshaken faith). With the public
arena of political action in a state of confused and dangerous
ferment, playwrights resorted increasingly to dramatizing a domestic sphere of private emotion now strenuously defined as its
antithesis, a move nowhere more influentially made than in the
next Shakespeare adaptation produced during the crisis, Thomas
Otway's *The History and Fall of Caius Marius* (1679), a play
destined to exert a lasting influence on subsequent conceptions of
both Shakespearean and contemporary tragedy.[29]

Otway's prologue to this play, like Dryden's prologue to *Troilus*,
implicitly identifies the divine Shakespeare with Divine Right, although the play which it introduces emerges as considerably less
conservative than this loyal trope might lead its audience to expect. To Otway, as to the adaptors of the 1660s, Shakespeare is
first and foremost a court writer, and his prologue, campaigning
busily for the continuation of Crown subsidy for the theatres,
attributes all the merits of his plays to the consistent royal patronage bestowed on their author:

Our *Shakespear* wrote too in an Age as blest,
The happiest Poet of his time and best.
A gracious Prince's Favour chear'd his Muse,
A constant Favour he ne'er fear'd to lose.
Therefore he wrote with Fancy unconfin'd,
And Thoughts that were Immortal as his Mind.[30]

Otway goes on to excuse his own play's reliance on Shakespearean
material (represented, as in Ravenscroft's earlier prologue, as a

---

[29] On *Caius Marius*, see Hazel M. Batzer, 'Shakespeare's Influence on Thomas
Otway's *Caius Marius*', *Revue de l'Université d'Ottawa*, 39 (Oct.–Dec. 1969),
533–61: John M. Wallace, 'Otway's *Caius Marius* and the Exclusion Crisis',
Modern Philology, 85 (May 1988), 363–72. On the emergence of the pathetic
heroine, see Laura Brown, 'The Defenceless Woman and the Development of
English Tragedy', *Studies in English Literature 1500–1900*, 22 (1982), 429–43:
on the connections between this development and the rewriting of Shakespeare, see
Jean Marsden, 'Rewritten Women: Shakespearean Heroines in the Restoration', in
Marsden (ed.), *The Appropriation of Shakespeare*, 43–56.

[30] Thomas Otway, *The History and Fall of Caius Marius* (London, 1680), A3^r.

harvest) on the grounds of Charles's temporary absence from the
theatrical scene (he was dangerously ill at the time of the première
of *Caius Marius*): apologizing to Shakespeare, Otway confesses
that

> Though much the most unworthy of the Throng,
> Our this-day's Poet fears h'has done him wrong.
> Like greedy Beggars that steal Sheaves away,
> You'll find h'has rifled him of half a Play.
> Amidst this baser Dross you'll see it shine
> Most beautifull, amazing, and Divine.
> To such low Shifts of late are Poets worn,
> Whilst we both Wit's and *Caesar*'s Absence mourn.
>
> $(A_3^r-^v)$

In fact this 'low shift' results more from the diseases of the body
politic than from those of the King's body natural: Otway, whose
previous successes had been in the now politically impossible
genre of the tragedy of state (notably *Don Carlos*, 1676), needed
to find a form of serious drama capable of surviving under the
immense pressures of the Exclusion Crisis. In Shakespeare he
found precisely what he needed: a tragedy dealing not with the
heroic ethical choices of political leaders, but with the sufferings
of helpless private citizens.

Neither an avowedly political Roman tragedy like Lee's banned
Lucius Junius Brutus (which it heavily influenced)[31] nor a simple
topical conscription of Shakespeare like Crowne's *The Misery of
Civil-War*, *Caius Marius* has a deliberately misleading opening.
The first speech of the play is grandly public, addressed by Metel-
lus to the Senators:

> When will the Tut'lar Gods of *Rome* awake,
> To fix the Order of our wayward State,
> That we may once more know each other; know
> Th'extent of Laws, Prerogatives and Dues;

---

[31] The chief source of pathos in Lee's play, the plot in which the tender Titus is
separated from his beloved Teraminta by the unbending republican commitment of
his father Brutus, owes much to Otway's delineation of the relations between
Young Marius (Romeo), Lavinia (Juliet), and Marius (Montague): it says much for
the discrepancy between Otway's affective form and his royalist politics that Lee's
imitation is, in Laura Brown's words, 'almost a manifesto of the Whig constitutional position during the exclusion controversy, and, except for its radical anti-
monarchism, a full expression of the dominant ideology of Britain after the
Glorious Revolution' (*English Dramatic Form*, 76–7).

The bounds of Rules and Magistracy; who
Ought first to govern, and who must obey?
(1)

In fact these are exactly the kind of questions which the play will
refuse to answer. Once Metellus has successfully persuaded his
faction to support Sylla for the consulship against the allegedly
corrupt Marius, he and his supporters are replaced on the stage by
the play's titular hero and his own cabal, and it is immediately
clear that neither side is morally superior to the other: indeed, the
original cause of the mortal hatred between Marius and Sylla is
throughout the play left as obscure as possible, their rivalry serving only as a general warning against civil conflict itself. As
Marius' rally disperses, and he begins to advise his son Young
Marius to abandon his love for Lavinia (the daughter of Metellus
to whom he had been betrothed before Metellus defected to Sylla),
the whole political plot of the play is relegated to the status of the
pointless background feud between the Montagues and the Capu-
lets, so much 'baser Dross', and the drama shifts decisively away
from the public arena to the celebration of its doomed young
lovers. In the following scene Metellus' patriotic enquiry is replaced as the central question of the play by quite another, posed
by Lavinia, as the first beautiful, amazing, and divine fragments of
Romeo and Juliet become visible: 'O, *Marius, Marius!* wherefore
art thou *Marius?*' (18).

However odd such of its lines sound now, this play marks a
decisive turning-point in the development of Augustan drama: it is
here that Otway discovered the formula for affective tragedy which
would be his most lasting contribution to the English theatre.
Lavinia is a virtuous, passive victim, the source of limitless pathos,
Young Marius an over-sensitive, vacillating juvenile lead, hope-
lessly caught up in events over which he has no control and
willing passionately to swear allegiance to whoever he happens to
be on stage with at the time. In Otway's reworking of the *Romeo
and Juliet* story, both lovers are denied all responsibility for their
fate: Young Marius forsakes no Rosaline for Lavinia, having
fallen in love with her in accordance with their parents' original
matrimonial plans, and kills no Tybalt, enduring banishment with
his father after another arbitrary political defeat. Reversing
Howard's Fletcherian alterations to the last act (by which the play

was granted a happy ending and became a parable about the healing of civil wounds), Otway adjusts the tomb scene to make the play still more tragic. In order to squeeze every possible drop of unadulterated pathos from the situation, he has Lavinia awaken before Young Marius has finished dying of the poison, and she then has to witness the death of her father at the hands of her father-in-law before being permitted to kill herself. In a spirit far from the consummation of 'This is thy sheath! There rust, and let me die,' Lavinia, like later Otway suicides, seems to choose death as the next best thing to destroying the world:

And now let Rage, Distraction and Despair
Seize all Mankind, till they grow mad as I am.
[*Stabs herself*]

(65)

By the end of the play this anarchic last wish seems well on the way to fulfilment: the repentant Marius immediately receives news that his apparent victory has been overthrown by a new rebellion, and the play's last words are spoken in senseless jest by the dying Sulpitius, Otway's violent Mercutio:

A Pox on all Mad-men hereafter. If I get a Monument, let this be my Epitaph:

Sulpitius *lies here, that troublesome slave,*
That sent many honester men to the Grave,
And dy'd like a Fool when h'had liv'd like a Knave.

(66)

Caius Marius is peculiarly hospitable to angry, nihilistic gestures of this nature, since in Otway's affective universe all is contingent, provisional, potentially disposable: cogency of plot and characterization are completely subordinated to the pity they are designed to evoke. Following Ravenscroft and Dryden, Otway produces a Shakespeare adaptation with a suffering, innocent woman at its centre, but his play goes further than either *Titus Andronicus* or *Troilus and Cressida* by making the pathos thereby elicited the play's chief *raison d'être* at the expense of political consistency, his interchangeable Marius and Sylla alternating arbitrarily in the audience's sympathies and only the plight of the blameless young

lovers remaining constant.[32] He discovered in rewriting *Romeo
and Juliet* that despite the stresses of the Exclusion Crisis he could
continue to produce viable tragedy by displacing decisive political
action and concentrating instead on the helpless, voluptuous sufferings of political victims, and despite his own loyalty to Stuart
absolutism he thereby struck a major blow for the *embourgeoise-
ment* of serious drama. After *Caius Marius*, tragedy would no
longer be the privilege of monarchs. Otway's next play, *The
Orphan*, 1680, is again set entirely among private citizens (as a
woman without powerful parents, its heroine Monimia has even
less social status than Lavinia), and it tellingly excuses its truancy
from affairs of state by further 'riflings' from Shakespeare, transplanting Belarius' lecture against court life from *Cymbeline*. Even
the most explicitly political of his subsequent tragedies, *Venice
Preserv'd* (1682), is again premissed on the reuse of Shakespeare
to dramatize the clash between corrupt public life and doomed
private sensibility, endlessly replaying the orchard scene of *Julius
Caesar* as it develops a central triangle of subversive Pierre
(Cassius), anxious newly recruited conspirator Jaffeir (Brutus),
and endangered wife Belvidera (Portia). In resorting to Shakespeare, Otway is searching like many readers after him for an
antidote to politics: but in fact the pathos-oriented tragedy he
finds proves to encode latently egalitarian political assumptions of
its own.[33]

   This emergence of a new form of tragedy more distanced from
matters of state than its early Restoration forebears is visible even
in the most notorious, and most obviously polemical, revisions of
Shakespeare that appeared during the Exclusion Crisis, those of
Nahum Tate, produced in swift succession a year after *Caius
Marius*, between late 1680 and late 1681. Tate's three adapta-
tions, despite the widespread view that he was motivated by blind
Augustan dogmatism, are just as conditioned by royalist politics

---

[32] Cf. Laura Brown on the limitations of affective tragedy: 'Pure formal pathos
seems to require the simplicity that permits an extensive development of the central
emotional scenes, and, for related reasons, it eschews an elaborate portrayal of
motivation or consistency . . . Perhaps the most graphic example of this concurrent
stifling of motivation and character consistency is in the Restoration adaptations of
Shakespeare's tragedies, which systematically substitute innocence for blame and
simple misunderstanding for responsibility'; *English Dramatic Form*, 100.
[33] On the emergence of affective tragedy in the late 1670s and the shift in
ideology it registers, see ibid. 69–101.

as those of Ravenscroft or Dryden, but like Otway's pathetic *Romeo and Juliet* they too contain the seeds of the more Whiggish forms which would dominate the theatrical repertory in the time of Rowe and Addison.[34] As his outraged preface to the printed edition of *The History of King Richard the Second* protests, his first Shakespearean experiment was intended as a piece of outright monarchist propaganda—'Every Scene is full of Respect to Majesty and the dignity of Courts, not one alter'd Page but what breaths Loyalty'[35]—but when it appeared in December 1680, Charles was facing a House of Commons potentially the most dangerous since 1640, and no play depicting the feasibility of deposing an English monarch could possibly be tolerated. Tate could not afford to make the same mistake twice, and his next offering, produced just when Whig demands for the legitimization of Monmouth were reaching their climax, more than makes amends. In this far more timely alteration of a Shakespeare play about British history, a bastard's rebellion is crushed and the legitimate monarch triumphantly restored. The play is, of course, *The History of King Lear*.

Tate's preface to this play is distinctly misleading, concentrating as it does on the love interest introduced between Cordelia and Edgar:

The Distress of the Story is evidently heightned by it; and it particularly gave Occasion of a New Scene or Two, of more Success (perhaps) than Merit. This Method necessarily threw me on making the Tale conclude in a Success to the innocent distrest Persons.[36]

This reason for altering the ending is a patent *non sequitur*: Dryden, after all, had heightened the distress of *Troilus and Cressida* by making Cressida as innocent as Troilus and killing both of

---

[34] On Tate's adaptations, see esp. Christopher Spencer, 'A word for Tate's *Lear*', *Studies in English Literature 1500–1900*, 3 (1963), 241–51; the 'Introduction' to Nahum Tate, *The History of King Lear*, ed. James Black (Lincoln, Nebr., 1975); Hume, *Development of English Drama*, 344–5, 350; Douglas Canfield, 'Royalism's Last Dramatic Stand: English Political Tragedy, 1679–89', *Studies in Philology*, 82 (1985), 234–63; Nancy Klein Maguire, 'Nahum Tate's *King Lear*: "the King's blest restoration"', in Jean Marsden (ed.), *The Appropriation of Shakespeare*, 29–42; Laura Rosenthal, '(Re)Writing Lear: Literary Property and Dramatic Authorship', in Susan Staves and John Brewer (eds.), *Early Modern Conceptions of Property* (London, forthcoming).

[35] Nahum Tate, *The History of King Richard the Second* (London, 1681), 'Epistle Dedicatory', A2.

[36] Id., *The History of King Lear* (London, 1681), 'The Epistle Dedicatory', A2^v–A3^r.

them. The real star of Tate's adaptation is in fact Edmund—the play begins with the 'Thou, Nature, art my goddess' soliloquy—and, shortly before his defeat at the hands of Edgar, Tate has him underline his kinship to the Duke of Monmouth in the most potentially controversial remark of the play:

> Thy mother being chaste
> Thou art assured thou art but Gloster's son.
> But mine, disdaining constancy, leaves me
> To hope that I am sprung from nobler blood,
> And possibly a King might be my sire.
>
> (Tate, *Lear*, 60)

Despite major additions to Edmund's role, including a plan to rape Cordelia in the storm, he is not mentioned once in Tate's preface—an omission probably dictated by prudence. An epilogue criticizing Monmouth led over a year later to the imprisonment of both Aphra Behn and the actress Mary Lee,[37] and Dryden and Lee's outlawed *Duke of Guise* probably could not have been published at all without its entirely mendacious preface insisting that any similarity to English dukes, especially Monmouth, was purely coincidental. Tate's prologue to *Lear*, characteristically, like Dryden's prologue to *Troilus and Cressida*, distracts attention from the political content of the adaptation to the venerable talents of Shakespeare:

> 'Twere worth our While t'have drawn you in this day
> By a new Name to our old honest Play;
> But he that did this Evenings Treat prepare
> Bluntly resolv'd before-hand to declare
> Your Entertainment should be most old Fare.
> Yet hopes, since in rich *Shakespear*'s soil it grew,
> 'Twill relish yet with those whose Tasts are True,
> And his Ambition is to please a Few . . .
>
> (A4ʳ)

Shakespeare thus serves for Tate, as for his colleague Dryden, as a stalking-horse for the topicality of his adaptations. The motives guiding his alterations to Shakespeare's 'old fare' are indeed made perfectly explicit in the preface to his next adaptation, *The Ingratitude of a Common-Wealth; or, The Fall of Caius Martius Corio-*

---

[37] On 10 Aug. 1682: see *The London Stage*, 1: 311.

lanus, premiered in November 1681, when the Tory reaction was well under way:

Upon a close view of this Story, there appear'd in some Passages no small Resemblance with the busie *Faction* of our own time. And I confess, I chose rather to set the *Parallel* nearer to Sight, than to throw it off at further Distance.[38]

Clearly, Tate's reasons for rewriting Shakespeare have far more to do with contemporary politics than with contemporary literary criticism, and any lingering belief in the old story that he gave *Lear* a happy ending because he was some kind of neo-classical cissy who couldn't stand the sight of stage blood can easily be dispelled by a quick glance at the orgy of gratuitous violence with which he chooses to conclude *Coriolanus*. The closing scene to what is otherwise a comparatively restrained treatment of the play begins with Coriolanus and Aufidius mortally wounding each other, and things go downhill from there. Aufidius tells Coriolanus that despite his mortal wound he is about to ravish Virgilia before his very eyes. Virgilia enters, having mortally wounded herself to preserve her chastity, and dies. Aufidius now dies, but his role as tormentor of the mortally wounded Coriolanus is taken over by his lieutenant, Nigridius. Nigridius describes mangling the limbs of Coriolanus' son Young Martius, who is then carried on to the stage, mortally wounded, by Volumnia. Volumnia, lapsing into insanity, mortally wounds Nigridius and runs off. Young Martius speaks pitifully to his mortally wounded father before dying of his mortal wounds: and finally Coriolanus, after delivering an understandably perturbed final speech, succumbs to his own. The main reason for this alteration to the play's ending seems to be the final tableau it enables Tate to create: Coriolanus dies with the dead Virgilia under one arm and the dead Young Martius under the other. Even this most openly political of Exclusion Crisis adaptations celebrates its hero's death as a poignant escape from public life into the family.

The History of King Lear, although as determinedly anti-Whig as its successor, similarly resorts to 'apolitical' domestic pathos at

---

[38] Nahum Tate, *The Ingratitude of a Common-Wealth; Or, The Fall of Caius Martius Coriolanus* (London, 1682), A2ᵛ. On this play, see esp. Ruth McGugan, *Nahum Tate and the Coriolanus Tradition in English Drama, With a Critical Edition of Tate's The Ingratitude of a Common-Wealth* (New York, 1987).

crucial moments, pathos which enabled it to survive by over a
century the dynasty it was produced to defend. The love affair
between Edgar and Cordelia which supplies the play with added
'Distress' and gives occasion of 'a New Scene or Two, of more
Success (perhaps) than Merit' also gives occasion for some incidental reflections on the universal superiority of private love and
virtue to public state, potentially at odds with Tate's professed
zeal for patrilineal monarchy. Cordelia, favouring the virtuous
heir of Gloster over her higher-ranking royal suitor Burgundy
(despite her father's commands), is already showing signs of bourgeois sensibility in the play's first scene, and these are made explicit
during the storm, when, rescued by Edgar from Edmund's hench-
men, she is hailed as a paragon for preferring a private relationship with her deliverer, even as Poor Tom, to her public role as a
princess:

CORD. Come to my Arms, thou dearest, best of Men,
   And take the kindest Vows that e're were spoke
   By a protesting Maid.
EDG. Is't possible?
CORD. By the dear Vital Stream that baths my Heart,
   These hallow'd Rags of Thine, and naked Vertue,
   These abject Tassels, these fantastick Shreds,
   (Ridiculous ev'n to the meanest Clown)
   To me are dearer than the richest Pomp
   Of purple Monarchs.
EDG. Generous charming Maid,
   The Gods alone that made, can rate thy Worth!
   This most amazing Excellence shall be
   Fame's Triumph, in succeeding Ages, when
   Thy bright Example shall adorn the Scene,
   And teach the World Perfection.
                        (Tate, *Lear*, 36)

Cordelia's priorities are endorsed in the play's last speech, when
Edgar, nominated as king (or at least regent) by his retiring future
father-in-law Lear, proves his inner worth by declaring the happy
ending to reside not in his elevation to the throne but in his
accession to domestic bliss:

Divine *Cordelia*, all the Gods can witness
How much thy Love to Empire I prefer!
                   (67)

In fact this entire concluding arrangement—by which Tate simultaneously secures the happiness of his 'innocent distrest Persons', saves the father-king from rebellion and secures the future of the state—is far from undilutedly high Tory in tendency. As Nancy Maguire has pointed out:

Although left alive at the end of the play, Lear sinks into a needed retirement instead of retaining the crown . . . The happy (and Whiggish) arrangement to have Cordelia and Edgar rule is, in a sense, elective monarchy rather than divine right, and their joint rule, of course, foreshadows the succession of William and Mary in 1688. Tate certainly catered to his Tory audience, but aspects of his adaptation . . . suggest that Tate, as well as members of his audience, hedged his bets.[39]

Following Dryden and Otway, Tate had revived Shakespeare as a court playwright, a time-honoured supporter of the English monarchy, but his adaptation's retreat from the troubled public issues of kingship and subjection into the celebration of private love and virtue betrays him into an implicit endorsement of quite different political assumptions. The Shakespeare who is revived to champion father-kings proves to be only imperfectly compatible with the Shakespeare invoked as the tender-hearted champion of private elective affinities (whether of Young Marius and Lavinia or of Edgar and Cordelia).

These contradictions are most apparent in the last Shakespeare adaptation produced during the crisis, Thomas Durfey's *The Injured Princess* (1682). Singling out a play already politically and generically ambivalent, *Cymbeline*, Durfey produces a tragicomedy (every bit as unstable as *The Female Prelate* or *The Coronation of Queen Elizabeth*) which inadvertently highlights the ideological exhaustion of existing Restoration dramatic genres, and, again, points very clearly towards the feminocentric domestic tragedies of the ensuing decades. Following Tate, Durfey (another devout royalist) chooses a Shakespeare play depicting the vindication of a virtuous British princess (this one with a happy ending, celebrating the ultimate military and political success of her royal father, already supplied), but like Otway and Tate he too produces an adaptation apparently less resoundingly in favour of absolute monarchy than its author intended. In its valorization of the private sphere—particularly its thoroughgoing treatment of Imogen

[39] Maguire, 'Nahum Tate's *King Lear*', 39.

as a wronged wife first and the heiress to the British state only second—Durfey's adaptation clearly anticipates the strategies by which Shakespeare's embarrassingly monarchist romances would be made fit for middle-class consumption in the time of *Cymbeline*'s next successful adaptors, William Hawkins and David Garrick, as I shall show in Chapter 5.

In the political and theatrical climate of the early 1680s, apparently, a Shakespearean romance like *Cymbeline* simply could not be brought up to date without exposing the inadequacies of the incongruous Restoration genres to which it had to be assimilated. Updating Posthumus as Ursaces, a bear-like, ranting protagonist of the heroic school, and his wife as Eugenia, an equally unsmiling heroine, *The Injured Princess* at first gives no clue as to its Shakespearean source, misleading its audience into expecting a clichéd heroic tragedy: however, these expectations are shattered by the arrivals firstly of Cloten, who becomes a superb, foppish Restoration bully (given to exclamations such as 'Gad any one that frowns at me is the Son of a Whore, and my Mother shall get him poyson'd'),[40] and secondly of Iachimo, who, renamed Shattillion ('an opinionated *Frenchman*', A2ᵛ) after the popular French restaurant Chateline's,[41] becomes a cynical rake straight out of libertine comedy. Thrown into unexpected proximity by the mixed genre of Shakespeare's romance, heroic tragedy and rake comedy proceed to expose each other as equally ridiculous and obsolete sets of postures. In a splendid expansion of Shakespeare's serenade scene (2. 3), for example, Durfey's Cloten tries to impress Eugenia by parodically aping the costume and attitudes of the Herculean hero:

I Gad this damn'd Armour is plaguy troublesom:
Does it become *Florio*? Hah! Do I look like one
That cou'd slay my ten thousand in a morning, and
Never sweat for't? Have I the sow'r Look of a Heroe?

.   .   .   .

---

[40] Thomas Durfey, *The Injured Princess, or the Fatal Wager* (London, 1682), 6.
[41] Cf. Durfey's spelling of this establishment in the prologue he supplied to his comedy *The Fool Turn'd Critick* (London, 1678): 'Next these we welcome such as briskly dine, | At *Locket's*, *Gifford's*, or with *Shatiline*. | Swell'd with Pottage, and the Burgundian Grape, | They hither come to take a kindly nap.' (In keeping with Durfey's reputation for plagiarism, this prologue had been published six years earlier: see *Covent Garden Drollery*, 26–7.)

Nay I know I shou'd look more like a Warrier,
If I were not so handsom; Pox on't, I have
Look'd so clear ever since I took Physick last,
That Gad I'me afraid people begin to think I paint.

.   .   .   .

Madam, I love and honour you in plain terms; pray
Give your consent, and let's be married; your Heroes hate delays.

$(21-2)^{42}$

Eugenia, needless to say, is not amused: but the play's greatest
conflict between comic levity and tragic seriousness is found in its
running combat between her solemn husband and the irresponsibly
ludic Shattillion. True to Restoration stereotype, Durfey's Iachimo
has already decided to visit Britain for the purpose of sampling its
women before the wager over Eugenia's fidelity is even proposed,
punningly remarking of the commoner Ursaces' marriage to its
princess that 'the Gentleman has giv'n us a good hint of the free
Constitution of his Countrey' (8), and, unlike the noble and comparatively immobile Ursaces, he, like his colleagues in the comedy
of intrigue, is permitted to address the audience in racy asides.
Undercutting Eugenia's outraged dignity, Durfey allows him to
turn the excuse he provides for his unsuccessful seduction attempt
(when Eugenia begins to call for help) into a comic feat of im-
provisation under stress—'"D's heart, this won't do, I must shift
quickly, or I'me ruin'd" (18)—and his response to Ursaces' furious
exit on being convinced that Eugenia has betrayed him is another
such aside:

I'le follow ye Sir, ha ha ha!
I am sensible this Lye will occasion some mischief;
But a Pox on't, I cou'd not for my life but make
The most on't, when my hand was in.

(26)

---

[42] Durfey's Cloten seems to have caught at least one contemporary imagination:
he is substantially plagiarized as 'Gayland', who has an almost identical death
scene, in Elkanah Settle's *The Heir of Morocco*, premièred at Drury Lane on 11
Mar. 1682. This second- (or third-) generation Cloten proved sufficiently popular
for Settle to publish his play as *The Heir of Morocco: With the Death of Gayland*
(London, 1682).

Even when recognized on the battlefield in Act V (despite another added comic ruse, a disguise)[43] and threatened by the enraged Ursaces with 'Death and Damnation', he coolly replies, 'A kind of an odd Reward for a man of my Parts' (48), and only a mortal wound and the demands of poetic justice can reduce him to repentant heroic diction. With the modes of tragedy and comedy established in the 1660s thus disabling one another on all sides, the play resorts to Otwayan pathos, with Eugenia explicitly opting out of public life in her first scene (much like Tate's Cordelia). Durfey expands Imogen's

> ... would I were
> A Neat-heards Daughter, and my *Leonatus*
> Our Neighbour-Shepheards Sonne
> (F1, 878)

into a lachrymose repudiation of her rank lasting some thirteen lines, in the course of which the royal oak of the Stuarts is reduced to mere affective décor:

> A Princess? O vain Title, and thou ingrate
> To mock my bitter Woes with Quality,
> The curs'd cause of my Grief—Ah wou'd I were
> Some Shepherd's Daughter, and my dear *Ursaces*
> The Darling of some neighb'ring Villager!
> That through the flowery Meadows sent him daily,
> His Scrip well fill'd with store of Rustick Viands,
> To treat me under some old shady Oak,
> The Monarch of the Grove: Then then should I be happy;
> There wou'd we look and smile, and talk and sing,
> And tell a hundred, hundred pretty Tales,
> Vow lasting passions all the live-long day,
> And sigh, and kiss the happy hours away.
> (Durfey, *The Injured Princess*, 4)

Durfey provides Eugenia with countless other such opportunities to point out how pitiable she is: he characteristically expands her

---

[43] See 48:

> *Enter* Shattillion *disguis'd like a* Britain.
> SHATT. Let *Roman* Fools give up themselves to Bondage,
> While I by Wit gain Freedom ...
> ... in safety
> I'le laugh at this Contrivance, and with pleasure boast
> Of my kind Fortune.

dialogue with Pisanio in the wilderness, for example, having Pisanio disbelieve her protestations of innocence so that she can suffer in isolation (and, after his exit, in prolonged soliloquy, 30–2). She-tragedy—the pathos generated by a suffering woman who owes her status as heroine to her misery rather than to her rank—rushes in where heroic tragedy and rake comedy are no longer confident to tread.[44]

Not entirely unlike *Cymbeline Refinished*, George Bernard Shaw's later adaptation of the same play, *The Injured Princess* emerges as a very sceptical piece of work. The fop and rake of comedy, notoriously indulged in Durfey's earlier plays,[45] are in the persons of Cloten and Shattillion made to appear genuinely evil, to the extent that Durfey tries to out-*Lear Lear* by having Cloten blind Pisanio:[46] meanwhile the hero, Ursaces, is exposed as laughably conventional, his standards of evaluation anachronistic and quite inappropriate to his situation. As for the implicit faith in the divine rightness of kings displayed by traditional heroic tra-gedy, the restoration of the legitimate heir to the throne of Britain is here, as in the original, relegated to the implausible fairytale sub-plot of the finding of the obnoxious princes; Ursaces and Eugenia, no longer in the political front line, are allowed to retreat with relief into a strictly private state of matrimonial bliss. As in Tate's *Lear* (but not in Shakespeare's *Cymbeline*), the closing speech of the play celebrates love rather than kingship, the happy ending having contracted from encompassing the entire British state to something far more private, represented primarily by an acute sensation in the hero's nervous system. To quote Ursaces' final ejaculation in full:

URSA. How like the Accent of some pitying God?
    The King then spoke:

---

[44] On Eugenia as an example of the new victim–heroine of affective tragedy, and the relation of this genre to contemporary domestic ideology, see Jean Marsden, 'Pathos and Passivity: D'Urfey's *The Injured Princess* and Shakespeare's *Cymbeline*', *Restoration*, 14: 2 (1990), 71–81.

[45] See esp. *Madam Fickle; or, The Witty False One* (London, 1677), *A Fond Husband; or, The Plotting Sisters* (London, 1677), and *Trick for Trick; or, The Debauched Hypocrite* (London, 1678).

[46] *The Injured Princess*, 39. There are numerous verbal parallels between *The Injured Princess* and *The History of King Lear*: cf. the blind Pisanio's pathetic appearance at the close of the play (53), a direct copy of Gloster's at the close of Tate's *Lear* (66).

> I swear you have outdone the Deities,
> Giv'n me the brightest Jewel of Perfection.
> O my fair Love! Was ever Joy like mine?
> Did ever Raptures touch a Heart so nearly,
> Or shoot with so much fierceness through the Soul?
> The excess on't is so great, sure it will kill me.
> Thus as some wounded Hero,
> That where most danger was, press'd forward still,
> At last his Life owes to Physicians skill:
> So Love, the bless'd Physician of the Mind,
> Heals all my Griefs, immortal Joys I find,
> And Heaven on Earth, whilst my *Eugenia*'s kind.
>
> (55)

Closing thus in retreat, Durfey's reclusive version of *Cymbeline* is appropriately the last Shakespeare adaptation of the Exclusion Crisis. It is perhaps equally appropriate that almost immediately after staging this demonstration of the bankruptcy of its royalist theatrical genres, the King's Company itself went bust.

Shakespeare and She-Tragedy

The hectic events and violent arguments of 1678–82 simultaneously rehearsed, in the state, the expulsion of James II at the Glorious Revolution six years later, and, on the stages of the Theatres Royal, the new kinds of tragic drama which would dominate the repertory in its aftermath. As the heroic play fell into obsolescence during the 1670s and 1680s, Shakespearean tragedy arrived at the centre of the serious repertory, claimed via Lavinia, Cressida, Cordelia, and Eugenia as the ancestor of the she-tragedy with which it would share that position throughout the ensuing century. This point is made implicitly by Brian Vickers, when, lamenting the persistence of late Restoration attitudes to (and adaptations of) Shakespearean tragedy in the Georgian theatre, he points out that, right down to 1800, Shakespeare's tragedies were staged alongside dramas written, like the adaptations of Otway and Tate, between the mid-1670s and the mid-1710s, notably Nathaniel Lee's *Alexander the Great* (1677) and *Theodosius* (1680), Otway's own *The Orphan* (1680) and *Venice Preserv'd* (1682), William Congreve's *The Mourning Bride* (1697), Nicholas

Rowe's *The Fair Penitent* (1703) and *Jane Shore* (1714), and
Ambrose Philips's *The Distrest Mother* (1712).[47] It is possible,
indeed, to go further than Vickers here by suggesting that for the
eighteenth century the tragic Shakespeare is, in effect, an honorary
member of this group of writers. It is Nicholas Rowe himself, for
example, who is commissioned to produce the first 'scholarly'
edition of the Complete Works (1709) after the success of *The
Fair Penitent*, and his editorial labours on Shakespeare are followed
by *The Tragedy of Jane Shore*, a middle-class she-tragic gloss on
Richard III professedly 'written in Imitation of Shakespeare's
Style'. Rowe's prologue to this play offers a distinctive reading of
the familiar Shakespeare-as-Nature trope used by his precursors to
justify adaptation: here the 'natural' lack of verbal sophistication
displayed by Shakespeare and his fellow Elizabethans is emphatically valorized, as a guarantee of their supposedly apolitical and
unintellectual appeal to the emotions alone:

Their words no shuffling, double-meaning knew,
Their speech was homely, but their hearts were true.
In such an age, immortal Shakespeare wrote,
By no quaint rules nor hampering critics taught;
With rough, majestic force he moved the heart,
And strength and nature made amends for art.
Our humble author does his steps pursue;
He owns he had the mighty bard in view,
And in these scenes has made it more his care
To rouse the passions than to charm the ear.[48]

    If claimed here by Rowe as the Elizabethan precursor of his
own variant of she-tragedy, Shakespeare is equated even more
frequently during the eighteenth century with Otway. Alexander
Pope, for example, in *The First Epistle of the Second Book of
Horace Imitated* (1737), singles them out as the two English
writers who best exemplify English tragedy:

Not but the Tragic spirit was our own,
And full in Shakespear, fair in Otway shone:

[47] Vickers, *Returning to Shakespeare*, 227: 'One reason for the remarkable
homogeneity of style and feeling in sentimental tragedy from Otway and Tate to
Cumberland is that many of the most performed plays throughout the whole of the
eighteenth century were, in fact, Restoration tragedies or the Restoration adaptations of Shakespeare.' On the later 18th-cent. repertory, see 228.
[48] Rowe, *The Tragedy of Jane Shore*, 9.

But Otway fail'd to polish or refine,
And fluent Shakespear scarce effac'd a line.[49]

Like Rowe, Pope recognizes Shakespeare as a rough, unpolished
Poet of Nature, and here he portrays Otway as his successor in
just this respect (although in this instance the comparison is not
intended to flatter). On other occasions, Otway occludes Shakespeare altogether in considerations of native tragedy: *Caius Marius*,
for example, is quoted more frequently than any Shakespeare
play, adapted or not, in the *Thesaurus Dramaticus* of 1724 (a
digestion of canonical plays into quotable fragments, listed by
topic).[50] Otway's hyper-affective version of the tomb scene is
elaborated and retained in all eighteenth-century acting versions of
Romeo and Juliet, and would continue to be part of most performing texts of the play as late as 1875.[51] Indeed, according to
Macnamara Morgan, writing in 1753, Otway had here beaten
Shakespeare at his own game, producing 'perhaps, the finest Touch
of Nature in any Tragedy, ancient or modern... none but that
Genius, who comes next to SHAKESPEAR's self, cou'd draw so fine
a Stroke'.[52]

[49] *The Twickenham Edition of the Poems of Alexander Pope*, ed. John Butt *et
al.* (6 vols. in 7; London, 1954–61), iv. 219. (Hereafter Pope, *Poems*.)

[50] Its 39 citations are matched only by the 38 achieved by Dryden's *Troilus*
(*Hamlet* comes next with 33, then *Othello* with 27); see *Thesaurus Dramaticus*
(London, 1724).

[51] See Theophilus Cibber, *Romeo and Juliet, a Tragedy, Revis'd and Alter'd
from Shakespear* (London [1748]): David Garrick, *Romeo and Juliet*, in *Plays*, iii.
Francis Gentleman, commenting on Garrick's elaboration of this scene, is characteristically enthusiastic, wondering, indeed, whether this pitiful stroke might not
render the play *too* moving for those of a nervous disposition: 'The waking of
Juliet before *Romeo*'s death, is exceedingly judicious; it gives an opportunity of
working the pathos to its tenderest pitch, and shows a very fine picture, if the
performers strike out just and graceful attitudes... Criticism could not wish, nor
ever met more melting incidents or expression, than the catastrophe of this piece
furnishes. We deem it rather too great a strain for tender sympathy'; John Bell
(publ.), [Francis Gentleman, (ed.)], *Bell's Edition of Shakespeare's Plays, as they
are now performed at the Theatres Royal in London...* (8 vols.; London, 1774),
ii. 148–52. On the 19th-cent. career of this particular alteration, see William Poel,
The Stage-Versions of Romeo and Juliet (London, 1915).

[52] Macnamara Morgan, *A Letter to Miss Nossiter Occasioned by her First
Appearing on the Stage, in Which is Contained Remarks on Her Playing the
Character of Juliet* (London, 1753), 49–50. On the identification of Otway with
Shakespeare, see Aline Mackenzie Taylor, *Next to Shakespeare; Otway's Venice
Preserv'd and The Orphan, and their History on the London Stage* (Durham, NC,
1950).

If Otway is thus perceived as a slightly inferior version of Shakespeare, it is also true that Shakespeare has come to be seen as simply a superior, elder version of Otway. Or, indeed, of Tate: such was the success of Tate's more privately inclined additions to *King Lear* that by the same point in the eighteenth century it was possible to regard the entire play as a primarily domestic tragedy, and a heated debate (with self-evident political overtones) was conducted between Joseph Wharton in the *Adventurer* and Arthur Murphy in the *Gray's Inn Journal* as to whether Lear's madness had anything to do with the loss of his kingship or was caused entirely by his familial difficulties with Goneril and Regan.[53] After the adaptations of the Popish Plot years, for all their ostensible monarchism, it would be possible to treat the royalty of Shakespeare's tragic protagonists as a mere stage convention, and to treat the plays themselves as discussions of 'universal' human suffering rather than as contributions to specific Renaissance debates about political legitimacy. (When Garrick replaced Davenant's pro-Restoration version of *Macbeth* with his own adaptation in the 1740s, for example, he costumed the Thane of Cawdor not as an armour-plated Herculean hero or a robed and bejewelled pseudo-Stuart but as a prosperous, red-coated Georgian general.)[54] As a writer of British histories, Shakespeare, as Tate and Crowne realized, could usefully provide playwrights with ways into contemporary politics: but as a master of pathos, as Otway recognized, he could equally provide ways of rendering politics apparently incidental.

Something of the extent to which the tragedians of the Exclusion Crisis set the pattern for subsequent approaches to Shakespearean tragedy and history is perhaps suggested by the next

[53] See *Adventurer* 132 (5 Jan. 1754): *Gray's Inn Journal* (12 Jan. 1754). Cf. 'On the Character of Cordelia in Shakspeare's King Lear', *London Magazine*, 2nd ser. 1 (1783), 293–5: in this essay, which makes no reference to her royal status whatsoever, Cordelia is prescriptively deployed as a paragon of proper womanliness, the patron saint of the private sphere into which Tate's adaptation places her play: 'There are few instances in any poet where the influences of contending emotions are so nicely balanced and distinguished: for while in this amiable picture, we discern the corrected severity of that behaviour which a sense of propriety dictates, mitigated and brought down by fine sensibility, and the softness of female character, we also see this softness upheld, and this sensibility rendered still more engaging, by the influences of a sense of propriety' (295).

[54] On Garrick's Macbeth costume, see esp. Stephen Orgel, 'The Authentic Shakespeare', *Representations*, 21 (1988), 1–25.

alterations of these plays produced, which despite widely differing political agendas repeat the adaptive strategies of Otway and Tate. The most important is the 'Whig' version of *Julius Caesar*, which became the standard London acting text of the play from around the time of the Glorious Revolution to the end of the eighteenth century: by comparatively minor cuts and additions to his role (including a final dialogue on the battlefield at Philippi with Caesar's ghost, which fails to shake his republican stoicism), Brutus is in this rendition of the play celebrated unambiguously as a freedom-loving patriot, and he kills himself in defiance rather than apology.[55] Opposed in its principles as this *Julius Caesar* is to Otway's royalism, its alterations to these last scenes none the less make its Brutus resemble the Jaffeir of *Venice Preserv'd* (another defiantly self-slain revolutionary), and in fact by the 1730s *Venice Preserv'd* itself, the politics of its form displacing those of its intended content, was being read alongside *Julius Caesar* as an analogous specimen of libertarian, constitutionalist tragedy in the pages of the anti-Walpole periodical, the *Craftsman*.[56]

Similarly, Colley Cibber's enduringly successful *Richard III* (1699) profits considerably from the example of Otway, enlarging the role of the unfortunate and unhappy Lady Anne (who, in a completely new scene, is allowed to speak Henry Bolingbroke's soliloquy on sleep from 2 *Henry IV*): but the strategies of the Exclusion Crisis adaptations are even more comprehensively rerun by the whole batch of topical revisions of Shakespeare which appeared in the wake of the Jacobite rebellion of 1715. A two-part version of *Julius Caesar* composed around 1716 by the disgraced Jacobite statesman John Sheffield, Duke of Buckingham (*The Tragedy of Julius Caesar, altered* and *The Tragedy of Marcus Brutus*), largely designed to counter the Whig view of the play, is pervasively indebted to Otway, attempting to reclaim she-tragedy for Stuart loyalism by emphasizing the value of the private realm embodied by Portia over the abstract ideals which lead Brutus to

[55] Published as *The tragedy of Julius Caesar: with the death of Brutus and Cassius. Written originally by Shakespear, and since alter'd by Sir William Davenant and John Dryden, late Poets Laureat* (London, 1719). The attribution to Davenant and Dryden is almost certainly false. On this acting text of *Julius Caesar* and its later 18th-cent. descendants, see John Ripley, *Julius Caesar on Stage in England and America, 1599–1973* (Cambridge, 1980), 24–34.
[56] See 'EXTRACTS *from several Political Plays, with* OBSERVATIONS', in *Craftsman*, 668 (28 Apr. 1739).

betray an unusually paternal and kingly Caesar.[57] Lewis Theobald's *The Tragedy of King Richard the II* and John Dennis's *The Invader of his Country; or, The Fatal Resentment*, both performed in 1719, rewrite Tate's unsuccessful adaptations of *Richard II* and *Coriolanus*, plays which admittedly serve rather better to offer guarded laments for the necessary passing of Stuart autocracy in the 1710s than they had done to defend it in the 1680s (although, again, neither proved especially popular, Dennis's receiving only three performances and Theobald's disappearing after 1721).[58] Theobald's *Richard II* is even more pathos-oriented than Tate's, adding a Young Marius and Lavinia love-plot between Aumerle and Northumberland's daughter Lady Piercy (who kills herself during the last scene after her lover's execution), and having Richard's death immediately follow his forced parting from Queen Isabella (to whom in this version he is tenderly loyal), a figure of unswerving virtue in distress who remains on stage to witness her husband's murder and speak the epilogue.[59]

---

[57] These two plays were never performed: they can be found in John Sheffield, *The Works of His Grace John Sheffield Duke of Buckingham* (2 vols.; London, 1723), 1. On Sheffield's adaptations and their participation in the Restoration and 18th-cent. assimilation of *Julius Caesar*, see Michael Dobson, 'Accents Yet Unknown: Canonisation and the Claiming of *Julius Caesar*', in Marsden (ed.), *The Appropriation of Shakespeare*, 11–28.

[58] *Richard II* becomes a cautious exercise in Jacobite pathos, as Theobald's prologue makes clear:

Our Author labours in an humbler strain,
But hopes to sooth you with a pleasing Pain;
To move your hearts, and force your Eyes to flow
With Tears, drawn from an ENGLISH *Monarch's Woe.*
Justly his pen's mistaken Task he'll own,
If you can see a Prince, without a Groan,
Forc'd by his Subjects to renounce his Throne.

Theobald, *The Tragedy of King Richard the II*, Bb3ʳ.

[59] Something of the same technique is shared by the last adaptations of this group, two surprisingly plangent repetitions of John Crowne's deployment of the *Henry VI* plays as sermons about the misery of civil war, both performed in 1723. In Ambrose Philips's *Humfrey Duke of Gloucester, a Tragedy* (London [1723]), Lady Eleanor becomes a blameless paragon who returns from the Isle of Man in time pitifully to discover her husband's murdered corpse, keeping King Henry off the stage entirely. Theophilus Cibber's *An Historical Tragedy of the Civil Wars in the Reign of King Henry VI* (London, 1723) supplements its redaction of *2* and *3 Henry VI* with, among other things, a tender new scene between York and his son, little Rutland, an equally poignant parting dialogue between Prince Edward and his wife Lady Anne Neville, and an extended dialogue between the latter and her distressed sister, Lady Elizabeth.

The only one of this group of adaptations to outlive its immediate political context, Aaron Hill's chauvinistic *King Henry the
Fifth: or, the Conquest of France by the English* (premièred in
1723 and last performed in 1746), is significantly the one which
goes furthest in its Otwayan modifications to Shakespeare's history, completely restructuring its original in domestic terms by
substituting she-tragedy for its entire comic sub-plot. Replacing
the spurned Falstaff with a spurned ex-mistress (similarly pensioned-
off after the coronation), this version of the play has Henry followed to France not by his ex-tavern companions but by Scroop's
seduced niece, Harriet, who, disguised as a page and employed *à
la* Cesario as a go-between to her royal rival, vies in person as an
object of pity with Princess Catherine, whose horror at the prospect of being married off against her wishes Hill endorses to the
extent of giving her the bitter reflections on ceremony voiced in
the original by Henry on the eve of Agincourt. (The bantering,
slightly gauche waiting-gentlewoman Alice is replaced as her companion, accordingly, by the dignified tragic confidante Charlot.)
Only one of this play's two potential tragic heroines, needless to
say, can be granted a happy ending: Catherine abandons her
objections to her royal match after discovering that Henry is in
fact the Englishman who wooed her incognito a year earlier (presumably during a lull in his liaison with Harriet), and Harriet,
after betraying the Scroop–Masham–Grey conspiracy, stabs herself at the close of a last tender dialogue with her former lover.
With the battle of Agincourt itself banished from the stage (nar-
rated in song by the Genius of England), it is the distresses and
intrigues of these two justly incensed women which occupy the
play's major action: Henry, rendered obviously perfidious despite
Hill's best attempts to launder his indiscretions, is of dramatic
interest primarily as a singularly untrustworthy potential husband,
his conquest of France an extension of his conquest of Catherine
rather than vice versa.[60]

Shakespeare's canonization as a stable figure of authority, ironically, profits enormously from this bewildering multiplicity of
contingent appropriations carried out between the Exclusion Crisis

---

[60] Cf. Brian Vickers on Colley Cibber's later *Papal Tyranny in the Reign of
King John* (1745): 'to a striking degree Cibber, like Hill and Theobald, in intensi-
fying the emotional level, recreates the style of Tate or Otway'; *Returning to
Shakespeare*, 221.

and the Jacobite uprisings. Despite the wide range of positions to which these alterations busily strive to conscript Shakespeare's histories and tragedies—Whig constitutionalism, Divine Right royalism, and all kinds of variously militant and quietist shades in between—their sheer proliferation seems to confirm the disingenuous claims of Ravenscroft and Dryden that Shakespeare's plays transcend mere politics: cumulatively the adaptations seem to demonstrate the timeless value of the plays they individually set out to rewrite and replace. In their shared use of the formulae for alteration developed during the Exclusion Crisis, they confirm in the process how much more at home Shakespeare's plays could appear, or could be made to appear, in a tragic repertory now dominated by female pathos. Whether pro- or anti-Stuart, Tory or Whig, the playwrights of the late seventeenth and early eighteenth century share a growing perception and promotion of Shakespeare as both a national father and a domestic one, his plays amenable to readings and rewritings stressing their private pathos, or their patriotic morals, or perhaps both. Lewis Theobald, indeed, conflates the two in *The Tragedy of King Richard the II*: the play's dedication to the Earl of Orrery fully combines Dryden's construction of Shakespeare as a father-figure with Otway's discovery of Shakespeare as the inventor of affective tragedy, suggesting, indeed, how neatly they might collude. Just as he has modified Shakespeare's history by supplying it with additional familial pathos, Theobald casts the play itself as an innocent Eugenia or Cordelia (or, indeed, Monimia), a blameless, powerless woman travelling in disguise through a perilous world, and its reception becomes a she-tragedy in itself, as the text pleads pitiably for succour in the name of its absent father:

MY LORD,

IT is owing to your Lordship's great Condescension, that I now presume to recommend to your Care an Orphan Child of *Shakespear*; who throws her Self at your Lordship's Feet, in the State of a Vertuous Woman in a Vicious Age, whose Innocence may be generally commended, tho' it be but sparingly incourag'd. Whatever Disguise I may have put upon Her, I hope, She retains those strong Lines of her Family, which may entitle Her, as a Descendant from that Great Parent, to Your generous Protection.[61]

---

[61] Theobald, *The Tragedy of King Richard the II*, A2^r–^{v}.

Shakespeare's tragedies and histories have themselves come to be seen as poignantly appealing tragic heroines, certain of tender regard in the coming days of the Shakespeare Ladies' Club, and, given their frequently British subject-matter, equally certain of increasing attention in a period of rising nationalism. In the process, Shakespeare has begun to acquire the prestige of England's greatest dramatist, a development decisively confirmed between the Glorious Revolution and the 1730s by the redemption of his comedies. As my next chapter will show, even Shakespeare's less elevated plays are henceforward proudly advertised as his own literary property—even while being rewritten in the interests of Augustan social propriety.

3

Property and Propriety

THE conditions of political censorship which did so much
both to dictate the form of the adaptations produced during and
after the Exclusion Crisis and to motivate their promotion as
works of the divine Shakespeare contributed also, in one instance,
to an unprecedented assertion and display of the Bard's intellectual
property not just in whole plots but in specific words and phrases.
Colley Cibber's *The Tragical History of King Richard III*, as well
as expanding the poignant role of Lady Anne, as we have seen,
adds a new first act to Shakespeare's play drawn from the end of *3
Henry VI*, so that the play's career of intrigue and bloodshed can
begin with the murder of the deposed Henry; when Cibber sub-
mitted his script to Queen Anne's Lord Chamberlain in 1699,
however, he was dismayed to receive instructions to omit this
material entirely from performance on the grounds that 'Henry
the Sixth being a Character Unfortunate and Pitied, wou'd put the
Audience in mind of the late King James'.[1] In the printed edition
of the play, published in the following year, Cibber takes elaborate
steps to clear himself of Jacobitism (insisting that the supposedly
offensive parts of the play are not his), and in the process disavows
any imputed willingness to claim authorial credit for those parts
of Shakespeare's text with which he has not mingled his labour:

I . . . leave it to the Impartial Reader how far [the first act] is offensive,
and whether its being Acted would have been as injurious to good
Manners, as the omission of it was to the rest of the Play.

Tho' there was no great danger of the Readers mistaking any of my
lines for *Shakespear's*; yet, to satisfie the curious, and unwilling to assume
more praise than is really my due, I have caus'd those that are intirely
Shakespear's to be printed in this *Italick Character*; and those lines with
this mark (') before 'em, are generally his thoughts, in the best dress I
could afford 'em: What is not so mark'd, or in a different Character is

---

[1] Colley Cibber, *The Tragical History of King Richard III* (1700), 'The Preface',
in Spencer (ed.), *Five Restoration Adaptations*, 279.

intirely my own. I have done my best to imitate his Style, and manner of thinking.[2]

Plainly separated from Cibber's own innocent contributions, the passages he has taken over from *3 Henry VI* and *Richard III* are here explicitly treated as the distinctive expressions of William Shakespeare's individual mind, Cibber merely compensating here and there for their obscurity or lack of decorum by putting Shakespeare's 'thoughts' into 'the best dress [he] could afford 'em'. The typographical strategy by which Cibber signals which thoughts are his own and which are Shakespeare's, furthermore, distinguishes as crucially between the stage and the study as it does between Cibber and Shakespeare: imitating Shakespeare's 'style, and manner of thinking', Cibber does his best to make the differences between the adapted and unchanged sections of the play imperceptible to theatre audiences, but then makes sure that they will be as visible as possible to readers.[3] Adaptation here becomes a process as much literary as theatrical, simultaneously catering to audiences and beguiling them, only capable of being fully recognized and appreciated by 'the curious' in the privacy of their own libraries.

In this respect Cibber's adaptation is entirely characteristic of its period. Between the 1680s and the 1730s, a new insistence on the separation of 'popular' from 'literary' drama makes itself felt, a separation which is in part a symptom of the repositioning of the stage in relation to what has been termed the emergent bourgeois public sphere, with its increased emphasis on print culture rather than oral. In this climate some of Shakespeare's hitherto neglected plays are rewritten, according to contrasting rationales, on both sides of this newly policed boundary: on the 'popular' side, Shakespeare provides at first the sources, and later the ostensible legitimation, for a variety of ephemeral entertainments; on the 'literary' side, often while being purged of just those 'low' elements which

---

[2] Colley Cibber, *The Tragical History of King Richard III* (1700), 'The Preface', in Spencer (ed.), *Five Restoration Adaptations*, 279.

[3] In fooling audiences, Cibber was extremely successful—there are still many people who would recognize 'Off with his head. So much for *Buckingham*' and 'Conscience avaunt; *Richard's* himself again' as quotations from *Richard III* without knowing that Shakespeare did not compose either line (ibid. 331, 339). Supplied without inverted commas, the former line may have misled contemporary readers too: whether Cibber intended to attribute it to Shakespeare or simply lost credit for it through a printer's error we may never know.

appealed to the popular entertainers, Shakespeare is constructed as a fully decorous Enlightenment author.[4] Although from the 1690s through the 1710s Shakespeare's characters are for many playwrights still common property, available for reuse and recombination in all manner of illicit theatrical contexts, by the 1730s the character most frequently and importantly abstracted from the Complete Works is Shakespeare himself, the implied author whose 'thoughts' and 'manner of thinking' Cibber seeks simultaneously to imitate and to appropriate in his version of *Richard III*. Once deduced from his own dramas, Shakespeare-as-author, posthumously professionalized by the editorial endeavours of Nicholas Rowe (1709) and Alexander Pope (1723–5), can be declared fully to possess them, and the adaptation and appropriation of Shakespeare's plays merely as a body of old texts begins to give place to the adaptation and appropriation of 'Shakespeare'. Summoned from the dead with ever more frequency to appear as a prologue, the Bard's spectre returns to the London stage in order to endorse, in particular, a series of prescriptive and corrective rewritings of his comedies: once their author has achieved the status of a monitory ghost, Shakespeare's plays too must be purged of their fleshly, earthly lapses.

Plagiarism and Indecency

One of the most striking features of the literary criticism which begins to emerge as such in England after the Glorious Revolution is its overwhelming interest in matters of intellectual property, a concept (frequently associated with other kinds of social decorum) destined to exert an increasing influence on ways of using Shakespeare both within and outside the theatres.[5] This development is especially apparent in the case of the last Shakespearean adaptor of the Exclusion Crisis, Thomas Durfey, whose status is utterly transformed over the decades following the première of his 1682

---

[4] On the Enlightenment concept of authorship, see Michel Foucault, 'What Is An Author?', in Josue Harari (ed.), *Textual Strategies* (Ithaca, NY, 1979).

[5] On the rise and function of literary criticism in the Enlightenment, see Peter Uwe Hohendahl, *The Institution of Criticism* (Ithaca, NY, 1982), 44–82: on its conceptions of literary property, see Mark Rose, 'The Author as Proprietor: *Donaldson* v. *Becket* and the Genealogy of Modern Authorship', *Representations*, 23 (1988).

version of *Cymbeline, The Injured Princess*.[6] A prolific and remorselessly mainstream playwright from his debut with the heroic
The Siege of Memphis; or, The Ambitious Queen in 1676 to his
final publication *New Operas, with Comical Stories and Poems* in
1721, Durfey is increasingly held up to ridicule towards the end of
his career as a violator of both property and propriety, until, after
his death, he comes to enjoy a shadowy existence in the discourse
of eighteenth-century criticism as the very personification of derivative smut. In this respect he is only one of the more conspicuous
victims of what Peter Stallybrass and Allon White have identified
as a general movement within early eighteenth-century culture to
stigmatize and repudiate the expressions of earlier popular culture,[7]
a development with far-reaching effects for both the treatment of
Shakespeare's texts and conceptions of his status as an author.

In 1682 Durfey is already being represented, largely on the
grounds of his devout royalism, as 'a *Debauchee, Buffoon*, a
Knave, a *Dunce*',[8] but his work is subjected to far more detailed
and punishing scrutiny in Gerard Langbaine's *Momus Triumphans: or, the Plagiaries of the English Stage*, an ownership-
obsessed catalogue of the printed English drama, published, highly
appropriately, in the year of the bourgeois revolution, 1688.[9] The
writings body-searched for stolen plots in this symptomatic publication are meticulously catalogued by author: as well as including the first full-scale exercise in Shakespearean source-hunting,
this pamphlet enacts an important and in many cases new separation between Shakespeare and the adapted versions of his plays,
listing the adaptations among the plays of their adaptors and
labelling them as such, even when the adaptations, like *The Injured
Princess*, do not themselves confess to deriving from Shakespearean
originals. Langbaine summarizes his view of Durfey in his next
book, *An Account of the English Dramatick Poets*, 1691—'Mr.
Durfey like the *Cuckow*, makes it his business to suck other Birds

---

[6] For a fuller and more general account of Durfey's critical reception, see Jack
Knowles and J. M. Armistead, 'Thomas D'Urfey and Three Centuries of Critical
Response', *Restoration*, 8: 2 (1984), 72–80.

[7] See Peter Stallybrass and Allon White, *The Politics and Poetics of Transgression* (Ithaca, NY, 1986), ch. 2: 'The Grotesque Body and the Smithfield Muse:
Authorship in the Eighteenth Century', 80–124.

[8] *The Tory Poets: A Satyr* (London, 1682), sometimes attributed to Thomas
Shadwell.

[9] Gerard Langbaine, *Momus Triumphans: or, the Plagiaries of the English Stage*
(London, 1688).

Eggs'[10]—an opinion developed at greater length by the first critical pamphlet devoted entirely to Durfey, *Wit for Money, or, Poet Stutter*, published in the same year. Ratifying its assault on Durfey's venal lewdness, this pamphlet, significantly, cites as his ultimate transgression his willingness to martyr the classics of English drama:

> Witness his laying violent hands on Shakespeare and Fletcher, whose plays he hath altered so much for the worse, like the Persecutors of Old, killing their living beauties by joining them to his dead lameless [*sic*] deformities.[11]

The assault is renewed in *Poeta Infamis: or, a Poet not worth Hanging*, published the following year: Durfey is here accused both of political slipperiness ('I wonder how a Man that has always been such a Grand *Tory*, should comply and turn *Whigg* at last')[12] and of literary vulgarity (the diction of his plays is 'mere *Billings-gate* Discourse, instead of Poetical Adornments in Conversation', 'more fit for *Bartholomew Fair*, than the *Theatre*', *Poeta Infamis*, 4, 12), and such is his treatment of other people's writings that the tract's anonymous author declares that: 'I cannot accuse you of being a Plagiary, because the greatest, and best part of all thy Works are stolen; but I can never (with a safe Conscience) allow thee to be a Poet' (ibid. 5).

Lacking in proper integrity, socially and morally transgressive, and showing inadequate respect for the literary work of others, Durfey is less than a true author. The attack is memorably taken up by Jeremy Collier, whose *A Short View of the Immorality and Profaneness of the English Stage* (1698), identifying the entire corpus of Restoration comedy with sexual corruption, singles out Durfey's popular three-part adaptation of *Don Quixote* (*The Comical History of Don Quixote*, 1694–6) for meticulous castigation, along with, in particular, Dryden's *Amphitryon* and Vanbrugh's *The Relapse*.[13] Collier's assault on Durfey is completed by a highly revealing quotation from a French neo-classical critic:

---

[10] Langbaine, *English Dramatick Poets*, 179.

[11] *Wit for Money, or, Poet Stutter* (London, 1691), 10.

[12] *Poeta Infamis: or, a Poet not worth Hanging* (London, 1692), 15. On Durfey's political compromises after 1688, see also Loftis, *Politics of Drama*, 23–4.

[13] Jeremy Collier, *A Short View of the Immorality and Profaneness of the English Stage* (London, 1698), 177–232.

I shall conclude with Monsieur *Boileau*'s *Art* of *Poetry*, This citation may possibly be of some service to Mr. *Durfey*; For if not concern'd in the Application, he may at least be precaution'd by the Advice.

The Translation runs thus.

I like an Author that Reforms the Age;
And keeps the right Decorum of the Stage:
That always pleases by just Reasons Rule:
But for a tedious Droll a Quibbling Fool,
Who with low nauseous Baudry fills his Plays;
Let him be gone and on two Tressels raise
Some *Smithfield* Stage, where he may act his Pranks.
And make *Jack-puddings* speak to Mountebanks.
                                             (208)

According to Collier, the kind of comedy at which Durfey excels, formerly the delight of the court, should be banished from the position of privileged cultural centrality it enjoys on the stages of the Theatres Royal to that definitive site of lowness and transgression, the fair. In that more appropriate setting, Collier implies, Durfey will be exposed for what he is: not a true author at all, but a kind of licensed flasher.

Durfey's name, indeed, soon becomes synonymous with this violent rejection of Restoration comedy. A character in the anonymous dialogue *A Comparison Between the Two Stages*, written by an avid theatre-goer who none the less expresses a surprising degree of support for Collier,[14] sneeringly dismisses the run of contemporary playwrights in one breath, lamenting that theatregoers nowadays have to tolerate the efforts of 'D[enni]s, D[urfe]y, G[ildo]n, S[ettl]e, B[urnab]y, and who not?' (54).[15] Durfey is singled out for particular condemnation: 'he's the very Antipodes to all the Poets, Antient and Modern', declares this tract (29). Tellingly, one of the few older Durfey plays still in the repertory

---

[14] *A Comparison Between the Two Stages* (London, 1702), 93–4.

[15] Interestingly, all these writers had experimented unsuccessfully with the adaptation of Shakespearean comedies, Dennis, Gildon, and Burnaby within the last three seasons. Immediately hereafter, Farquhar is added to this catalogue, and his *The Constant Couple; or, A Trip to the Jubilee* is castigated in characteristic terms as a perfect specimen of the low, carnivalesque comedy of which all these writers are accused; Critick admits that he laughed at the play, but only 'With scorn, contempt and derision; I wou'd ha'done the same at the merry Tricks of a Monkey, or the Wit of a Jack-pudding, and think it the more entertaining Farce of the two' (*A Comparison*, 56).

was henceforward cleared of its association with this increasingly disreputable writer: from 1702 onwards, revivals of *The Injured Princess* advertise the play only as *Cimbiline, King of Brittain. Written by the Famous Author William Shakespear.*[16]

Twenty-five years after Durfey's death, the scapegoating of Durfey as a writer synonymous with disreputable dramatic forms and the redefinition of Shakespeare's plays as their absolute antithesis are made key points in Garrick's celebrated manifesto speech, Dr Johnson's *Prologue Spoken by Mr Garrick at the Opening of the Theatre in Drury-Lane, 1747*. Opening with a famous paean to Shakespeare not as a Stuart father-king but as the great paternal originator of the theatre itself ('When Learning's triumph o'er her barb'rous foes | First rear'd the Stage, immortal Shakespeare rose ...'), this poem goes on to contrast the achievements of the Renaissance stage against the sins of its Restoration successor, sins personified, once more, by Durfey:

The Wits of *Charles* found easier Ways to Fame,
Nor wish'd for Johnson's Art, or Shakespear's Flame;
Themselves they studied, as they felt, they writ,
Intrigue was Plot, Obscenity was Wit.
    .   .   .   .   .   .

Till Shame regain'd the Post that Sense betray'd,
And Virtue call'd Oblivion to her Aid.
    .   .   .   .   .   .

But who the coming Changes can presage,
And mark the future Periods of the Stage?—
Perhaps if Skill could distant Times explore,
New *Behns*, new *Durfeys*, yet remain in Store.[17]

The process of disowning and reviling Durfey and his drama comes full circle from *Wit for Money*'s righteous indignation at *The Injured Princess* a decade after this horrified speculation, when Garrick, in another famous prologue, scorns those critical members of his audience who for all their pretensions to discrimination are 'So blindly thoughtful and so darkly read, | They take Tom Durfey's for the Shakespeare's Head'.[18]

---

[16] *The London Stage*, 2: 26–7.
[17] Samuel Johnson, *The Complete English Poems*, ed. David Fleeman (Harmondsworth, 1971), 83–4.
[18] Prologue to *Catharine and Petruchio*, 1756, in Garrick, *Plays*, iii. 190–1.

As Bergmann and Pedicord's notes on this passage point out, 'Garrick is anxious to establish his theatre as the home of Shakespeare's plays . . . since D'Urfey represents decadence and indecency to the public, Garrick wishes to draw a distinction between D'Urfey's theatre and his own reformed stage at Drury Lane.'[19] Shakespeare's comedy and Durfey's, which had coexisted at Drury Lane in one play in 1682, are now defined as polar opposites: Shakespeare has been redefined as a classic author, Durfey as an anti-author, a Smithfield prankster.

The divorce between Shakespeare and the kinds of low entertainment represented here by Durfey, prefigured in *Wit for Money* as early as 1691, was by no means complete at the turn of the eighteenth century, and there were still writers perfectly willing to treat Shakespeare's plays as raw material for their own reworkings: increasingly, however, this attitude to adaptation is associated only with low theatrical forms and low theatrical venues. A good example is provided by a fairground droll, the first record of which, an advertisement for a performance at Parker's Booth, Bartholomew Fair, dates from 1703.[20] Called *The Famous History of Dorastus and Fawnia* (reappearing in a bill of 1729 as *Dorastus and Fawnia, or the Royal Shepherdess* and another of 1749 as *Dorastus and Fawnia, or, The Royal Shepherd and Sheperdess*),[21] this playlet, no text of which survives, has been identified by Stanley Wells (from surviving cast lists) as an adaptation of *The Winter's Tale*, a conflation of Shakespeare's play and its source, Greene's *Pandosto*;[22] it may lie behind Macnamara Morgan's more up-market version *The Sheep-Shearing* (1754), which in its turn, ironically enough, would be imitated in one of the very plays introduced by the impeccably respectable prologue quoted above, Garrick's *Florizel and Perdita* (premièred in 1756). To the performers at Parker's Booth, apparently, *The Winter's Tale* remained part of the common stock of old stories and plays from which such entertainments might be generated; blissfully oblivious to the stirrings of Bardolatry, the bills name no author (the very idea of

[19] Ibid. 430, l. 9 n. and l. 35 n.
[20] See Sybil Rosenfeld, *The Theatre of the London Fairs in the Eighteenth Century* (Cambridge, 1960), 16.
[21] Ibid. 33, 119–120.
[22] Stanley Wells, 'A Shakespearean Droll?', *Theatre Notebook*, 15 (1961), 116–17.

authorship being quite irrelevant to this genre), and the droll probably neither sought nor achieved the dignity of print. Here for a while at least the lesser-known among Shakespeare's plays remained an integral part of popular culture, unclaimed for literary respectability.

The survival of this attitude to Shakespeare and the question of authorship is made explicit in the preface to another unpretentious entertainment derived in part from one of his plays, namely Charles Molloy's *The Half-Pay Officers*, first performed at Lincoln's Inn Fields on 11 January 1720. This short farce—which Molloy modestly refrains from distinguishing even by that label, referring to it merely as a 'Thing'—was cobbled together at short notice as the vehicle for a superannuated Restoration actress called Mrs Fryar, who happened to retain in her memory the widow's role she had once played in Davenant's *Love and Honour*; Molloy merely abbreviated Davenant's play, and supplied Mrs Fryar with two new wooers in the persons of Fluellen and Pistol.[23] (Pistol, rechristened Culverin, takes over the role of Vasco in Davenant's play, but still ends up being forced to eat Fluellen's leek.) In the Preface, Molloy treats neither himself nor Shakespeare as 'authors' proper: he refuses the title himself, and grants Shakespeare no proprietorship over his characters, considering Fluellen simply as a well-esteemed 'Thing' available for reuse much as one might retell a good joke:

THIS Thing was brought upon the Stage with no other Design, but that of shewing Mrs. *FRYAR*, the House being willing to encourage any thing, by which it might propose to entertain the Town; therefore the Author, or rather the Transcriber, did not think himself in any way concerned in its success, as to the Reputation of a Writer; I say Transcriber, the greatest Part of it being old: The Part of Mrs. *Fryer* is in an old Play, call'd, *Love and Honour*, which she acted when she was young. . . .

THE Character of *Fluellin* has been esteem'd (next to that of Sir *John Falstaff*) the best and most humorous that *Shakespear* ever wrote; there are many other Things in this, that have been reckon'd good Comedy: This we may venture to say, without incurring the censure of vain; for it

---

[23] 'Principal Part by Peg Fryer, it being the first time of her Appearing on any Stage since the Reign of King Charles II', proclaim the bills. Quoted in *The London Stage*, 2: 563. On Peg Fryer and her performance in this play, see John Harold Wilson, *All the King's Ladies*, 144–5; *BDA* v. 419–20.

can be no Offence to Modesty, for a Man to commend what is not his own.[24]

Writing purely to oblige a performer and please the public, Molloy disclaims all pretence to authorial originality; the old jokes and situations he has strung together (which include a comic duel probably derived from *Twelfth Night*) are resources available to anyone, and his play is confessedly as much the arbitrary result of a coincidence of actress and public demand as it is the product of Molloy's distinctive individual labour. The title page of *The Half-Pay Officers* proclaims that it offers the play 'As it is Acted at the Theatre in Lincoln's-Inn Fields', and Molloy's preface really only glosses the implications of what by 1720 was already an old-fashioned approach to dramatic publishing; for Molloy, the text of such a play represents not an author's finished literary product but a necessarily imperfect souvenir of performance, the surviving memento of a collective experience. *The Half-Pay Officers* is neither Molloy's, nor Shakespeare's, nor Davenant's; its characters and scenes belong to the theatre, not to any single proprietor, and can thus be combined and adapted at will.

This blithe lack of interest in Shakespeare's original authorship, rare by 1720, seems gradually to have become impossible over the course of the early eighteenth century, and the trend towards at least greater lip-service to a more exalted view of the individual writer is apparent even in a series of adaptations as shamelessly opportunistic and generically impure as *The Half-Pay Officers*. The change is especially marked in the case of two inventive reworkings of *A Midsummer Night's Dream*, produced in 1692 and 1716 respectively. The text of *The Fairy-Queen*, a lavish semi-opera with music by Purcell (produced at Drury Lane in 1692), is less concerned with the issue of authorship even than *The Half-Pay Officers*, mentioning neither Shakespeare nor the adaptor (probably Settle);[25] the play, having offered its audience every special effect of which the Theatre Royal was capable, concludes not with Puck's 'If we shadows have offended . . .' but with Titania merely assuring the audience that they have had their money's

---

[24] Charles Molloy, *The Half-Pay Officers* (London, 1720), 'Preface', pp. iii, v.

[25] The ascription was first made by Frank C. Brown in *Elkanah Settle*, 95–6, and has been generally accepted since. Brown quotes from a pamphlet, *Reflexions on Settle's Narrative* (1683), which suggests that Settle may have first produced this opera in the form of a fairground droll in the early 1680s.

worth and ought to be grateful—'If all this will not do, the Devil's in ye.'[26] Twenty-four years later, however, when Richard Leveridge set about profitably ridiculing the continuing vogue for opera with another entertainment drawn from the same play, *Pyramus and Thisbe. A Comic Masque*, such dramatic hybrids seemed to require some apology rather than this kind of confident boast. Significantly, Leveridge chooses to justify his variety turn not only on the grounds that it is entertaining in the theatre, but by pointing out that it derives from a Shakespearean original which is itself a specimen of sheer low comedy:

As Diversion is the Business of the Stage, 'tis Variety best contributes to that Diversion. The Reader therefore, or *Auditor rather*, tho' the severest Critick, 'tis hoped will accept of the following *Entertainment*.

The ARGUMENT

    ...This Tragical Tale the great *Shakespear* thought fit to turn into a most Comical Interlude, in a Play of his call'd *The Midsummer Night's Dream*, as Perform'd by a Company of Rusticks, set out in the lowest Air, and Style of downright Farce and Doggrel.

    From that Immortal Author's Original, I have made bold to Dress out the same in Recitative, and Airs, after the present *Italian* mode, hoping I have given the same Comical Face, though in a Musical Dress.[27]

Leveridge, as a musician, is even keener than Molloy to have his adaptation judged in the theatre rather than on the page (hence his desire to treat the reader as an 'Auditor rather'), but unlike Molloy he feels the additional need to present his indulgence in broad humour as an example of fidelity to Shakespeare's original 'Interlude', the vulgar 'Air' of which he insists upon as if anticipating readers unaccustomed to thinking of 'great' Shakespeare as an exponent of 'downright Farce and Doggrel'. Shakespeare is here invoked to legitimize and indeed sell low comedy (by 1716 there is presumably more commercial gain to be made by advertising an adaptation of *A Midsummer Night's Dream* as deriving from Shakespeare than there was in 1692), but apparently by now he

---

[26] [Elkanah Settle], *The Fairy-Queen: an Opera* (London, 1692), 52. In fact the show lost money: see Hume, *Development of English Drama*, 405, 407.

[27] Richard Leveridge, *Pyramus and Thisbe. A Comic Masque* (London, 1716), 'Preface'. *A Midsummer Night's Dream* still having failed to achieve popularity in its entirety, Leveridge's comic masque was imitated 30 years later in John Frederick Lampe's *Pyramus and Thisbe: a mock opera* (London, 1745).

can only do so at the risk of tarnishing his reputation as an 'Immortal'.

In the same year as this preface, two competing part-Shakespearean farces appeared which are revealingly divided on this question of whether to acknowledge Shakespeare as a past master of the Smithfield prank. Early in 1716, Charles Johnson began work on a topical elaboration of the Induction to *The Taming of the Shrew*, turning Christopher Sly into a Jacobite shoemaker. Before his *The Cobler of Preston* had opened at Drury Lane, however, the comedian Christopher Bullock, having heard rumours of the source, title, and plot of the play, had written, rehearsed, and premièred his own *The Cobler of Preston* at Lincoln's Inn Fields.[28] Vindicating this somewhat unethical coup, Bullock adopts a casual attitude to dramatic authorship which in some respects seems to resemble those of Molloy or the producers of *Dorastus and Fawnia*: 'I hope I may be allow'd (without Offence) to take *Shakespear*'s *Tinker* of *Burton-Heath*, and make him the *Cobler* of *Preston*, as well as another; for no single Person has yet pretended to have a *Patent* for plundering Old Plays.'[29] It is telling, however, that Bullock is already imagining the possibility of such reuse of old texts falling under the sway of some kind of copyright legislation (imagining a 'Patent' being issued that might copyright plagiarism itself), and, unabashed as he is about his theft of Johnson's idea ('I thought it might be of as good Service to our *Stage* as to the *other*,' Bullock, *Cobler*, ix), it clearly is not possible for Bullock to treat Shakespeare's comedies as just any 'Old Plays'. In publishing his farce he avails himself of a convention imitated from more self-consciously literary adaptations: 'I have the Story as it was wrote by *Shakespear* in the *Taming of the Shrew*: and part of his Language I have made use of, with a little Alteration (which, for the satisfaction of my Readers, I have distinguish'd by this Mark ' before each Line)' (ibid. vi.)

Low comic actor as he is, Bullock clearly feels, despite his unashamed unoriginality, that in publishing his farce he is aspiring to a kind of authorship incompatible with disrespect for the play-

---

[28] Bullock's play appeared on 24 Jan. (as an afterpiece to Vanbrugh's *The Confederacy*), Johnson's on 3 Feb. (as an afterpiece to Vanbrugh's *The Relapse*). See *The London Stage*, 2: 386–7.

[29] Christopher Bullock, *The Cobler of Preston. And the Adventures of Half an Hour* (4th ed.; London, 1723), 'Preface', pp. vi–vii.

wright he is 'plundering', and thus he chooses to come clean with
his readers about the precise extent of his debt to Shakespeare. In
the play's prologue, as in Leveridge's preface, Shakespeare is invoked as an authority for the farce's ignoble subject-matter, fea-
turing as 'Old Shakespear', a source of timeworn common sense
here contrasted against the narrowly political orientation of
Johnson. According to Bullock, the topical reference to the Jacobite
defeat at Preston in Johnson's title has only been retained as a
ploy to attract more paying customers: disavowing any political
motive, he declares that,

> though our Scene's at *Preston*, we've no Plot,
> But what Old *Shakespear* made—to ridicule a Sot.
> Indeed I can't deny—
> But th'Underplot was laid with a Design
> To please some Friends—and draw the Vulgar in.
> (Bullock, Cobler, 'Prologue')

Bullock's willingness to confess his debt to Shakespeare, as well as
suggesting a divided halfway stage between a completely happy-
go-lucky view of dramatic authorship (treating all plots and old
plays as fair game) and a more deferential attitude to literary
property, is also probably derived in part from a desire to embar-
rass Johnson. Johnson's rival *The Cobler of Preston* nowhere
confesses its Shakespearean source: its prologue, indeed, denies
that the kind of entertainment this skit represents is remotely
compatible with literary reputation. The product of a 'Heimskirk
Muse', playing 'in Life's low Business', such a play can aim to
receive only vulgar belly-laughs, defined as the very antithesis of
literary fame:

Names that could never rise to Epic Verse
May furnish out a Ballad, or a Farce.
Our Author has a Comick Rebel stole
To make you Mirth; a drinking, noisy Fool:
His Heimskirk Muse in Life's low Business plays,
And hopes in Laughter to receive your Praise.[30]

Johnson's decision not to record Shakespeare's contribution to
this tawdry amusement in fact represents not the cheerful plagiar-

---

[30] Charles Johnson, 'The Cobler of Preston', in Leo Hughes and Arthur H.
Scouten (eds.), *Ten English Farces* (Austin, Tex. 1948), 151.

istic indifference of Parker's Booth (as Bullock implicitly suggests by conspicuously proclaiming his own debt to the Bard) but its opposite. It is not that Johnson does not care that Shakespeare wrote the original from which his farce is taken but that he wishes actively to suppress this piece of information in the interests of Shakespeare's authorial honour, just as in preparing *As You Like It* for the stage in 1723, as we shall see, he would save Shakespeare from vulgarity by excising virtually all its characters beneath the rank of courtier.[31]

By the time of Richard Worsdale's version of *The Taming of the Shrew*, however, *A Cure for a Scold* (1735), Shakespeare's status is so well established that there is no question of concealing his original authorship, which is indeed offered as the chief selling-point of Worsdale's play on its title page ('Founded upon SHAKE-SPEAR's taming of a Shrew'), in its preface ('If the Publick are so kind to believe that the Great Author, whose Work I have attempted to abbreviate, is not extreamly injured by this Undertaking, my greatest Fear is over'), and in its prologue, which goes so far as to represent Worsdale's play as the direct utterance of a Bard presented in the image of a morally uplifting Mark Antony:

'Tis *Shakespear* speaks, let ev'ry Ear attend,
The Good we're sure to please—the Bad may mend.[32]

The division between 'low' adaptations largely uninterested in Shakespeare's authorship and 'literary' ones concerned above all to portray him as a great exemplar has by now broken down: indeed, by the middle of the century, as Garrick would discover to his great profit, the invocation of the great Shakespeare would be capable of legitimizing virtually anything. The inherently improving

---

[31] Similarly, William Taverner and Dr Brown, adapting Shakespeare's most purely farcical play *The Comedy of Errors* as *Every Body Mistaken* (acted at Lincoln's Inn Fields just a month after Johnson's play), not only follow Johnson's example in not attaching Shakespeare's name to the entertainment, but refrain, like the producers of *Dorastus and Fawnia*, from publishing the script at all. See Hogan, i. 98.

[32] Richard Worsdale, *A Cure for a Scold. A Ballad Farce of Two Acts* (London, [1735]). A year before Worsdale's play another adaptation of *The Comedy of Errors* appeared, the anonymous *See If You Like It* (the very title of which presupposes a new degree of familiarity with the Shakespeare canon), which, although, like *Every Body Mistaken*, unpublished, was proudly advertised as 'A Comedy of Two Acts, Taken from Plautus and Shakespeare'. See Hogan, i. 99.

qualities of Shakespearean drama are now virtually indisputable, and can even survive association with this 'Ballad Farce of Two Acts' (despite its silent retention of substantial portions of Lacy's *Sauny the Scott*). Shakespeare has now been fully acknowledged as the author even of such a farcical comedy as *The Taming of the Shrew*, and even of this adapted version. This process, whereby both author and plays are redeemed for Augustan culture, is made still clearer by a series of more avowedly 'literary' treatments of his texts carried out over the same period.

Property and Propriety

As well as participating enthusiastically in the fall of Durfey, Collier's *A Short View of the Immorality and Profaneness of the English Stage* and its unknown sympathizer's *A Comparison Between the Two Stages* contribute their share to the rise of Shakespeare. While the religious and political allegiances of Collier's tract have often been remarked upon (not least by the writers it attacks),[33] what has usually escaped comment is the fact that these views coexist in Collier's work with both a new strain of neo-classicism and a new emphasis on the textuality of drama: as a result, its treatment of Shakespeare prefigures several of the adaptations produced during the ensuing decades in claiming the Bard as in every sense a classic, and a library classic at that. Spared the worst of Collier's lash, Shakespeare features in *A Comparison Between the Two Stages* as one of the last respectable props of a crumbling and discredited repertoire: between them, the two essays suggest something of both how and why the revival and alteration of Shakespeare was of such interest to the playwrights of the early eighteenth century.

The idea that *A Short View of the Immorality and Profaneness of the English Stage* can be read not simply as an all-out assault on literature but as part of a general movement within the literary

[33] Cf. William Congreve, *Amendments of Mr. Collier's False and Imperfect Citations* (London, 1698); Sir John Vanbrugh, *A Short Vindication of The Relapse and The Provoked Wife from Immorality and Profaneness* (London, 1698); John Dennis, *The Usefulness of the Stage, to the Happiness of Mankind, to Government, and to Religion. Occasioned by a late Book, written by Jeremy Collier, M.A.* (London, 1698).

culture itself towards a prudish neo-classicism should not be a surprising one. Collier's book, after all, despite its scorn of 'the *Heathen* Religion' (Collier, *Immortality and Profaneness*, 'The Contents', A4), begins and ends with appeals to classical precept and example; chapter I ('The *Immodesty* of the *Stage*') devotes most of its length to demonstrating that the Roman and Greek theatres were '*more* inoffensive than *the* English' (ibid.), praising Terence, Seneca, Aeschylus, Sophocles, and Euripides in turn, and the final chapter, 'The Opinion of *Paganism*, of the *Church*, and *State*, concerning the *Stage*', prefaces its minute scrutiny of the Church Fathers' opinions on the subject with an equally thorough explication of the 'Opinion of the *Heathen* Philosophers, Orators, and Historians concerning the *Stage*', and a proof that the theatre was outlawed by 'the *Constitutions* of *Athens*, *Sparta*, and *Rome*' (A4^v). As learned in the classical dramatists as any other educated man of his day, Collier proves to be just as deeply read in the vernacular tradition. For all his disapproval of acting, he clearly feels that no particular shame should attach to perusing plays in the study; excelling at a species of close reading which is the antithesis of drama criticism, he delights in citing playwrights in support of his own anti-theatrical viewpoint. Anticipating Tonson and Rowe's inception of the Shakespearean editorial tradition a decade later, Collier's tract is already treating Shakespeare's plays as texts to be read rather than performed.

Shakespeare appears twice in the course of Collier's attempts to excavate a tradition of classical purity in the English theatre, once unfavourably and once as a paragon. After Collier's initial trawl through the writings of antiquity, Shakespeare is cited as the first and most reprehensible of the native pre-Civil War triumvirate:

To come Home, and near our own Times: The *English* Theatre from Queen *Elizabeth* to King *Charles* II. will afford us something not inconsiderable to our purpose.

   As for *Shakespear*, he is too guilty to make an Evidence: But I think he gains not much by his Misbehaviour; He has commonly *Plautus*'s *Fate*, where there is most Smut, there is least Sense.

(50)

Collier for the time being imports the chaster Corneille to take Shakespeare's place, but a hundred pages later he returns to Shakespeare, changing his mind and admitting him to the court as a prosecution witness against Dryden, in whose *The Mock-Astrologer*, according to Collier (148), 'we see what a fine time Lewd People have on the *English Stage*':

In the mean time I shall take a Testimony or two from *Shakespear*. And here we may observe the admir'd *Falstaffe* goes off in Disappointment. He is thrown out of Favour as being a *Rake*, and dies like a Rat behind the Hangings. The Pleasure he had given, would not excuse him. The *Poet* was not so partial, as to let his Humour compound for his Lewdness. If 'tis objected that this remark is wide of the Point, because *Falstaffe* is represented in Tragedy, where the Laws of Justice are more strictly observ'd. To this I answer, that you may call *Henry* the Fourth and Fifth, Tragedies if you please. But for all that, *Falstaffe* wears no *Buskins*, his Character is perfectly Comical from end to end.

(154)

Collier can ultimately forgive Shakespeare because at heart, as the disciplining of Falstaff shows, his comedy is that of a neo-classical moralist: reclaiming him from his lapses into obscenity and from his lapses into nonsense amounts to the same thing, and this short, punitive abstraction of a morally instructive biography of Falstaff from the Henriad is in a sense a direct critical precursor of the corrective Shakespeare adaptations which appear over the next twenty years. Collier's aesthetic preference for classical dramatic decorums and his moral insistence on Christian social decorums are revealed in these citations of Shakespeare as two aspects of the same movement to reject and expel the vulgar and the disorderly (appropriately represented here by the unregenerate comic body of Falstaff), a movement in which Shakespeare's literary adaptors soon enlist themselves as enthusiastic collaborators.

Shakespeare features again as a potential saviour in *A Comparison Between the Two Stages*, although here it is Shakespeare himself who is abstracted from the Henry plays rather than Falstaff. At the climax of the pamphlet's conspectus of the recent history of the two rival companies, Betterton is depicted in crisis. His breakaway troupe at Lincoln's Inn Fields is threatened by the popularity of Drury Lane's unregenerate operatic spectaculars (for which *The Fairy-Queen* had established a precedent),[34] with which Betterton's Lincoln's Inn Fields has not the scenic resources to compete. With no popular dramatic formulae coming to hand to

[34] *A Comparison*, 34.

replace the outdated and increasingly despised dramatic modes of his existing repertory,[35] he retires to his study and falls to his knees in prayer.

O *Shakespear, Shakespear*! What have our Sins brought upon us! We have renounc'd the wayes which thou hast taught us, and are degenerated into Infamy and Corruption: Look down from thy Throne on *Mount Parnassus*, and take commiseration on thy Sons now fallen into Misery: Let down a Beam of thy Brightness upon this our forlorn *Theatre*; let thy Spirit dwell with us, let thy Influence be upon our Poets, let the Streams of thy *Helicon* glide along by *Lincolns-Inn-Fields*, and fructifie our Soil as the Waters of the *Nile* make fruitful the barren Banks of *Egypt. He rose, and rose much comforted*: With that he falls to work about his Design, opens the Volume and picks out two or three of Shakespears Plays; and now, says he, I'll feague it away ifaith.

(*A Comparison*, 42)

Betterton proceeded to mount a whole series of Shakespeare revivals, beginning with both parts of *Henry IV*, and, as *A Comparison Between the Two Stages* puts it, 'Shakespear's Ghost was rais'd at the New-house, and he seem'd to inhabit it for ever' (45).[36] Even a more hostile commentator, George Farquhar, shares this sense of Betterton's contact with the Author's shade: his prologue to *The Constant Couple: or, A Trip to the Jubilee*, performed at rival Drury Lane in 1700, similarly presents the Lincoln's Inn Fields run of Shakespearean revivals as a feat of necromancy:

To Engage the Fair, all other Means being lost,
They Fright the Boxes with Old *Shakespeare*'s GHOST.
    .   .   .   .

Their Case is Hard, that such Despair can show;
They've Disoblig'd all Powers Above, they know;
And now must have Recourse to Powers below.
Let *Shakespeare* then lye still, *Ghosts* do no good;
The Fair are Better Pleas'd with Flesh and Blood:
What is't to them, to mind the *Antient*'s Taste?
But, the Poor Folks are Mad, and I'm in haste.
Runs off[37]

---

[35] On the decline of Restoration comedy in particular, see Laura Brown, *English Dramatic Form*, 102–44.
[36] On Betterton's Shakespeare revivals, see Hume, *Development of English Drama*, 441–2.
[37] George Farquhar, *Dramatic Works*, ed. Shirley Strum Kenny (2 vols.; Oxford, 1988), i. 232–3.

By the early eighteenth century, clearly, to revive Shakespeare's works is not merely to reuse some old scripts but to call up the spirit of their author, newly promoted to the status of an 'Antient'.

Significantly, within a few seasons of thus summoning Shakespeare's ghost to the stage, Betterton would be helping summon him into print, collaborating with Nicholas Rowe on the first-ever biographical preface to the Complete Works.[38] Rowe's epoch-making 1709 edition shares *A Comparison*'s impulse to supply Shakespeare's works with an author, deduced from his plays, as Margreta de Grazia points out, in the image of their troublesome, wanton irregularity: the apocryphal anecdotes of Shakespeare's youth retailed by Rowe's preface (stealing deer, declaiming elegies over dying calves, seducing Burbage's mistress, and so on) register 'a certain unease about his particular bent of genius: its unruliness, or, in the terms repeated in commentary of this period, his "extravagance" and "licentiousness"'.[39] However, on attaining authorship of acknowledged masterpieces such as *Hamlet*, Shakespeare began to achieve, even in his own lifetime, a properly bodiless, dignified, and even royal status: 'I could never meet with any further account of him ... than that the top of his own performance was the Ghost in his own *Hamlet*,' reports Rowe.[40] The impact of this newly pervasive, if ghostly, authorial presence on attitudes to rewriting his works is revealed by a supplement to Rowe's edition, the spurious seventh volume of poems and commentary contributed to Edmund Curll's piracy the following year. Charles Gildon's 'REMARKS on the Plays of *Shakespear*' devotes much of its energy to vindicating Shakespeare's plays against the less respectable of their stage adaptations (three of which, residual traces of the 'As it is Acted' approach to Shakespearean publishing which Rowe's edition, following the Folios, supplants, manage unwitting marginal appearances in frontispiece illustrations to the earlier volumes).[41] In his first commentary on an individual play,

[38] See Samuel Schoenbaum, *Shakespeare's Lives* (Oxford, 1970), 129–35. Cf. Colonel Hart's remarks, quoted in the Introd.

[39] '"Extravagance" characterized accounts of Shakespeare's life just as "irregularity" distinguished his works, during the Restoration and beyond.' De Grazia, *Shakespeare Verbatim*, 75–7.

[40] Nicholas Rowe, 'Some Account of the Life, &c., of Mr. William Shakespeare', in *The Works of Mr. William Shakespear* (6 vols.; London, 1709), i. vi. On Rowe's edition, see esp. Gary Taylor, *Reinventing Shakespeare*, 69–81.

[41] The frontispiece to *A Midsummer Night's Dream* derives from stage designs for *The Fairy-Queen*, that for *The Taming of the Shrew* depicts a scene from Lacy's adaptation *Sauny the Scott*, and that for *The Tempest* derives from the

Gildon sets about carefully defending *The Tempest* against the transgressive and spurious *The Enchanted Island* (despite elsewhere giving his verdict in favour of Dryden's *Troilus and Cressida* and Tate's *King Lear*): according to Gildon, the added scenes are 'scarce guilty of a Thought, which we could justly attribute to *Shakespear*. I have given Instances enough I hope to show what I propos'd, that the Alteration has been no Benefit to the Original.'[42]

Gildon, clearly, does not disapprove of adaptation *per se*, but he believes that it only benefits Shakespeare's texts when its exponents supply thoughts 'which we could justly attribute to Shakespear'— presumably to replace those of Shakespeare's original thoughts which we would rather not attribute to Shakespeare. Shakespeare is thus positioned as the ultimate figure of authority behind original and adaptation alike, and Gildon goes on to abstract him from the text he has been discussing in the image of its most powerful character. After his attack on *The Enchanted Island*, Gildon closes his remarks on *The Tempest* by citing one passage for special praise, marking the first appearance as such of what has become perhaps the most famous of all Quotations from Shakespeare:

His Reflections and Moralizing on the frail and transitory State of Nature, is wonderfully fine.

'PROSP.   —These our Actors,
'As I foretold you, were all Spirits, and
'Are melted into Air, into thin Air,
'And like the baseless Fabrick of the Vision,
'The cloud-capt Towers, the gorgeous Palaces,
'The solemn Temples, the great Globe it self;
'Yea, all which it inherit, shall dissolve,
'And, like this insubstantial Pageant faded,
'Leave not a Track behind. We are such Stuff
'As Dreams are made of, and our little Life
'Is rounded with a Sleep.'[43]

---

operatic *The Tempest; or The Enchanted Island*. See Akpofure Oduaran, 'The First "collected edition" of Shakespeare: A Study of Nicholas Rowe's Edition of 1709', Ph.D. thesis (University of New Brunswick, 1985), 283.

[42] Nicholas Rowe [and Charles Gildon] ed., *The Works of Mr. William Shakespeare* (7 vols., London, '1709' [1710]), vii. 272. As Stephen Orgel points out in 'The Authentic Shakespeare': 'This is quite different from arguing that what is wrong with the Davenant text is that it is inauthentic.' (12).

[43] Rowe [1710], vii. 273–4.

What is striking about Gildon's introduction to this quotation is the ambiguity of the word 'His': are these 'Reflections' being held up for our admiration as Prospero's, or Shakespeare's? Gildon reprints the same passage from *The Tempest* in 1718, when, emphatically attributed to its author rather than its dramatic mouthpiece, it features in 'Shakespeariana: or Select Moral Reflections, Topicks, Similies, and Descriptions from SHAKESPEAR,' part of Gildon's *Complete Art of Poetry*, and the earliest example of this particular manner of commodifying Shakespearean drama for domestic consumption.[44] Prospero's speech (quoted identically, save for the alteration of 'the Vision' to 'their Vision' and 'Track' to 'Wrack') is here first printed under the tendentious heading beneath which it has been brandished so many times since: it is offered as Shakespeare's definitive statement on '*Humane Nature*'. Imaginable as the royal magician Prospero or the royal ghost Old Hamlet, Shakespeare has been converted from vulgar showman to otherworldly philosopher, his texts at their most exalted moments representing his own unmediated thoughts.

Gildon's own contribution to the purification of Shakespeare in the theatre, his adaptation *Measure for Measure, or Beauty the Best Advocate*, performed by Betterton's company at Lincoln's Inn Fields in February 1700, is accordingly framed by an explicit rejection of theatrical vulgarity and an explicit endorsement from a suitably righteous manifestation of Shakespeare's ghost. Its prologue (written by Oldmixon), like Collier's remarks on Durfey, scorns contemporary comic playwrights at length as 'Smithfield-Bards',[45] indeed at such length that the task of introducing the adaptation itself is postponed to a three-line postscript:

> [*Going, Comes Back:*
> Hold; I forgot the Business of the Day;
> No more than this, VVe, for our Selves, need Say,
> 'Tis *Purcels* Musick, and 'tis *Shakespears* Play.
>
> (A4ʳ)

Purcell's music (not to mention Nahum Tate's libretto) is featured in the form of 'The LOVES of *Dido* and *Aeneas*, a MASK, in Four MUSICAL ENTERTAINMENTS' (7), which Angelo has performed by

---

[44] Charles Gildon, *The Complete Art of Poetry* (2 vols.; London, 1718).
[45] Id., *Measure for Measure, or Beauty the Best Advocate* (London, 1700), A4ʳ.

instalments in an unsuccessful attempt to take his mind off Isabella, but despite this formal irregularity (which might at first glance appear to class the play with *The Fairy-Queen* as a transparently mercenary excuse for some crowd-pleasing operatic choruses), Gildon regards the adaptation as laudably Aristotelian, indeed as a tragedy: in 'REMARKS on the Plays of *Shakespear*' he writes of *Measure for Measure* that

The Main Story or Fable of the Play is truly *Tragical* for it is Adapted to move Terror, and Compassion, and the Action is one. Its having a Fortunate Catastrophe, is nothing to the purpose for that is in many of the Greek Tragedies...the Unities of Action and Place are pretty well observed in this Play, especially as they are in the Modern Acceptation.[46]

Gildon's 'Modern Acceptation' is throughout entirely consonant with both this self-congratulation on its classicism and the de-nunciation of Smithfield bards carried out by its prologue. Al-though he draws heavily on Davenant's *The Law Against Lovers*, Gildon is far more insistent than his predecessor on making Shakespeare's play less indecent and more socially exclusive: not only are Mistress Overdone, Froth, Elbow, Abhorson, and the offstage Kate Keep-down absent, but Pompey Bum, Barnardine, and Davenant's winsome nymphet Viola have also disappeared completely, and Lucio has become a polite well-wisher.[47] Pre-sumably delighted to have thus been re-created at Lincoln's Inn Fields as a respectable Augustan, Shakespeare rises from the grave to speak the epilogue. Cursing the rival company at Drury Lane (alluding in particular to Cibber's *Richard III*), Shakespeare blesses Betterton (whose performance as Angelo followed a recent success as Falstaff), and seconds the prologue's attack on contemporary dramatists (incidentally confirming Otway's status as his natural successor):

My Plays, by *Scriblers*, Mangl'd I have seen;
By Lifeless *Actors* Murder'd on the *Scene*.
Fat *Falstaff* here, with Pleasure, I beheld,
Toss off his Bottle, and his *Truncheon* weild:
Such as I meant him, such the *Knight* appear'd;

---

[46] Rowe [1710], vii. 293.
[47] For a more detailed account, see the edition of the play by Edward A. Cairns, *A Critical Edition of Charles Gildon's Measure for Measure, or Beauty the Best Advocate* (New York, 1987), 40–64.

He Bragg'd like *Falstaff*, and, like *Falstaff*, fear'd.
But when, on yonder *Stage*, the Knave was shewn
Ev'n by my Self, the Picture scarce was known.

 . . . . . .

Let me no more endure such Mighty VVrongs,
By *Scriblers* Folly, or by *Actors* Lungs.
So, late may *Betterton* forsake the *Stage*,
And long may *Barry* Live to Charm the *Age*.
May a New *Otway* Rise, and Learn to Move
The *Men* with *Terror*, and the *Fair* with *Love*!
Else may your Pleasure prove your greatest Curse;
And those who now *Write dully*, still *Write worse*.
    (Gildon, *Measure for Measure*, A4ᵛ)

Gildon's adaptation—never signalled as such in its prologue, which nowhere qualifies its claim to be offering 'Shakespears Play'—is by implication, like Betterton's Falstaff, true to the real Shakespeare's real intentions. As in Collier's paragraph on Falstaff, Shakespeare is presented by this adaptation as at heart a neo-classicist and a moralist, present in the smut-free essence of his text (which Gildon has obligingly distilled) as the fully responsible proprietor and guarantor of its authenticity and its meanings.

Gildon's strategy of exhuming Shakespeare as a ghost to confer posthumous approval on his adaptation is of course derived from Dryden's prologue to *Troilus and Cressida*, and it is thus especially appropriate that when the Bard's shade next treads the boards of Lincoln's Inn Fields (courtesy of George Granville, Lord Lansdowne) it should be in the recently deceased ex-laureate's company. To herald the appearance of Granville's *The Jew of Venice* in 1701, 'the Ghosts of *Shakespear* and *Dryden* arise Crown'd with Lawrel',[48] and once more the provision of a reputably spiritual author for the play and the excoriation of carnivalesque theatrical vulgarity form part and parcel of the same claim to literary

---

[48] George Granville, Lord Lansdowne, *The Jew of Venice* [1701], in Spencer (ed.), *Five Restoration Adaptations*, 345–402, 'Prologue', 348. (Subsequent references to Granville relate to this edition.) Granville, a prominent Jacobite (in *The Jew of Venice* Portia's alcoholic offstage German suitor becomes '*Myn Heer van Gutts*, the Dutchman' as a posthumous insult to King William), originally intended the play as a benefit for his literary and political colleague: 'The Profits of this *Play* were design'd for Mr. *Dryden*; but, upon his Death, given to his Son,' explains a footnote to this prologue. On Granville, see Elizabeth Handasyde, *Granville the Polite: The Life of George Granville Lord Lansdowne, 1666–1735* (Oxford, 1933): on *The Jew of Venice*, see 54–64.

probity. This prologue, contributed to the play by Granville's cousin Bevill Higgons, is more outspoken even than Collier in its denunciation of transgressively low comedy, the popularity of which is cited by Dryden's ghost as a symptom of rampant homosexuality among contemporary playgoers: not for the last time the author of the *Sonnets*—and, even more ironically, the creator of Antonio and Bassanio—is figured as the patron of an exclusively heterosexual version of normality;

[DRYD.] Their sickly Judgments, what is just, refuse,
And French Grimace, Buffoons, and Mimicks choose;
Our Scenes desert, some wretched Farce to see;
They know not Nature, for they tast not Thee.
          .   .   .   .

Thro' Perspectives revers'd they Nature view,
Which give the Passions Images, not true.
Strephon for *Strephon* sighs; and *Sapho* dies,
Shot to the soul by brighter *Sapho*'s Eyes:
No Wonder then their wand'ring Passions roam,
And feel not Nature, whom th'have overcome.
For shame let genal Love prevail agen,
You Beaux Love Ladies, and you Ladies Men.
                                        (348)

In the world of Higgons and Granville, real literature, such as the drama of Dryden and Shakespeare, inhabits a contracted, orderly space, beyond which all is grotesquerie, Frenchness, the fair, the masquerade, the unnatural, the inverted. Shakespeare proves his worthiness to inhabit this space by expressing horror and disgust at Dryden's report ('These Crimes [were] unknown, in our less polisht Age'; ibid.) and offering his plays as a contribution to the internal policing which is the proper and unique function of literature:

The Law's Defect, the juster Muse supplies,
Tis only we, can make you Good or Wise,
Whom Heav'n spares, the Poet will Chastise.
                                        (349)

If more sexually innocent than the early eighteenth century, Shakespeare's age was also less accomplished in polite letters, and the ghost's final remarks express a gratified amazement at Granville's flawlessly classical adaptation:

These Scenes in their rough Native Dress were mine;
But now improv'd with nobler Lustre shine;
The first rude Sketches *Shakespear*'s Pencil drew,
But all the Shining Master-strokes are new.
This Play, ye Criticks, shall your Fury stand,
Adorn'd and rescu'd by a faultless Hand.

(ibid.)

Needless to say, the clowning, plebeian Gobbos are conspicuously absent from the rescued version of *The Merchant of Venice* which follows. In fact the adaptation continues its prologue's crusade not only against low comedy but against sexual abnormality: identifying capitalism itself as a form of sexual perversion, Granville presents Shylock as a fetishistic precursor of Auric Goldfinger who, for once accepting Antonio's invitation to dinner, toasts the sole object of his desires:

'I have a Mistress, that out-shines 'em all—
'Commanding yours—and yours tho' the whole Sex:
'My Money is my Mistress! Here's to
'Interest upon Interest.

[*Drinks*
(364)[49]

Despite Granville's lordly horror at the unnatural reproduction of interest upon interest, however, he has no reservations about the unnatural reproduction represented by the technology of the printing press: although its title-page promises that the play is printed 'As it is Acted at the THEATRE in *Little-Lincolns-Inn-Fields*', it is clear that Granville's adaptation has been written with the discriminating reader at least as prominently in mind as the corrupt theatre-goer. Like Cibber's preface to *Richard III*, Granville's 'Advertisement to the Reader' registers a widening separation between adaptations of Shakespeare and the rest of the contemporary repertory. Whereas earlier adaptors had modernized Shakespeare's language to make it blend in with their own (a

---

[49] On Granville's Shylock, see John Harold Wilson, 'Granville's "Stock-Jobbing Jew"', *Philological Quarterly*, 13 (1934), 1–15. Laura Rosenthal has pointed out the connection between the play's anti-homosexual prologue and its presentation of Shylock in her unpublished essay 'Disembodied Shakespeare: The Author as Ghost' (1991): she further argues that the representation of Shakespeare as a ghost promotes him to a status above the literary marketplace which Granville and his contemporaries are so interested in decrying.

procedure still followed in William Burnaby's curiously dated redaction of *Twelfth Night, Love Betray'd; or, the Agreeable Disappointment*, which flopped at Lincoln's Inn Fields in 1703),[50] Granville, again following Cibber, alters his own diction to imitate that of Shakespeare. With a punctiliousness far removed from the world of *Dorastus and Fawnia*, the text of his adaptation typographically discriminates Shakespeare's work from his own, but, unlike Cibber, Granville chooses to label his own share of the play rather than Shakespeare's:

The Reader may please moreover to take Notice, (that nothing may be imputed to *Shakespear* which may seem unworthy of him) that such Lines as appear to be markt, are Lines added, to make good the Connexion where there was a necessity to leave out; in which all imaginable Care has been taken to imitate the same fashion of Period, and turn of Stile and Thought with the Original.[51]

'Shakespeare' has clearly become a category unto itself within the theatrical repertory; his plays are henceforward not so much modernized as corrected retrospectively.

Granville's willingness both to revive the spirit of Shakespeare and to imitate his style should not be interpreted, however, as a symptom of uncritical Bardolatry. The evident admiration behind Granville's concern 'that nothing may be imputed to *Shakespear* which may seem unworthy of him' coexists uneasily with its obverse: in the first sentence of his 'Advertisement', Granville suggests on the contrary that Shakespeare's play may in many fundamental respects seem unworthy of its adaptor: 'THE Foundation of the following Comedy being liable to some Objections, it may be wonder'd that any one should make Choice of it to bestow so much Labour upon.'[52]

---

[50] 'PART of the Tale of this Play, I took from *Shakespear*, and about Fifty of his Lines; Those that are his, I have mark'd with Inverted Comma's, to distinguish 'em from what are mine. I endeavour'd where I had occasion to introduce any of 'em, to make 'em look as little like Strangers as possible'; William Burnaby, *Love Betray'd; or, the Agreeable Disappointment* (London, 1703), 'Preface'.

[51] Spencer, *Five Restoration Adaptations*, 347. It seems entirely appropriate that during the first few seasons in which the property-conscious adaptations of Cibber and Granville were being performed, Jacob Tonson was busily negotiating the copyright to the Shakespeare corpus in readiness for the preparation of Rowe's edition. See Giles Dawson, 'The Copyright of Shakespeare's Dramatic Works', in Charles T. Prouty (ed.), *Studies in Honor of A. H. R. Fairchild* (Columbia, Mo., 1956).

[52] Spencer, *Five Restoration Adaptations*, 347.

A year after the appearance of Granville's play, John Dennis found his own less successful contribution to the classicization of Shakespearean comedy, *The Comical Gallant: or the true Amours of Sir John Falstaffe*, caught between precisely these two viewpoints. In a critical climate dominated by the increasing execration of farce and the increasing veneration of Shakespeare, to both of which Granville's play makes such signal contributions, Dennis's adaptation of *The Merry Wives of Windsor* was doomed, even before it was composed, to please no one:

When I first communicated the design which I had of altering this Comedy of *Shakespear*, I found that I should have two sorts of People to deal with, who would equally endeavour to obstruct my success. The one believed it to be so admirable, that nothing ought to be added to it; the others fancied it to be so despicable, that any ones time would be lost upon it.[53]

To many critics engaged in the cultural decontamination project of the 1700s, clearly, *The Merry Wives of Windsor* deserved oblivion on the grounds of its contemptibly low subject-matter alone, and Dennis's version, premièred at Drury Lane early in 1702, does not seem to have achieved a third night.[54] Significantly, Dennis promptly turns from adaptation to literary criticism proper: he avenges himself by prefacing its published text with 'A Large Account of the Taste in Poetry, and the Causes of the Degeneracy of it', and his most important and widely read contributions to the Augustan assimilation of Shakespeare hereafter are made not in the theatre but in other critical disquisitions, notably *An Essay upon the Genius and Writings of Shakespeare* (1712).[55] Meanwhile, until the wave of adaptations produced between 1719 and 1723 (all of which are scrupulously purified of cheap laughs, as will become clear in the case of Charles Johnson's *Love in a*

[53] John Dennis, 'A Large Account of the Taste in Poetry, and the Causes of the Degeneracy of it', [1702], in *The Critical Works of John Dennis*, ed. Edward Niles Hooker (2 vols.; Baltimore, 1939), i. 279.

[54] *The London Stage*, 2: 19: Hogan, i. 320. On this play, see David Wheeler, 'Eighteenth Century Adaptations of Shakespeare and the Example of John Dennis', *Shakespeare Quarterly*, 36 (1985) 438–49.

[55] This latter tract is credited (?) with being the first-ever critical work devoted entirely to Shakespeare. On Dennis's last foray into adaptation, *The Invader of his Country; or, The Fatal Resentment* (performed in 1719), his unsuccessful post-Jacobite *Coriolanus*, see Ch. 2, above.

Forest), the campaign to turn Shakespeare into respectable literature similarly adopts other media.

Cibber's and Granville's new desire to make superior provision
for the reader and Dennis's turn away from adaptation to literary
criticism both participate, as I have suggested, in a general movement in early eighteenth-century culture towards the usurpation
by the printing press of the previous authority of the stage. This
movement is decisively enacted by two famous publications directly
contemporary with Rowe's edition, the *Tatler* and the *Spectator*
(1709–12), a glance at which can contribute significantly to our
understanding of the rationales behind the treatment of Shakespeare in print and on stage alike. The views on Shakespeare
expressed in the pages of the *Tatler* and the *Spectator* have been
sufficiently discussed and anthologized to require little comment
here;[56] what I should like to draw attention to are the implications for the theatrical treatment of his plays of the novel perspective from which these periodicals view the stage at all. Unlike
earlier pamphlet critiques of the contemporary theatre such as *A
Comparison Between the Two Stages*, which assume the personae
of dedicated playgoers who claim authority by purporting to represent the theatre audience's own consensus, Addison and Steele
prefer to ground their comments on the theatre by assuring their
readers that they are essentially outsiders: they make similar claims
to speak for 'the Town', but the Town and the theatregoing public
are no longer synonymous. 'Isaac Bickerstaff''s discussions of
theatrical affairs in the *Tatler* claim simply to retail, with comment, the relevant views heard in Will's Coffee House; judgement
and discernment reside here, in this hygienic, select, semi-private
space (closer to a study or a library than to a theatre), rather than
among the democratic, promiscuous crowd in the theatre audi-
torium itself.[57] Prefacing a Collierite attack on Etherege's *The
Man of Mode*, Steele may concede that 'The Seat of Wit, when

---

[56] See esp. the persuasive analysis in Gary Taylor, *Reinventing Shakespeare*,
62–8. The most important Shakespearean criticisms from the two periodicals are
conveniently reprinted in Vickers, *Critical Heritage*, ii. 203–14, 269–80.

[57] See *Tatler*, 1 (12 Apr. 1709): 'All Accounts of GALLANTRY, PLEASURE and
ENTERTAINMENT, shall be under the Article of WHITE'S CHOCOLATE-HOUSE: POETRY,
under that of WILL'S COFFEE-HOUSE; LEARNING under the Title of GRAECIAN;
FOREIGN and DOMESTICK NEWS, you will have from ST. JAMES'S COFFEE-HOUSE;
and what else I have to offer on any other Subject, shall be dated from my own
APARTMENT.'

one speaks as a Man of the Town and the World, is the Play-house' (*Spectator*, 65: 15 May 1711),[58] but it is the underlying ambition of his periodicals to supersede it as such, to bring it under the jurisdiction of the very different audience—or, rather, readership—convened by the coffee-houses.[59] Although Bicker-staff's successor Mr Spectator assures his readers that his face is 'very well known ... in the Theatres both of *Drury-lane* and the *Hay-market*' (*Spectator*, 1: 1 Mar. 1711), the most famous *Spectator* essays on the stage—Steele's puffs for Ambrose Philips's she-tragedy, *The Distressed Mother* (previewed by Mr Spectator at a private rehearsal, endorsed by the approval of the non-theatregoing rustic Sir Roger de Coverley; *Spectator* 290: 1 Feb. 1712; ibid. 335, 25 Mar. 1712) and Addison's account of the 'Trunk-maker' —betray a marked unwillingness to allow the theatre audience the final (or even the first) say on which plays deserve encouragement. Describing the activities of the Trunk-maker (a mysterious fre-quenter of the upper gallery who, 'when he is pleased with any thing that is acted upon the Stage, expresses his Approbation by a loud Knock upon the Benches'; ibid. 235: 29 Nov. 1711), Addison indulges in some patent wish-fulfilment, developing a comic fantasy in which a single discriminating critic (anonymous or pseudony-mous like himself) is able to exercise absolute power over the opinions and behaviour of his fellow auditors:

[h]is Blow is so well timed, that the most judicious Critick could never except against it. As soon as any shining Thought is expressed in the Poet, or any uncommon Grace appears in the Actor, he smites the Bench or Wainscot. If the Audience does not concur with him, he smites a second time: and if the Audience is not yet awaked, looks round him with great Wrath, and repeats the Blow a third time, which never fails to produce the Clap ... I cannot but take notice of the great use it is to an Audience, that a Person should thus preside over their Heads, like the Director of a Consort, in order to awaken their Attention, and beat Time to their Applauses.

(Ibid.)

---

[58] All citations for the *Spectator* are from the Oxford edition, ed. Donald F. Bond (5 vols., Oxford, 1965).

[59] See Stallybrass and White, *Politics and Poetics*, 99: 'Although it was an "addition" to the cultural map, the coffee house presented itself not so much as an addition as a replacement, an alternative site and part of an alternative and superior network in the stratification of the city.'

Already a far more 'judicious Critick' than the rest of the audience, the Trunk-maker is to be succeeded, according to the terms of the facetious proposal with which this essay concludes, by a line of similar monitors who will combine equal pit-subduing strength with more explicitly elitist standards:

[T]o the End that this Place should always be disposed of, according to Merit, I would have none preferred to it, who had not given convincing Proofs, both of a sound Judgment and a strong Arm, and who could not, upon Occasion, either knock down an Ox or write a Comment upon *Horace*'s Art of Poetry.

(Ibid.)

A succession of university-educated dictators compelling the stage to uphold the standards of the study, these imagined future Trunk-makers, muscle-bound Colliers all, are to discipline the theatre's soul as relentlessly as they belabour its woodwork. Significantly, they are to do so in the name of Shakespeare, or at least in the cause of the more elevated portions of his *œuvre*: one of the current Trunk-maker's highest recommendations is that he 'seldom goes away from a Tragedy of *Shakespear*, without leaving the Wainscot extreamly shattered' (ibid.). For Shakespeare to continue to function as a figure of authority in the new cultural environment of the early 1700s (as he does in this essay), the campaign to purify his works, initiated by Gildon and Granville, must continue; as Stallybrass and White point out, the coffee-houses and the publications located there inculcated the imperative 'that participation in the public sphere—and therefore participation in the serious public realm of debate—demanded a withdrawal from popular culture and its translation into negative and even phobic representations'.[60]

This imperative is nowhere more luridly obeyed than in the work of Hogarth, who in 1724 follows Addison in representing Shakespeare as the complete antithesis of the ignoble theatrical trends which the Trunk-makers are to oppose. *A Just View of the British Stage* caricatures the Drury Lane management (the 'Triumvirate'—Cibber, Booth, and Wilks) and the plays they have been producing: the managers are depicted rehearsing what the print's caption describes as 'a new Farce that will include [th]e two famous Entertainments *Dr. Faustus* & *Harlequin Shepherd* to wch

[60] Ibid.

will be added *Scaramouch Jack Hall* the Chimney-Sweeper's Escape
from Newgate through [th]e Privy, with [th]e comical Humours of
Ben Johnsons Ghost . . . The Bricks, Rubbish &c. will be real, but
the Excrements upon *Jack Hall* will be made of Chew'd Ginger-
bread to prevent Offence.' Beside the privy which forms part of
the set on which the managers are rehearsing, the title pages from
discarded scripts of *Hamlet*, *Macbeth*, and *Julius Caesar* hang on
a peg, as lavatory paper. As well as the attractions listed in the
caption, the performance will include rope-dancing, puppetry (including Mr Punch), Italian music, a mock-hanging, and a pantomime dragon.[61] To prefer contemporary popular comic forms to
Shakespeare, clearly, as in Higgons's prologue to *The Jew of
Venice*, is to be plebeian, puerile, treasonous, semi-human, and, if
not homosexual, coprophiliac.

In this continuing intellectual climate, the repressed vulgar elements of Shakespearean comedy might occasionally return around
the margins of the theatrical repertory in disreputable entertainments such as *Dorastus and Fawnia* or *Pyramus and Thisbe*, but
clearly no playwright or critic with any pretensions to literary
reputation (or any care for Shakespeare's) could afford to celebrate him as the creator of, say, Lance and Crab, and it is perhaps
not entirely surprising that Alexander Pope's *The Works of Shakespeare, Collated and Corrected*, published the year after Hogarth's
engraving, should display such singular intolerance towards
Shakespeare's clowns. Pope's edition reveals more clearly than any
other Augustan publication the connection between the desire to
rescue Shakespeare from the theatre in the interests of print culture
and the urge to delete his plays' lapses into vulgarity. Identifying
moral corruption and textual corruption alike as symptoms of
Shakespeare's unfortunate association with the public stage, Pope
blames the errors in Shakespeare's texts on 'the ignorance of the
Players, both as his actors and as his editors',[62] and his edition
accordingly combines Granville's twin strategies of excising 'low'
passages and marking non-Shakespearean ones by relegating many
of Shakespeare's passages of low humour to the foot of the page
as vulgar theatrical interpolations, unworthy of the great poet this

---

[61] This work is reproduced in *Engravings by Hogarth* ed. Sean Shesgreen (New
York, 1973), no. 4.
[62] Alexander Pope (ed.), *The Works of Shakespeare, Collated and Corrected* (6
vols.; London, 1723–5), vol. i, p. xiv.

monumental edition hopes to redeem. At the same time, the edition
combines Cibber's strategy of typographically labelling Shakespeare's own 'Thoughts' with Gildon's treatment of the Complete
Works as a mine of quotations attributable directly to the Author,
marking Shakespeare's most 'Shining Passages' with marginal inverted commas so that the reader will always be able to recognize
the elevated moments at which Shakespeare is most fully present
in his own text.[63] That this edition is designed, like the adaptations of Gildon and Granville, to refashion the Complete Works in
the image of a respectablized Shakespeare is made explicit in the
seventh volume of poems and commentary appended to this edition
(like Gildon's to Rowe's) by George Sewell. According to Sewell,
all previous editions of Shakespeare have reproduced his classic
authorial spirit only in defaced form: 'A fine Writer thus treated
looks like *Deiphobus* among the Shades, so maim'd by his pretended Friend that the good *Aeneas* hardly knew him again.'
(Pope, *The Works of Shakespeare*, vol. vii [by George Sewell],
viii). However, Pope's edition, transfusing Pope's talent into Shakespeare's hitherto mangled and inert text, will infallibly restore
Shakespeare's image: after all, '[w]hen a Genius of similar Fire
and Fancy, temper'd with a learned Patience, sits down to consider what SHAKESPEARE would *Think*, as well as what he could
Write, we may then expect to see his Works answer our Idea of
the Man' (ibid.).[64]

Adaptation and canonization are here plainly revealed as completely mutual activities: to present Shakespeare's plays in forms
that, free of all transgressive blemishes, display 'such Thoughts as
we could justly attribute to Shakespeare' and to confirm and
promulgate a suitably elevated 'Idea of the Man' are complementary aspects of the same process. These connections between the
purifying of Shakespeare's works from low comedy and the promotion of Shakespeare as a true author, finally, are further revealed by two successive versions of *As You Like It*, the last of
which makes their implications for the theatre ominously clear.

[63] On this practice, see Margreta De Grazia, 'Shakespeare In Quotation Marks',
in Marsden (ed.), *The Appropriation of Shakespeare*, 62. On Pope's edition in
general, see John Butt, *Pope's Taste in Shakespeare* (London, 1936).

[64] It is worth drawing attention to the increasing use of the term 'Works' to
describe Shakespeare's plays at this time: in Pope's edition, as in Rowe's, the
'Comedies, Histories and Tragedies' of the Shakespeare folio have become classical
'Works', as finished as the contents of the Jonson folio.

The first of these, Charles Johnson's *Love in a Forest*, produced in 1723 while Pope's edition was in preparation, ringingly evokes its author in a sonorous prologue which manages slyly to infer that Johnson's alterations are part of a natural maturing process; the fact that *As You Like It* has had to be 'refin'd' for 'this learn'd Age' somehow manages to be implicit in a tribute to Shakespeare's timeless greatness. Shakespeare, fully present in this purified text, 'treads the stage' in spirit at its performance, thanks to the 'superiority' which enables his intelligence to survive even flirtations with low comedy such as *The Merry Wives of Windsor*:

IN Honour to his Name, and this learn'd Age,
Once more your much-lov'd SHAKESPEAR treads the Stage.
Another Work from that great Hand appears,
His Ore's refin'd, but not impar'd by *Years*.
  .   .   .   .

If into lower Life his Pencil strays,
Still his unrivall'd Wit demands the Bays;
Superior still, the Comic Force survives
In *Falstaff, Shallow* and the *Merry Wives*.[65]
          (Charles Johnson, *Love in a Forest* (London, 1723), 'Prologue')

Despite this acceptance of *The Merry Wives*, Johnson remorselessly erases all traces of such 'straying' from the text of *As You Like It*; his version of the play completely excludes the vulgar Touchstone, Audrey, Corin, Phebe, Silvius, and William, who are represented as weeds, dangerously fecund intruders no longer permissible in the grounds of polite literature. The natural space of Shakespeare's unadapted work, tellingly, has been promoted from being the untended garden referred to by Flecknoe to something both grander and more cultivated:

Forgive our modern Author's Honest Zeal,
He hath attempted boldly, if not well:

---

[65] *The Merry Wives of Windsor* had been revived at Lincoln's Inn Fields in 1720 after a disappearance of 15 years; see Hogan, i. 320.

Johnson's play was not a great success (after an initial run of six performances it was never revived: see Hogan, i. 90–1), but that he was right in judging that by now the public might be interested in even superficially unpromising plays as long as they were offered as being from 'that great Hand' is demonstrated by the minor sensation created by Lewis Theobald's *Double Falshood; Or, the Distrest Lovers* (London, 1728), (which may or may not be, as Theobald claimed, a lost adaptation of a lost Shakespeare play), on its première in 1727.

Believe, he only does with Pain and Care,
Presume to weed the beautiful Parterre.
                                        (Ibid.)

For Johnson in 1723, it seems, the beauty of Shakespeare's 'comic
force', like that of an Augustan aristocrat's parterre, is still premissed, however widely it may be celebrated, upon the exclusion
of the peasant classes. The only lower-class characters permitted
to enter Johnson's play at all are the rude mechanicals from *A
Midsummer Night's Dream*, grudgingly allowed to adorn the fifth
act with their deferential performance of *Pyramus and Thisbe*
before the restored Duke Senior. Johnson's prologue may be prepared to celebrate Shakespeare as a wonderfully fertile comic
writer, but as such he is only to tread the stage on condition that
his plays are meticulously pruned first.
   Johnson's drastic banishment of all the original natives from the
Forest of Arden is outdone, however, in the play's next incarnation, which, imitating and redoubling the strategies deployed by
Love in a Forest, represents in many ways the *reductio ad absurdum*
of early eighteenth-century adaptation. In 1739, John Carrington
composed his own version of *As You Like It*, an adaptation which
not only excludes the vulgar from its cast but denies them access
to the play altogether. Expensively 'Printed for the Author' by
subscription, *The Modern Receipt: or, A Cure for Love* goes one
better than Cibber's *Richard III* or Granville's *The Jew of Venice*
by not only appealing to the discriminating reader over the heads
of the theatregoing public but disdaining to address the theatre-
going public altogether; the play is the first closet adaptation of
Shakespeare (unless, as one well might, one regards Pope's edition
as such), intended not for performance at all but solely for the
perusal of 'the *polite* world'.[66] Carrington, instead of polishing
and moralizing Shakespeare that he may join the campaign against
lewdness and frolic in the theatre (alongside the likes of Sir Roger
de Coverley), produces a play which can instead compete solely
against printed editions of *As You Like It*. For Carrington, making
Shakespeare into the right class of author virtually involves saving
him from being a playwright at all. At this extreme of the process,
refining the Bard almost comes full circle to the kind of serene

---

   [66] J.C. [John Carrington], *The Modern Receipt: or, A Cure for Love* (London,
1739), 'TO THE LOVERS of both SEXES'.

indifference to Shakespeare represented by *Dorastus and Fawnia*. A connoisseur of adaptation as an art form in itself, Carrington has deliberately chosen a play which in order to be distilled into polite literature needs to be rewritten almost beyond recognition, and, eschewing Bardolatry, he comes close to suggesting that it is his incomprehension and dislike of the original which best qualify him to adapt it:

[F]rom the Nature of Alterations, every one will readily expect to find my great Original in a Dress more agreeable, and becoming, than any he has hitherto appeared in: That this was the Ground of my Undertaking, no one, I think, will dispute ... in order to my better Succeeding, [I] made Choice of a Play, the most proper for my Design, as being chiefly different from the reigning Taste, and least conspicuous for modern Beauties ... if I have omitted any of [Shakespeare's] most shining Passages, I will ingenuously confess it to be owing to my Want of Judgment in distinguishing them. I have taken the Liberty to make some alterations in the Plot, and Catastrophe, as well as in great Part of the Language.

(Carrington, *The Modern Receipt*, 'Preface')

Carrington's well-bred adaptation, in most respects a caricature of Johnson's, is perhaps of negligible importance in itself, but it certainly demonstrates how successfully Lord Lansdowne and the other respectablizing adaptors of the early eighteenth century had saved Shakespearean comedy, despite the prevailing hysteria against farce, as something both polite and publishable—had saved Shakespeare, potentially, from his own disfiguring penchant for the theatre.

By the 1730s, clearly, Shakespeare is fully established as the 'great Original' behind all of his texts, whether corrected for the stage or for publication, and all subsequent uses of his plays must appropriate not only their contents but their author. Accordingly, it is with two influential attempts to claim Shakespeare's newly established authority by fixing and embodying what Sewell terms 'our Idea of the Man' that my next chapter will be concerned, projects which dramatize the continuing conflict between the stage and the study revealed by these two versions of *As You Like It* in their rival bids to present Shakespeare 'in a Dress more agreeable, and becoming, than any he has hitherto appeared in'.

4

Embodying the Author

ONCE Shakespeare has been abstracted (or even rescued) from his texts by the likes of Pope and Dennis, and personified as a true author in Rowe's biography or the necromantic prologue to *The Jew of Venice*, the adaptation and appropriation of Shakespeare's plays begins to decline in importance compared to the adaptation and appropriation of Shakespeare himself. Changing Shakespeare's words becomes only one among many ways of establishing what their author means, of promoting his authority, and of claiming him as an ally: from the 1730s onwards, the political and cultural arguments enacted in the adaptations of the preceding fifty years —with their various conscriptions of Shakespeare's plays in support of royal prerogative or British liberty, fairground comedy or literary refinement—overflow into other media, as Shakespeare the Author, just as much as his *œuvre*, becomes the centre of a struggle for the right to speak for the core of the national culture. In this chapter I shall be examining the ways in which this conflict takes place, in particular, around two competing figures which seek to embody and thus secure the authorial spirit of Shakespeare himself. One of these is the statue of Shakespeare erected in Westminster Abbey in 1741, conceived by its sponsors as an affirmation of the national poet's resistance to ministerial corruption, but variously treated by contemporaries as a monument to Jacobite nostalgia, to female patronage, and to the supremacy of the study over the theatre. The other embodiment is not an artefact but an actor, David Garrick, whose entire career, beginning in the same year in an entertainment which repossesses this very statue on behalf of a newly regenerate stage, enacts a rival bid to pose as the century's definitive embodiment of Shakespeare, claiming him in the process not only for live drama but for domestic virtue.

The Statue

Patriot King

The first published intimation that Shakespeare had acquired sufficient national importance to warrant commemoration in Westminster Abbey occurs in the *Weekly Register* for 26 January 1734. 'I believe', writes an anonymous correspondent, 'that everyone that visits this sacred Repository of the illustrious Dead, cannot help looking round, like me, for the divine *Milton*, and the immortal *Shakespear*; Names which are the Honour of their Country, and yet have receiv'd no Honour from it.'[1] This writer's interest both in defining a national literary pantheon (as the locus of the country's honour) and in commissioning monuments by way of reparation to its members (generally represented as either neglected or betrayed) is characteristic of the mid-1730s, when a mounting propaganda campaign against Sir Robert Walpole's government, conducted across an extraordinary range of media, explicitly politicized questions of culture to an unusual degree. By the time this letter was composed, Shakespeare and his republican admirer had in fact already been sculpted side by side as part of just such an exercise in politically motivated canon-formation, albeit in a less accessible and more evidently partisan setting than the Abbey. This was the Temple of British Worthies, commissioned for the elaborate allegorical gardens at Stowe by their owner Richard Temple, Viscount Cobham, who since turning against Walpole over the Excise Bill in 1733 had been the leader of the Opposition coalition group loosely known as the Patriots.[2]

The bust of Shakespeare included in this extraordinary building is the first monument to the playwright to celebrate him in a national context, and it is worth noting that the version of cultural nationalism of which Shakespeare is here invoked as a father is

---

[1] Reprinted in the January issue of the *London Magazine*, 3 (1734), 30. The cause was taken up by James Ralph: see his *A Critical Review of the Public Buildings, Statues, and Ornaments In, and about London and Westminster* (London, 1734), 79–80.

[2] On the Patriots, see esp. Christine Gerrard, 'The Patriot Opposition to Sir Robert Walpole: A Study of the Politics and Poetry, 1725–42', D.Phil. (Oxford, 1986); Bertrand Goldgar, *Walpole and the Wits* (Lincoln, Nebr. 1976); Isaac Kramnick, *Bolingbroke and his Circle: The Politics of Nostalgia in the Age of Walpole* (Cambridge, Mass., 1968).

one specifically opposed to the government of the day: however he may have been deployed since, Shakespeare became national poet in the 1730s as an Opposition playwright rather than an Establishment one. The Temple of British Worthies is only one of a series of monuments at Stowe built for this Patriot headquarters as a composite statement about the current deplorable condition of the realm and Cobham's ideals for its restoration; nearby, for example, are the Temple of British Liberty (one of the earliest and most influential Gothic follies, its architectural style, pseudo-Saxon monuments, and pseudo-Druidic effigies reflecting the nostalgic traditions of Whig history), a neo-classical Temple of Ancient Virtue, and the less august Temple of Modern Virtue—satirically, a ruin, dominated by a fat, headless statue usually assumed to represent Walpole himself.[3] The Temple of British Worthies, designed by William Kent and completed in 1735, incorporates sixteen busts, executed by the Dutch sculptors Peter Scheemakers and Michael Rysbrack, depicting exemplary Britons (fourteen historical figures, with two heroic contemporaries framing them) chosen to constitute a gallery of the great national achievements, both political and intellectual, which the current regime was supposedly betraying. Representing the active life are Alfred the Great, Edward the Black Prince (selected in complimentary allusion to the current Prince of Wales, Frederick, who was rapidly becoming the focus of the Patriots' campaign), Elizabeth I, William of Orange, Raleigh, Drake, Hampden, and, perhaps bathetically, Sir John Barnard, the City MP who was at the time Walpole's most outspoken critic in the Commons; on the contemplative side are Bacon, Newton, Locke, Shakespeare, Milton, Inigo Jones, Sir Thomas Gresham (founder of the Royal Exchange), and, as their living heir and spokesman, Alexander Pope. Pope's presence in this predominantly Whig pantheon may suggest something of the wide range of opinions represented among the Patriots (whom the pro-government press indiscriminately vilified as either Levellers or Jacobites, or both), and it may also suggest the extent to which

---

[3] On Cobham's Stowe monuments, see George Bickham, *The Beauties of Stow* (London, 1750), esp. 38–45; Margaret Whinney, *Sculpture in Britain, 1530 to 1830* [1964], rev. John Physick (London, 1988), 172; George Clarke, 'Grecian Taste and Gothic Virtue: Lord Cobham's Gardening Programme and its Iconography', *Apollo* 97 (1973), 566–71; Michael I. Wilson, *William Kent, Architect, Designer, Painter, Gardener, 1685–1748* (London, 1984), 210–11.

Shakespeare and Milton are here being claimed as anti-ministerial writers, antitheses of the Grubstreet hacks bribed to write on behalf of Walpole. In the words of one loyal panegyrist on Stowe, Samuel Boyse, they are enshrined in the Temple as 'Poets who scorn'd the Muses to profane, | Nor courted vice, nor wrote for sordid gain'.[4] In this respect the monument performs in stone one of the favourite rhetorical strategies of the Patriots' journal, the *Craftsman*, which, regularly justifying its scurrility by appeal to *Areopagitica*, specialized in quoting carefully chosen satirical passages from Shakespeare (such as descriptions of Wolsey and Angelo) and inviting their application as prophetic portraits of Walpole.[5]

Of the three incorruptible poets commemorated at Stowe, one, however, soon appeared to succumb to posthumous governmental bribery. In April 1737, partly fulfilling the hopes of the *Weekly Register*'s correspondent, a bust of Milton appeared in Poets' Corner in Westminster Abbey, the identity of the poet virtually upstaged on the marble tablet beneath it by that of the loyal servant of Walpole's government who had commissioned it:

> In the year of our Lord Christ
> One thousand seven hundred and thirty seven
> This Bust
> of the Author of PARADISE LOST
> was placed here by William Benson Esquire
> One of the two Auditors of the Imprests
> to his Majesty King George the second
> formerly
> Surveyor General of the Works
> to his Majesty King George the first.

In the same month as this conspicuous display of governmental munificence, however, the Opposition response got under way. 'SIR', begins 'A.Z.' in the *London Daily-Post and General Advertiser* of 26 April,

I Perceive with the utmost Pleasure, that there is a great *Spirit* for promoting the Design of erecting SHAKESPEAR'S Monument, by acting his Play of

---

[4] Samuel Boyse, *The Triumphs of Nature, a Poem* (1742), in *The Works of the English Poets, from Chaucer to Cowper* (21 vols.; London, 1810), xiv. 534–8.
[5] On this publication's use of Shakespeare, see Bate, *Shakespearean Constitutions*, 64–70.

JULIUS CAESAR the 28th of this month. I am persuaded, this will appear still more, when it is known, that the Right Hon. the Earl of *Burlington*, Dr. *Mead*, Mr. *Pope*, and Mr. *Fletewood* are the *Trustees*, and will have the sole Direction of the Monument.

The committee A.Z. names held impeccable Patriot credentials: its leader Burlington had, like Cobham, gone into opposition during the Excise Crisis, and alongside his client and ally Pope he had soon also recruited Benjamin Martyn, author of the anti-Walpole play *Timoleon* (1730).[6] Their campaign to commemorate Shakespeare in Westminster Abbey is essentially a continuation of the statuary project initiated by Cobham's Temple of British Worthies —as is suggested by Burlington's commissioning of the same architect to design the monument, William Kent (along with one of the same sculptors, Peter Scheemakers)—and it is throughout characterized by an explicit claiming of Shakespeare as both a foe to tyranny and a genuinely national hero, above the reach of bribery or invidious patronage. Martyn's prologue to this benefit performance of *Julius Caesar*, for example, in true *Craftsman* fashion, invokes Shakespeare on the side of heroic resistance to an overweening Great Man, implicitly making the public's unforced support for the raising of his monument into an anti-Walpole demonstration:

While Brutus bleeds for liberty and Rome,
Let Britons crowd to deck his Poet's tomb.
To future times recorded let it stand,
This head was lawrel'd by the publick hand.[7]

The Honourable James Noel's epilogue to this benefit is even more explicit about the political allegiances of Burlington's campaign, deliberately using the opposition's buzzword of the moment:

When Portia weeps, all gentle breasts must mourn,
When Brutus arms, all gen'rous bosoms burn.
When Rome's firm Patriots on the stage [are] shown,
With pride we trace the Patriots of our own...
                    (*A General Dictionary*, ix. 189)

---

[6] On *Timoleon*, see Gerrard, 'Patriot Opposition to Walpole', 42: on Opposition drama in general see Loftis, *Politics of Drama*, 94–127.

[7] Printed, along with James Noel's epilogue (quoted below), in [Pierre Bayle, *et al.*] *A General Dictionary, Historical and Critical* (10 vols.; London, 1734–41), ix. 189. For a similarly libertarian reading of *Julius Caesar*, see *Craftsman*, 28 Apr. 1739.

Such authentic national feelings on behalf of Shakespeare and Britain are placed by Martyn into pointed contrast with Benson's effrontery in co-opting Milton:

No single hand durst claim to rear his stone,
And fix in Shakespeare's monument his own.
                                                    (Ibid.)

This theme is taken up elsewhere by Pope, who threw himself into the Abbey project with gusto: 'After an hundred and thirty years' nap, | Enter Shakespear, with a loud clap,' quips one couplet on the proceedings.[8] In more serious vein, he composed the Latin inscription originally planned for the scroll to which Scheemakers' sculpted figure of Shakespeare points ('AMOR PVBLICVS POSVIT') and, more satirically, he suggested an expanded English translation in which both Benson and another such patron (Alderman Barber, whose name is glorified on the monument to Samuel Butler nearby) are attacked: 'Thus *Britain* lov'd me; and preserv'd my Fame | Clear from a *Barber*'s or a *Benson*'s name.'[9]

However devoutly Whiggish Martyn's prologue and Noel's epilogue to *Julius Caesar* may be in their reading of the play as wholly on the side of Brutus against Caesar, the 'politics of nostalgia' which the Patriot group promulgated was not without its monarchist strain,[10] and this too is visible throughout the commissioning and execution of Shakespeare's Abbey memorial, which can be seen as, among other things, a monument to lost royalty, or at very least to lost royal patronage. The association between divine Shakespeare and Divine Right is still highly visible in the

[8] Pope, *Poems*, vi. 395. On this epigram, see Mary Granville, *The Autobiography and Correspondence of Mary Granville, Mrs. Delany*, ed. Lady Llanover (3 vols.; London, 1861), ii. 139 (21 Dec. 1740).

[9] Pope, *Poems*, vi. 395. On Pope's involvement in Burlington's Abbey project, see Morris R. Brownell, *Alexander Pope and the Arts of Georgian England* (Oxford, 1978), 354–6; David Piper, *The Image of the Poet: British Poets and their Portraits* (Oxford, 1982), 78–82. Appropriately, statuettes of Pope imitating the pose of Scheemakers' Shakespeare would be produced after his death, along with similar depictions of their fellow literary Worthy, Milton: see Piper, *The Image of the Poet*, 90, 206 n. 48.

[10] See esp. Henry Saint John, Viscount Bolingbroke, *The Idea of a Patriot King* (written in 1738–9, and finally published in *Letters, on the Spirit of Patriotism: on the Idea of a Patriot King: and on the State of Parties at the Accession of King George the First*, London, 1749), aimed at Frederick, Prince of Wales (and arguably equally applicable to Charles Edward Stuart). On this aspect of opposition politics and literature, see Gerrard, 'Patriot Opposition to Walpole', 243 ff.: Kramnick, *Bolingbroke and his Circle*, 205–35.

1730s, even in the most libertarian of writings on the Bard's
behalf. Martyn's prologue, for example, imagining Shakespeare
'lawrel'd by the publick hand', seems to picture the Bard in the
role of the kingly Caesar, posthumously achieving, through the
rhetorical efforts of Mark Antony, the 'monarch's voice' denied
him in life. More strikingly, Lewis Theobald's prologue to the
second and last benefit performance to raise money for the statue,
a revival of *Hamlet* at Covent Garden in April of 1739, repeats
this identification of Shakespeare with the royal ghost of Caesar
while conflating this spectre with another paternal spirit. It was
spoken by the actor Ryan, who played the Prince:

> [*The Curtain drawn up to solemn Musick,
> shews the Stage in Mourning.*]

Immortal SHAKESPEAR! we thy Claim admit;
For, like thy *Caesar, thou art mighty yet*!
Thy Spirit walks abroad; and at our hands
The Honorary Tomb, thy Right, demands . . .[11]

Mourned at this play's opening and demanding vindication at the
hands of Ryan/Hamlet, Shakespeare, as in many earlier prologues,
is once more playing Old Hamlet, the ghost of the legitimate
monarch. Even when invoked in support of vengeful, reforming
Brutuses, apparently, Shakespeare comes to occupy the position of
'our king of English literature' (as one guidebook to the Abbey
monuments aptly registers one subtext of his memorial),[12] potentially a locus for Jacobite idealizations of the lost days of Stuart
rule as much as for Whig dreams of Gothic or Elizabethan liberty.[13]
Theobald's prologue, in this respect not unlike Otway's to *Caius
Marius*, goes on to look back wistfully to the days when British
kings patronized native literature, representing his audience as
engaged, in effect, in belatedly performing Shakespeare's royal
state funeral:

[11] Printed in the *London Daily Post and General Advertiser*, 12 Apr. 1739.
[12] Violet Brooke-Hunt, *The Story of Westminster Abbey* (London, 1902), 225.
[13] On the Jacobite resonances of *Hamlet* in the mid-18th cent., see Douglas
Brooks-Davies, '*Tom Jones*: Encountering the King', in id., *Fielding, Dickens,
Gosse, Iris Murdoch and Oedipal Hamlet* (New York, 1989), 1–59: John Allen
Stevenson, '*The Castle of Otranto*: Political Supernaturalism', in *The British Novel,
Defoe to Austen* (New York, 1991), 90–109. Theobald's elegy for the last *de facto*
Stuart monarch, Queen Anne, intriguingly, echoes Hamlet's elegies for his dead
father: see Lewis Theobald, *The Mausoleum* (London, 1714), esp. 20.

Britons, with virtuous pride your merit know;
You've done, what kings, of old, were fond to do:
Then, when the poet died, the monarch mourn'd;
And, by command, his ashes were inurn'd.
  (*London Daily Post and General Advertiser*,
   12 Apr. 1739)

In the event, however, this congratulation of the virtuous Britons assumed to have turned out for the occasion proved premature, and Shakespeare's commemorators had to resort, like Barber or Benson, to private patronage. The *London Daily Post and General Advertiser* for 11 April reports that:

Last Night was perform'd the Tragedy of Hamlet, at the Theatre-Royal in Covent-Garden, toward raising a Fund for the Erecting a Monument to the Memory of SHAKESPEAR; on which Occasion 'twas expected there would have been a greater Audience than there appear'd to be. But the Lord Burlington was pleased, out of his Regard to the Memory of so great a Man, to give Ten Guineas for himself.

None the less, work proceeded to schedule on the statue, and it was finally unveiled, to enormous public interest, early in 1741.

Scheemakers' figure soon became, and has remained, one of the best-known and most widely reproduced of all likenesses of Shakespeare: in some sense it is still the official portrait of Shakespeare as national poet, as distinct from the mere Mr William Shakespeare recorded by Droeshout's frontispiece to the Folio or Janssen's bust beside the grave in Stratford. Possibly even before its completion it had been engraved by James Hulett for use as the frontispiece to an edition of Shakespeare's poems (Plate 1),[14] and more prominently a sumptuous engraving by Gravelot claims equal authority with the Droeshout portrait and the Janssen bust in the preliminary materials to Sir Thomas Hanmer's edition of the Complete Works in 1744 (Plate 2). Yet another such engraving is reproduced in the *London Magazine* for 1751 as the sole illustration to a new biography of the poet (Plate 3), and until very recently another propped the national economy by adorning and valorizing the twenty-pound note.[15] Within a few years of its

---

[14] William Shakespeare, *Poems on several occasions* (London, n.d. [1740?]). On this engraving, see below.
[15] On this use of the Scheemakers likeness, see Graham Holderness, 'Preface: "All this"', in Graham Holderness (ed.), *The Shakespeare Myth* (Manchester, 1988), pp. xi–xx.

1. Frontispiece to *Poems on several occasions. By William Shakespeare* (London, [1740?]). *James Hulett.* (Bodleian Library shelfmark Malone. I. 396; reproduced by courtesy of the Bodleian Library.)

unveiling, indeed, Scheemakers' figure had in large measure superseded the merely personal or local representations provided by
Shakespeare's contemporaries, a feat it apparently owes not only
to its position in a national temple but to its proper *gravitas*. One
J.G. of Stratford, writing to the *Gentleman's Magazine* in 1759,
remarks that since the installation of the Abbey memorial, many
visitors to Shakespeare's grave have been unable to accept the bust
in Holy Trinity as a true likeness of the poet at all, although its
expression suggests 'a chearfulness of thought, which, I hope, it
will be allowed *Shakespear* was no stranger to', but he none the
less approves of Scheemakers' statue, admitting that it 'is really in
a noble attitude, and excites an awful admiration in the beholder;
the face is venerable, and well expresses that intenseness of serious
thought, which the poet must be supposed to have sometimes
had'.[16] Noble, awe-inspiring, venerable, and intensely serious, this
is a monument aptly identified with the ghosts of Caesar and King
Hamlet, worthy of proximity to the tombs of the Plantaganets and
Tudors with which its pedestal, bearing portraits of Elizabeth I,
Henry V, and Richard III, cannot help but identify it. As J.G.
implicitly recognizes, this is the creator of the histories and tragedies (as the dagger suspended among the laurel wreath elsewhere
on the pedestal suggests) rather than that of the comedies: the
proximity of the laurel wreath to the triad of sovereigns from the
histories further suggests that Shakespeare is being claimed as an
honorary epic poet, the British Worthy who immortalized his
nation's heroic golden age.[17]

But what is the Shakespeare thus embodied thinking so seriously
about? What vatic message does this accusing ghost bring to the
corrupt world of Hanoverian London? The statue's free hand
gestures severely towards a scroll which hangs down in front of
the pedestal, as if to indicate some graven wisdom—but when the
memorial was unveiled in February 1741, this scroll, the focus of
the entire monument, was left completely blank. (Pope's Latin
inscription appeared only on a plaque behind the figure itself.)
This extraordinarily suggestive state of affairs (the National Poet
at last enshrined in the temple of the Establishment, pointing
solemnly at a completely empty piece of paper—a symbol of

[16] *Gentleman's Magazine* (June 1759), 257.
[17] On the design of this statue, see also Michael I. Wilson, *William Kent*, 140–2;
Whinney, *Sculpture in Britain*, 189–90.

2. Engraving from Sir Thomas Hanmer (ed.), *The Works of Shakespeare, Revised and Corrected* (6 vols.; Oxford, 1744), vol. i. *H. Gravelot.* (Reproduced by courtesy of the Governing Body, Christ Church, Oxford.)

3. Illustration to 'A New Account of the celebrated Shakespear', *London Magazine*, 20 (1751), 151. (Reproduced by courtesy of the Special Collections Department, Northwestern University Library, Evanston, Illinois.)

nihilism? of writer's block? of Shakespeare's availability for multiple appropriation?) did not go unremarked. An anonymous contributor to the *London Evening Post* for 7–10 February recognizes the absurdity of the situation in general terms, offering a wearily exasperated Shakespeare who blames his bathetic inanity on ecclesiastical incompetence:

On this blank Scroll what I'd express,
In vain must the Spectator guess:
For though I earnest point below,
No Meaning does the Tablet show.
Some Thought express'd had sure been apter,
Had it so pleas'd the *Dean* and *Chapter*;
But why at last I nothing mean,
Ask the wise *Chapter* and the *Dean*.

Two others, however, commented more pointedly, providing mottoes entirely in keeping with the convictions of Burlington's committee. Remarkably, the first engraving of the statue, James Hulett's frontispiece, recognizes this monument to the national poet as a reproach to Walpolean patronage, supplying Shakespeare's scroll with Pope's couplet attack on Benson and Barber (Plate 1). A much more thorough explication of one of the statue's main political sub-texts, however, was provided by an anonymous writer who, very much in the manner of the *Craftsman*, represents Shakespeare as an angry victim of government censorship, a vengeful satirist summoned from an age of plain speaking only to be silenced by a dean afraid of incurring the wrath of the repressive prime minister. The March edition of the *London Magazine* prints:

An Inscription wrote with a Black Lead Pencil, on the Blank Scroll on *Shakespear's* MONUMENT.

When *Burleigh's* counsels *Britain* bless'd I wrote,
Free was my heart, and unconfin'd my thought;
Of *publick crimes* I shew'd the *publick hate*,
And mark'd *bad ministers*, and told their fate:
When W[alpole]'s counsels rule *Britannia's* land,
Living again, erected here I stand;

Again my thoughts should on this marble rise,
But fearing what I'd say, the d[ea]n denies ...[18]

In the event the dean ultimately defused the statue's potential as a focus for sedition by converting it, in May, into an orthodox *memento mori*, reverting to Dryden and Gildon's association of Shakespeare with Duke Prospero by filling the blank scroll with a misquotation from *The Tempest*:

The Cloud cupt Tow'rs,
The Gorgeous Palaces,
The Great Globe itself
Yea all which it Inherit,
    Shall Dissolve;
And like the baseless Fabrick of a Vision
Leave not a wreck behind.

This hasty, botched piece of work infuriated Pope, who in his notes to the 1743 revision of *The Dunciad* calls it 'that Specimen of an Edition ... which indeed Shakespeare has great reason to point at'.[19]

Ladies' Man

Given the epic solemnity of the statue—whether engaged in irate proof-reading, anti-ministerial satire, or aphasic sententiousness— it cannot have pleased its designers much better that within a decade of its unveiling it would be reproduced in the form of a porcelain scent bottle.[20] While Burlington's committee may have regarded the positioning of Elizabeth I's head on Shakespeare's pedestal as a symbol of his unquestionable loyalty to constitutional purity, another group active in the cause of installing Shakespeare in the Abbey may have felt that it represented more importantly

[18] A manuscript version of this poem appears in Bodleian Library MS Rawl. Poet 152, fo. 185. Despite its claim, Shakespeare was in fact more a beneficiary than a victim of Walpole's censorship: one of the reasons for the increase in Shakespeare revivals during the late 1730s was the discouraging effect of the 1737 Stage Licensing Act on the production of new plays. See Bate, *Shakespearean Constitutions*, 26: Arthur H. Scouten, 'The Increase in Popularity of Shakespeare's Plays in the Eighteenth Century: A Caveat for Interpreters of Stage History', *Shakespeare Quarterly*, 7 (1956), 189–202.

[19] Pope, *Poems*, v. 267. The belated carrying out of the inscription is recorded in *Gentleman's Magazine*, 11 (1741), 276.

[20] See Piper, *The Image of the Poet*, 90, 206 n. 48.

the Bard's dependence on specifically female patronage.[21] If there was a tradition dating back at least as far as Dryden's prologue to *The Enchanted Island* of associating Shakespeare with father-kings, there was equally a tradition, dating back to Margaret Cavendish's letters or Aphra Behn's preface to *The Dutch Lover*, of associating him with women, and as recently as 1726 Lewis Theobald had observed that 'there is scarce a Poet that our English tongue boasts of, who is more the subject of the Ladies' reading'.[22] This association was institutionalized in the late 1730s by the establishment of the Shakespeare Ladies' Club (for whose members or successors the scent bottle was presumably intended), an informal association of 'Ladies of Quality' who in addition to supporting the Abbey project petitioned theatre managements to revive more Shakespeare in place of both the libertine excesses of Restoration comedy and the irrational insipidity of Italian opera. Such was their conspicuous success that some contemporaries give them sole credit not only for the decade's enormous increase in Shakespearean performances but for Burlington's entire project. Eliza Haywood, for example, records in the *Female Spectator* that:

SOME ladies indeed have shewn a truly public Spirit in rescuing the admirable, yet almost forgotten *Shakespear*, from being totally sunk in oblivion:—they have generously contributed to raise a monument to his memory, and frequently honoured his works with their presence on the stage:—an action, which deserves the highest encomiums, and will be attended with an adequate reward; since, in preserving the fame of the dead bard, they add a brightness to their own, which will shine to late posterity.[23]

---

[21] The tradition of regarding Elizabeth as Shakespeare's patroness, promulgated by Rowe's biography, first reaches print via John Dennis, whose 1702 preface to *The Comical Gallant* supplies the anecdote of her commissioning of *The Merry Wives of Windsor* (perhaps in order to justify his own adaptation of the play on the grounds that Shakespeare had been compelled to work too hastily): 'I knew very well, that it had pleas'd one of the greatest Queens that ever was in the World, great not only for her Wisdom in the Arts of Government, but for her knowledge of Polite Learning, and her nice taste in the Drama, for such a taste we may be sure she had, by the relish which she had of the Ancients.' See John Dennis, 'To the Honourable George Granville, Esq.', in *The Comical Gallant: or the Amours of Sir John Falstaffe* (London, 1702), A2. On this tradition, see Schoenbaum, *William Shakespeare*, 144–5.

[22] Lewis Theobald, *Shakespeare Restored* (London, 1726), v–vi.

[23] Eliza Haywood, *The Female Spectator* (5th edn., 4 vols.; London, 1755), i.

Haywood's praise would be echoed by the greatest of all experts on Shakespeare's eighteenth-century reputation twenty years later: '*It was You Ladies* that restor'd Shakespeare to the Stage,' remembered Garrick in 1769, 'you form'd yourselves into a Society to protect his Fame, and Erected a Monument to his and your own honour in Westminster Abbey.'[24]

Despite Haywood's prophecy, the Shakespeare Ladies' Club has by no means enjoyed the fame it deserves: investigating its activities in 1956, for example, Emmett Avery failed to discover the names of any of its members, a failure bemoaned by Jonathan Bate as 'vivid testimony of the erasure of women—even aristocratic ones —from the historical record'.[25] In this particular erasure, however, both these historians are perhaps guilty of a certain unwitting contributory negligence, since there exist not only a poem by Thomas Cooke (an editor of the *Craftsman*) devoted to the praises of a 'Lady of Quality' clearly identified as the leader of the Ladies' Club, but a manuscript poem and a published play by two contemporary women writers who fervently enlist themselves among its supporters. *An Epistle to the Right Honourable The Countess of Shaftesbury, with a Prologue and Epilogue on Shakespeare and his Writings*, published by Cooke in 1743, hails the Countess as the supreme benefactress behind Shakespeare's canonization in what is evidently a reference to the Club's activities two years earlier:

FAIR Patroness of long departed Worth,
O! Thou, who lately called our Genius forth!
Who, like a Guardian Angel, didst inspire
Thousands, and taught them what they should admire;
O! Thou, whose Spirit wak'd a drowsy Age
To pay a due Regard to *Shakespeare*'s Page,

265–6. James Miller, although elsewhere an advocate of the Club (see below), offers a more sceptical view of the Ladies' Club's enthusiasm for Shakespeare as a mere fad in his *Of Politeness. An Epistle to the Right Honourable William Stanhope, Lord Harrington* (London, 1738): 'Not less *Spadillia Shakespear* understands, | Yet runs each Night, and stares, and claps her Hands . . . | . . . For 'tis not what they like, or what they know, | But as the *Fashion* drives the Fop must go' (7).

[24] The text of this speech, delivered at the Jubilee, is preserved on a slip of paper pasted into Garrick's *MS Journal of a Journey to France and Italy, 1763–64*, now in the Folger Shakespeare Library: quoted in Johanne M. Stochholm, *Garrick's Folly* (London, 1964), 91–2.

[25] See Emmett L. Avery, 'The Shakespeare Ladies' Club', *Shakespeare Quarterly* (Spring 1958), 153–8: Bate, *Shakespearean Constitutions*, 25–6.

To thee the richest Gift of Fame we owe,
That Truth can give, or Fancy can bestow.[26]

The countess in question, Susanna Ashley-Cooper, who as first
wife of the 4th Earl of Shaftesbury belonged to the most celebrated
of all Whig dynasties, was a daughter of Baptiste Noel, Earl of
Gainsborough; the Honourable James Noel who composed the
libertarian epilogue to the benefit performance of *Julius Caesar* in
1737 was almost certainly a family connection.[27] She is known
to have been busy in artistic circles at the time of the Ladies' Club
(commissioning a new music room at her country house in
Wimborne St Giles, Dorset, and supporting Handel), and was
indeed already a well-known and highly regarded figure in London
society—Robert Dodsley cites her as a prominent example of
grace combined with intelligence in his *Beauty: or the Art of
Charming* (1735),[28] and Cooke, commenting elsewhere on her
devotion to Shakespeare, likens her to both the Venetian and the
Roman Portias.[29] Her husband was politically active in the late
1730s as an opponent of Walpole's government over the question
of war with Spain[30] (an issue frequently associated with the Ladies'
Club's campaign),[31] and they may both have been connected with
opposition writers since a decade earlier—they are probably the
'Florio and Clara' praised in *The Female Faction: or, The Gay
Subscribers* among the patrons who supported the publication of
John Gay's *Polly* after it was banned from the stage at the insistence of Walpole in 1729.[32]

[26] Thomas Cooke, *An Epistle to the Right Honourable the Countess of Shaftesbury* ... (London, 1743), 3. I am immensely grateful to the excellent Kathy Rowe
of Harvard for sending a photostat of this volume from the Houghton Library.

[27] It is interesting in this context that this performance was advertised as taking
place 'At the particular Desire of several Ladies of Quality'. See *The London Stage*
3: 663.

[28] See Robert Dodsley, *Beauty: or the Art of Charming* (London, 1735), 7–8.

[29] See Thomas Cooke, *A Demonstration of the Will of God by the Light of
Nature* (London, 1742), 'The Dedication', pp. v–vi.

[30] See e.g. *A New Miscellany for the Year 1739* (London, 1740), 26–9.

[31] See e.g. *A Seasonable Rebuke to the Playhouse Rioters* ... *To which is
prefixed, a Petitionary Dedication to the Fair Members of the Shakespear-Club*
(London, 1740), which, with a rallying cry of 'Friends! Britons! Countrymen'!
(13), urges the perpetrators of some recent disturbances at Drury Lane to stop
frightening female theatre-goers and fight the Spanish instead: for performing this
service on their behalf, the anonymous author facetiously hopes in his Dedication
to be rewarded with the post of Secretary to the Shakespeare Ladies' Club.

[32] See *The Female Faction: or the Gay Subscribers* (London, 1729), 7.

It is Pope rather than Gay, however, who features most prominently in both the poem and the play composed by Ladies' Club supporters. Mary Cowper's 'On the Revival of Shakespear's Plays by the Ladies in 1738', preserved in the *Cowper Family Miscellany*,[33] shows considerable, if ultimately qualified, enthusiasm for the poet, representing him (in the terms of the *Dunciad*) as the sole heroic guardian of sense active since the deaths of Addison and Steele: however, quietly avenging the pervasive misogyny of Pope's poetry, Cowper suggests that compared to the activities of the Ladies' Club his satiric crusade has achieved nothing—as members of Minerva's own sex, only the Club have been able fully to represent the goddess's wisdom and partake of her power, and it is only they who have successfully summoned Shakespeare back to life. To Cowper, the Shakespeare Ladies' Club provides a glimpse of a utopian future in which intelligent women, leading the way to a proper valuation of native literature and demanding a high level of intellectual achievement from their suitors, will redeem Britain from its servile cultural dependence on the Continent. Her poem, which brings together in vivid and condensed form most of the tropes associated with the Ladies' Club, has languished in obscurity for too long, and certainly deserves quotation in full:

See happy *Britain* raise her drooping *Head*,
Supported by the *Fair Ones* friendly *Aid*.
Dullness, that Opiate of the *Human Mind*,
Her *Reign* now ended, has to *Sense* resign'd.
See crowded *Theatres*, whose loud Applause
Was late bestow'd, but Oh! how *mean* the *Cause*!
Blush at their *Follies* past, & freely own
They feel a *Charm*, till now but rarely *known*;
A real, solid *Pleasure*, wch exceeds
All they receiv'd from **Riches*[34] Active *Deeds*.

---

[33] BM Add. MSS 28101: Mary Cowper's poem is on 93^v and 94^v. I am immensely grateful to Joanna Lipking of Northwestern University for alerting me to the existence of this splendid text. Mary Cowper was a daughter of William Cowper, MP, and an elder cousin of William Cowper the poet. In 1743 she married the brilliant lawyer William de Grey, later Lord Walsingham, who, according to contemporaries, 'strikingly resembled Garrick'. Charles Ryskab, *William Cowper of the Inner Temple, Esq.* (Cambridge, 1959), 75–6.

[34] '* The Master of the New House in Covent Garden—Famous for playing Harlequin—as well as fitting out *Pantomime* Entertainments' (Cowper's marginal note).

While *Addison* and *Steele* yet liv'd, in vain
Dullness essay'd to vindicate her *Reign*:
But when, by Fates *Decree*, of These *bereft*,
The Cause of *Wisdom* was defenceless left,
Then in our *Verse*, no *Energy* was found,
And as we sunk in *Sense*, we rose in *Sound*.[35]

In vain to *Pope Minerva* lifts her *Eyes*,
(He yet *untainted* the *Contagion* flys)
To Him she gives, what *Mortal* can, to do,
Against the many=headed *Senseless Crew*;
Who fond of *Noise* & gay *Impertinence*,
No longer listen to the *Voice* of *Sense*:
At last the Goddess *her own Sex* inspires,
Fills with her *Strength*, & warms wth all her *Fires*,
See *Wisdom*, like a *Stream*, whose rapid *Course*
Has long been stopp'd, now wth redoubled Force
Breaks out—the softer Sex redeems the Land
And *Shakespear* lives again by their *Command*.
For *Fashion's* Sake the very *Beaux* attend
And by their *Smiles* w^d seem to *comprehend*.

Pursue ye Gen'rous *Fair*! till all is done,
The *Task* you have so gloriously *begun*.
Nor to One *Bard* Alone your Aid *confine*,
Let *Each*, as *Merit* calls, alternate, *shine*:
Banish all *Tumblers*—*Farce*—& *Harlequin*—
The Work's but half *Compleat* while these *remain*,
And set us free from Follys num'rous Train.
Be it your *Bus'ness* to reform the *Stage*,
That *perfect*, by Degrees, will *Mend* the *Age*;
Reason and *Truth* so *Providence* decreed,
Once *listen'd to*—are certain to *succeed*:
Then shall our *Youth* prefer their Native *Home*
Nor after *Modes* to Foreign *Climates roam*.
And knowing *Worth* alone can *please* the *Fair*,
Their *Minds improvement*, be their only *Care*,
Good Sense shall rule to *Ages* yet *unborn*
And *Britain* cease to be her *Neighbour's Scorn*.

The recommendation to the Ladies in this poem of reforming the
stage was taken up the following year by the poet and novelist
Elizabeth Boyd, whose sole play *Don Sancho, or The Students*

---

[35] '* *Italian Operas*' (ibid.).

Whim (an oblique commentary on the Westminster Abbey project eloquently dedicated, in its prologue, to Pope) concludes, rather like this poem, with 'Minerva's Triumph, a Masque'.[36] Boyd (to whose 1732 novel *The Happy-Unfortunate* the Countess of Shaftesbury had subscribed)[37] clearly recognizes the plan to erect Shakespeare's statue as a bid to capture Shakespeare's ghost: in her play, three undergraduates and the aristocratic amateur necromancer who goes under the assumed name of Don Sancho summon the Bard's shade at midnight to the Botanical Gardens in Oxford, where Minerva herself causes his monument to appear as a substitute after the disdainful absent presence of the Author is wafted back to Elysium in a cloud. It is her own power over Shakespeare's ghost rather than Don Sancho's, however, which Boyd celebrates in the play's induction: casting her endeavours on the mercy of the Ladies, Boyd, like Cowper, clearly revels in the unaccustomed authority provided by her participation in this triumph of Minerva:

Ladies your Aid, or we shant win a Heart;
Be Just, be Kind, theres Mercy in those Eyes,
Minervas Triumph, be the Fair Ones Prize;
Whose Magick Charms, controul the learned Sage,
        .   .   .   .   .   .

And once again let Shakespear bless the Stage;
Soul-Soothing Shade, rouz'd by a Woman's Pen,
To Check the impious Rage of lawless Men.
        .   .   .   .

(Boyd, A^v–A2^r)

An admirer of Granville, Boyd follows the example of the prologue to *The Jew of Venice* by summoning this 'soul-soothing shade' in the company of one of his most gifted adaptors: at the close of Don Sancho's invocation 'the Earth trembles, and the Ghosts of *Shakespear* and *Dryden* rise as in Glory to a soft sweet Symphony' (11). Boyd, indeed, like Cowper, does not think the resurrection of poetic merit now in progress thanks to Minerva and her disciples should be confined to Shakespeare, and after the departure of Shakespeare and Dryden the stage is briefly occupied by 'Minerva's

---

[36] Elizabeth Boyd, *Don Sancho: or, The students whim...with Minerva's triumph, a masque* (London, 1739). On Boyd's career, see Janet Todd (ed.), *A Dictionary of British and American Women Writers* (London, 1985), 56.
[37] The novel was republished in 1737 as *The Female Page*, prefaced by the same list of subscribers.

Temple', a predominantly Tory analogue of the Temple of British Worthies, in which are represented not only these two writers but a whole canon of deserving moderns—Gay, Congreve, Addison, Waller, Sheffield, and Granville (15). Pope, not yet dead, is absent from this temple, but his work is represented, albeit in paraphrase, by the inscription Boyd chooses for Shakespeare's monument, which seems to derive from Pope's epigram on the Bard's 'hundred and thirty years' nap':

Six score Years, after Death upreard I stand,
The Wonder, as the Glory of the Land.
         William Shakespear.

                                  (18)

Sharing Pope's desire to classicize Shakespeare, Boyd actually represents this inscription as being carved in Greek (it is obligingly translated by one of the students), and she implicitly casts Dryden as Virgil to Shakespeare's Homer by having Dryden's nearby inscription carved in Latin (translated, it runs 'As *Shakespear*'s Friend, I here erect my Throne, | The grateful Burden, of Unfeeling Stone'). Despite this potential disregard for the English vernacular, however, her play is every bit as patriotic as Mary Cowper's poem, sharing Cowper's sense that the resurrection of Shakespeare (and, in this instance, Dryden) by Minerva is part of a general process of national renewal, something which Mercury's song during the manifestation of the monuments makes ringingly clear:

MER. See, oh see the rising Bust,
   Shakespear's Tomb, the Good, the Just;
   To his Country's endless Praise,
   See the Bard from *Lethe* raise;
   Joining worthy *Dryden*'s Urn,
   Social Pair see they return.
CHORUS. Once again, *Britannia*'s Fame,
   Letter'd Gold their Worth proclaim.
   Once again, &c.

                    (16)

It is this strain of virtuous patriotism above all which contemporary writers both for and about Shakespeare's Ladies choose to stress, often in flat defiance of the social and literary orientations suggested by the surviving evidence as to their identity. Championing the native sense of Shakespeare against foreign imports

such as opera and the harlequinade, the Ladies are repeatedly
claimed in the name of a distinctly middle-class version of domestic
virtue (despite the exalted station of at least their leader), and as
frequently represented (despite their gender) as engaged in the
restoration of British masculinity. An epilogue in their praise from
1738 (closer in spirit to Cowper's poem than to Boyd's play)
provides a characteristic example:

When worse than barbarism had sunk your taste,
When nothing pleas'd but what laid virtue waste,
A sacred band, determin'd, wise, and good,
They jointly rose to stop th'exotick flood,
And strove to wake, by *Shakespeare*'s nervous lays,
The manly genius of *Eliza*'s days.[38]

Notwithstanding its sovereign's inconvenient womanhood,
Elizabeth's reign is here invoked as the locus of morally upstand-
ing virility (using Shakespeare as a kind of potency-reviving spirit
guide), the historical site of the triumph of the Protestant virtues:
this epilogue is by George Lillo, who five years earlier, in the
pioneering middle-class tragedy *The London Merchant: or, The
History of George Barnwell*, had credited the virtuous brokers of
the City with the defeat of the Spanish Armada.[39] The Shakespeare
revival of the 1730s indeed thrived on anti-Spanish feeling, with
which Shakespeare had already been identified on several previous
occasions—in Dennis's prologue to a 1707 revival of *Julius Caesar*,
for example, which has Shakespeare's ghost proudly tell of how
his play inspired Elizabeth and her subjects alike to resist the
ambitions of Philip II.[40] Such anti-Hispanic sentiments ran par-

---

[38] George Lillo, *Marina*, 'Epilogue', in *The Plays of George Lillo*, ed. Trudy
Drucker (2 vols.; New York, 1979), ii. 127. For further examples of this strain of
rhetoric on the subject, see Avery, 'Shakespeare Ladies' Club'.

[39] Id., *The London Merchant: or, The History of George Barnwell*, ibid. i. 99–
190. See Thorogood's dialogue with Trueman in I. i. 103–5: arguing that merchants deserve greater public recognition, Thorogood explains that the international moneylenders of Genoa, preferring the custom of England's just and
worthy capitalists to that of their Spanish counterparts, have denied Philip II a loan
with which to equip his fleet, thereby buying time for English defensive prepara-
tions. On the popularity and influence of this play, see esp. Kathleen Wilson,
'Empire of Virtue: The Imperial Project and Hanoverian Culture, *c*.1720–1785', in
Lawrence Stone (ed.), *The British State and Empire in War and Peace* (London,
forthcoming).

[40] John Dennis, 'Prologue to the Subscribers for *Julius Caesar*', in *A Collection
and Selection of English Prologues and Epilogues* (4 vols.; London, 1779), iii. 1–2.
Cf. the anonymous epilogue to Theobald's *Double Falshood*.

ticularly high during the 1730s, especially among the merchant community, as a result of actions by Spanish coastguards against British shipping in the Caribbean. Walpole did not declare war until late 1739, but demands for military action from mercantile lobby groups had already reached hysterical levels by mid-1738: 'The general cry is War, Revenge on the SPANIARDS, *Restitution for our* PAST LOSSES, *satisfaction to our* NATIONAL HONOUR, and above all, ample Security to our FUTURE TRADE AND NAVIGATION,' reported the *London Evening Post* for 17–19 August, 1738.[41] In this climate, the cult of Elizabeth and things Elizabethan flourished, as a few lines from a poem published in the same year by an angry young man destined to become one of Shakespeare's greatest advocates may suggest:

On *Thames*'s Banks, in silent Thought we stood,
Where Greenwich smiles upon the silver Flood:
Struck with the Seat that gave Eliza birth,
We kneel, and kiss the consecrated Earth;
In pleasing Dreams the blissful Age renew,
And call Britannia's Glories back to view;
Behold her Cross triumphant on the Main,
The Guard of Commerce, and the Dread of *Spain* ...
  (Samuel Johnson, 'London', in *Complete English Poems*, 61)

The propagation of the spirit of 1588 among merchant groups in the sphere of political activism and Lillo's propagation of a middle-class version of Shakespeare in the theatre are clearly aspects of the same general demand for a closer alignment of both the national culture and the state with the interests of the trading classes: certainly the play offered to the Ladies' Club by Lillo's appeal to 'the manly genius of Eliza's days' presents an eminently bourgeois—and maritime—version of the Bard. *Marina* is an adaptation of *Pericles* which concentrates on presenting its heroine's adventures as what a newspaper puff describes as 'a remarkable Instance of the Triumphs and Rewards of Persever-ance in Virtue':[42] omitting everything prior to Leonine's balked assassination and Marina's subsequent abduction by the pirates, the play concentrates almost exclusively on its exemplary female

[41] Quoted in Kathleen Wilson, 'Empire, Trade and Popular Politics in Mid-Hanoverian Britain: The Case of Admiral Vernon', *Past and Present*, 121 (Nov. 1988), 73–109.
[42] *The Daily Advertiser*, 8 Aug. 1738.

protagonist. Lillo compensates for this abbreviation by protracting the brothel scenes, dwelling on the story they offer of virtue in distress and elucidating its moral lessons more fully by expanding the dialogue between Marina and the reformable rake Lysimachus. The prologue presents the result as a direct expression of Shakespeare's virtuous sensibility, a morally elevating tear-jerker:

> ... Shou'd as the soul,
> The fire of *Shakespeare* animate the whole,
> Shou'd heights, which none but he cou'd reach, appear,
> To little errors do not prove severe.
> If, when in pain for the event, surprize
> And sympathetick joy shou'd fill your eyes;
> Do not repine that so you crown an art,
> Which gives such sweet emotions to the heart:
> Whose pleasures, so exalted in their kind,
> Do, as they charm the sense, improve the mind.
>
> (Lillo, *Marina*, 'Prologue', in *Plays*, ii. 61)

The Shakespeare thus adapted to the tastes and concerns of the middle classes is recognizably a precursor of Samuel Richardson,[43] and it is not surprising to find the latter (a professed admirer of Lillo)[44] subsequently enrolling two of his paragons of virtue among the Ladies' Club's sympathizers. Pamela writes after her elevation to the theatre-going classes that England 'should not quit the manly nervous Sense, which is the Distinction of the *English* drama. One Play of our celebrated *Shakespeare* will give infinitely more Pleasure to a sensible Mind, than a dozen *English-Italian* Operas',[45] while Sir Charles Grandison's beloved Harriet Byron, describing the social amusements of London, urges her correspondent, 'If you find that I prefer the highest of these entertainments, or the Opera itself, well as I love music, to a good play of our favourite Shakespeare, then, my Lucy, let your heart ake for your Harriet'.[46]

---

[43] *Marina*, after all, depicting successful resistance to an aristocratic seducer who in the end offers marriage, and the imprisonment of a virtuous woman in a brothel, anticipates major plot motifs of *Pamela* and *Clarissa* respectively.

[44] See Samuel Richardson's first (anonymous) original publication *The Apprentice's Vade Mecum; or, Young Man's Pocket Companion* (London, 1733), 16. The tract is otherwise uncompromisingly anti-theatrical.

[45] Samuel Richardson, *Pamela, or, Virtue Rewarded* [1741–2], Shakespeare Head edition (!), (4 vols.; Stratford-upon-Avon, 1929), iv. 91.

[46] Id., *The History of Sir Charles Grandison* [1753–54], ed. Jocelyn Harris

The Shakespeare regularly imagined on the Club's behalf is himself something of a Sir Charles Grandison: the author not only of the uplifting and instructive *Marina* but of the impeccably polite *The Universal Passion* (a hybrid of *Much Ado About Nothing* and Molière's *Princesse d'Elide*, whose adaptor, the Revd James Miller, assures the Ladies' Club that 'sacred Decency's his constant Aim'),[47] his plays are always distinguished by 'Decency and good Manners' and give pleasure 'without the least Violence being offered to Virtue, Truth or Humanity'[48]—even if they have to be rewritten to prove it. It is the essentially genteel spirit of their author which counts, a spirit with whom the Ladies' Club are put in touch by an elaborate advertisement for a revival of *King John* printed on the front page of the *Daily Advertiser* for 4 March 1737. Consisting of a letter headed 'WILLIAM SHAKESPEAR, from Elisium, to the Fair Supporters of Wit and Sense, the Ladies of Great Britain,' this text again identifies the playwright with Old Hamlet, but, unlike the severe bard of Theobald's fund-raising prologue, this spectre has returned not out of a desire for post-humous vindication but out of his strict regard for the obligations of etiquette:

FAIR CREATURES,

... My Shade, this present Evening, intends to visit you at the New Theatre in the Haymarket, there, in the most suppliant manner a gener-ous Heart would desire in an oblig'd Dependent, to pay you my Devoirs, and to introduce my own Play of King John on that stage. ... The Favors

[1972] (3 pts. in 1; Oxford, 1986), 1: 22–3. Cf. Harriet's appropriation of Shake-speare as a native, feminized ally against the snobbish, aristocratically educated Oxford pedant Mr Walden: describing a tea-table dispute in another letter to Lucy, she remembers that 'Mr Walden ... would needs force into conversation, with a preference to our Shakespeare, his Sophocles, his Euripides, his Terence' (59).

[47] James Miller, *The Universal Passion* (London, 1737), 'Prologue'. Miller goes on to assure his audience that 'There's nought but what an *Anchoret* might hear, | No Sentence that can wound the chastest Ear ...' (ibid). Many of this play's performances were advertised as having been mounted 'At the Particular Desire of Several Ladies of Quality', a formula common on the playbills of the late 1730s and generally assumed to represent the activities of the Club. The première of Henry Fielding's *The Historical Register for the Year 1736* clashed with one such performance of Miller's play, on 21 Mar. 1737 (see *The London Stage*, 3: 650–1), which may explain its epilogue's rather dismissive reference to 'you Ladies, whether you be Shakespear's Ladies, or Beaumont and Fletcher's Ladies'; *The Works of Henry Fielding, Esq; with the Life of the Author*, 2nd edn. (8 vols.; London, 1762), iii. 208.

[48] Miller, *The Universal Passion*, 'Dedication'.

already heaped on me by the British Beauties, have emboldened me to entreat for more, and humbly to desire that they will . . . not suffer me to pay Respects to empty Boxes. I would, kind fair ones, have waited on you in Person to have made this request, but the time of my Excursion on Parole is limited to so short a Date, that such a Design is render'd Impracticable . . . I am well assur'd the Play will be conducted with . . . decency . . . and I give you the Word of a Ghost of Honour, that I'll endeavor to behave in such a manner as becomes,

> *Dear agreeable Ladies*
> *Your most obliged, and*
> *most devoted humble Servant,*
> W. SHAKESPEAR.

With flawless manners and one eye on his box-office profits, this, for all the puff-writer's irony, is a fitting depiction of the bourgeois Shakespeare, a master of polite letters from an age manly enough never to have heard of opera and respectable enough to have repulsed the Spanish by sheer force of moral credit. Within a few years, indeed, such a Shakespeare would even be perceived in the august Abbey memorial itself. Published during the same year as the last part of *Sir Charles Grandison*, in which the paragon of civil manliness finally marries his Shakespearean Lady Harriet, *An Historical Description of Westminster-Abbey, Its Monuments and Curiosities* describes Scheemakers' statue in terms far more suggestive of Richardson's exemplar for the bourgeoisie than of Burlington's epic British Worthy:

Both the Design and Workmanship of this Monument are extremely elegant; the Figure of *Shakespear*, and his Attitude, his Dress, his Shape, his genteel Air, and fine Composure: all so delicately express'd by the Sculptor, cannot be sufficiently admired.[49]

Stone Guest Appearance

Already the object of contending appropriations before its completion—simultaneously claimed by different commentators as the embodiment of an opposition Shakespeare, a royal Shakespeare, a women's Shakespeare, and a bourgeois Shakespeare—this statue also figures extensively in a sustained debate over whether the

---

[49] *An Historical Description of Westminster-Abbey, Its Monuments and Curiosities* (London, 1754), 107.

Shakespeare it presents belongs in the library or on the stage. This debate is enacted, often in very curious ways, by the metaphors in which contemporaries respond to Scheemakers' statue, which seem to indicate an inability to decide whether the Bard is as yet unborn, is returning to life in the live theatre, or is achieving only a shadowy afterlife among the undead of classic literature. Writing in 1739, Elizabeth Boyd sees Scheemakers as a midwife, assisting at the birth of the Poet of Nature: in the prologue to *Don Sancho* she hopes that her play may be performed as the statue nears perfection,

When rich vein'd Earth rob'd of immortal stone
Sees *Englands* pride, beneath the Artist Groan,
Then, whiles half form'd the beautious Embrio glows,
It would be just to say—thus *Shakespear* rose.

(A^r)

In a different context, James Miller's prologue to *The Universal Passion* uses a similar trope, commending his adaptation to the Ladies' Club as, in effect, their own illegitimate child by the Bard:

'Twas this gave Birth to our Attempt to-night,
Fond to bring more of his rich Scenes to light.
To your Protection *Shakespear*'s Offspring take,
And save the *Orphan* for the Father's Sake.

In the theatre, perhaps, this union might be considered fruitful: but as represented by the Abbey memorial, the labours of canonization might appear to offer Shakespeare at best the living death of official ghosthood. James Noel's epilogue to the 1738 benefit performance of *Julius Caesar* shares Boyd's sense of Scheemakers' statue as an embryo and Miller's metaphor of the Ladies' Club as mothers, but its celebration of the happy event of Shakespeare's addition to Britain's most distinguished cemetery cannot help but suggest not a glorious resurrection but something between a stillbirth and an exhumation:

But here what humble thanks, what praise is due,
Ow'd to such gen'rous virtue, ow'd to you!
With grief you saw a bard neglected lie,
Whom towring genius living rais'd so high.
With grief you saw your Shakespeare's slighted state,
And call'd forth merit from the grave of fate.

Let others boast they smile on living worth;
You give a buried bard a brighter birth.
                (*A General Dictionary*, 189)

The Abbey monument may birth the canonical Shakespeare, but it simultaneously enacts his funeral, relocating the corpus as it does so from the theatre to the study. Certainly there is nothing about the statue to suggest that it commemorates a mere working playwright: dressed in an expensive suit of clothes derived from the aristocratic portraits of Charles I's court, Shakespeare, meditating gravely in what appears to be a library, leans with one elbow on a lectern topped with a pile of immense leather-bound books—presumably his own works, in what can only be Pope's thoroughly anti-theatrical edition. Indeed, the monument's presentation of a strictly literary Shakespeare would be confirmed over the coming years, as the cast which Scheemakers mass-produced from his model for its head became one of the most popular library busts of the eighteenth century.[50] Lewis Theobald's prologue to the 1739 *Hamlet* benefit, again addressed to the Ladies' Club, tries anxiously to reclaim Burlington's funerary project for the cause of live drama, but it is only able to do so at the cost of representing the theatre itself as a rival mausoleum, preserving the emphatically dead body of Shakespeare's plays:

For the dead Bard, receive our thanks and praise,
And make us Sharers in the Tomb you raise.
Ye Fair, who have distinguish'd Favours shewn,
And made this Poet's Patronage your own;
Urge those, whose gen'rous Hearts confess your Sway,
To follow, where your Virtues point the way:
Then think, this Pile his honour'd Bones contains,
And frequent Visit—here—the lov'd Remains.
    (*London Daily Post and General Advertiser*,
    12 April 1739)

Boyd, more inventively, solves this problem by actually dramatizing the canonization performed by the Abbey project in *Don Sancho*, appropriating the statue as an inert prop which merely substitutes for the dramatic character of Shakespeare's ghost; but unfortunately *Don Sancho*, although provisionally accepted at Drury Lane, was never produced (see Boyd, '*Advertisement*'). In her

[50] See Whinney, *Sculpture in Britain*, 453 n. 29.

induction, Boyd expresses the fear that her script may be plagiarized, a fear which was, in fact, multiply realized. Theobald himself
borrowed Boyd's resurrection of Shakespeare's ghost as a performer to speak for the statue on 9 April 1741: a puff in that day's
London Daily Post and General Advertiser offers a revival of *King
John* at Covent Garden complete with 'a New Epilogue in the
Person of Shakespeare (ushered in by Solemn Musick) on Occasion
of the Monument erected by the Publick to his Memory. Written
by Mr. Theobald. With an exact Representation of the said Monument.' No other trace of this text survives: however, a much more
extensive reworking of Boyd's idea, complete with Minerva's
triumph, was both staged and printed, and its sensational success
was to initiate a whole series of bids to reclaim Shakespeare, in
Scheemakers' effigy, on behalf of the theatre. 'We are informed
that last Night a new Entertainment call'd Harlequin Student was
rehears'd at the late Theatre in Goodman's Fields,' reported the
Daily Advertiser for 26 February 1741 'when several Persons
who were present generally concurr'd in Opinion it had the Preference of any yet perform'd there, and more particularly that Part
of it in which the Monument of Shakespear is introduc'd.'

The canonization of Shakespeare was becoming such a widespread pursuit that even his supposed adversaries on the illegitimate popular fringes of the drama were willing to get in on the
act: the same winter that saw the unveiling of Scheemakers' monument saw versions of *Richard III*, *Henry VIII*, and *Henry IV*
played by puppets, the last starring Mr Punch as Falstaff.[51]
Partly thanks to the activities of the Ladies' Club, the unveiling of
the Westminster Abbey memorial coincided with an unprecedented
amount of Shakespearean activity in the theatres: during the 1740/1
season, one in every four performances given in London was of a
Shakespeare play (a record which even during Garrick's professedly
Bardolatrous management of Drury Lane was never challenged).
Of the three principal houses, only two, the licensed Theatres
Royal of Drury Lane and Covent Garden, were operating strictly
within the law: the third, Goodman's Fields, evaded the Licensing

---

[51] These productions were mounted by Charlotte Charke; see her autobiography, *A Narrative of the Life of Mrs. Charlotte Charke*, (*youngest daughter of
Colley Cibbler* [sic], *Esq.*). *Written by herself* (2nd edn.; London, 1755), 75, 82;
George Speaight, *A History of the English Puppet Theatre* (London, 1955),
102–8.

Act by advertising its performances as concerts in two parts 'at the *late* [i.e. former] theatre in Goodman's Fields' [my italics], during the intervals of which plays would be performed 'gratis, by persons for their diversions'. Defying the law of the realm, its manager, Henry Giffard, specialized also in defying the established canons of the theatrical profession, reviving forgotten and unfashionable plays (in 1740/1 he staged unrevised texts of *All's Well That Ends Well* and *The Winter's Tale*, the first known London productions of either play since Shakespeare's lifetime), employing unconventional and inexperienced performers (making theatrical history by hosting Garrick's triumphant first performance as Richard III the following season), and putting together generically irregular shows (such as his catchpenny dramatization of *Pamela*, also in 1741/2) to capitalize on passing fads. Premièred at Goodman's Fields on 4 March 1741, *Harlequin Student*, although published without Giffard's name, is a typically eccentric example of his work, a hastily written commercial exploitation of the interest aroused by the Abbey monument, derivative in form and distinctly suspect in content.

The full title of this 'Entertainment' identifies it as the celebration of a change of faith: *Harlequin Student: or the Fall of Pantomime, with the Restoration of the Drama*,[52] a formula probably mimicked, appropriately enough given the head on Scheemakers' pedestal, from the illicit fairground play *The Coronation of Queen Elizabeth, With the Restauration of the Protestant Religion: or, The Downfal of the Pope*.[53] This allusion both royalizes Shakespeare by association with Elizabeth and claims him for virtue by association with militant Protestantism, but the conversion to these earnest values of which it boasts proves to be a very belated one, and less than wholehearted. The play is in fact a lavish, hedonistic, and perfectly orthodox harlequinade, a virtually wordless orgy of farce, slapstick, and special effects (with Harlequin and Pierrot pursuing Colombine through a variety of gadget-ridden scenery) excused only at the last minute by its highly compromised panegyric on Shakespeare. After the bulk of the performance is complete, with Harlequin celebrating his marriage to Colombine in the company of Pierrot, Scaramouche, and Punch, the play is incongruously interrupted by the arrival of Jupiter, who has come to harangue the audience for tolerating the show so far:

[52] Published in London in 1741.
[53] Published in London in 1680; see ch. 2, above.

Too long, *Britannia*, hast thou blindly err'd,
And Foreign Mimes to *English* wit preferr'd!
Eunuchs to Sloth your senses have betray'd,
And *British* spirits (as they sung) decay'd.
But see, behold! a better Time returns,
Each Bosom now, with nobler Rapture burns!
Immortal SHAKESPEAR's matchless Wit revives,
And now the Bard in speaking Marble lives:
Numbers each Night, his endless Beauties praise,
Each day with Rapture on his Statue gaze;
For ever thus th'unequall'd Bard adore,
Let Mimes and Eunuchs lull the Sense no more,
But with his Muse, your own lost Fame restore.
    [*It thunders*, Harlequin *trembles, and
        immediately Incantation Sounds are
  heard. . . . The Scene draws, and discovers the
 monument of Shakespear, exactly represented, as
     lately erected in* Westminster Abbey . . .]
           (*Harlequin Student*, 22)

The Bard may now 'live' on stage in 'speaking Marble', but his
dumb idol needs intermediaries if his intrusive imputed message is
to be heard. Ironically, the voice he is supplied with, as Mercury
proceeds to banish pantomime on his behalf, is not that of 'the
Drama' at all, but of opera: every word of the remaining portion
of the play is sung. Mars warns the audience that 'Eunuchs taint
the soundest [heart] | Weaken Man in every Part,' and, following
Burlington's notion of the epic Bard, claims that:

SHAKESPEAR's Soul-exalting Muse
Will raise your Thoughts to nobler Views,
Read but o'er his matchless Verse,
Soon you'll prove the sons of *Mars*.

           (24)

For her part, Minerva, in the best tradition of Mary Cowper's
poem, urges the audience to

Banish Foreign Songsters hence,
Doat on *Shakespear*'s manly Sense.
Send th'Invading Triflers Home,
To lull the Fools of *France* and *Rome*!

           (Ibid.)

—all to music by a Frenchman (Prelleur) on a set designed by an Italian (Devoto).[54] Giffard may have been a genuine admirer of Shakespeare, but he knew that his audience were not about to abandon the pleasures of low comedy and music overnight: his play cannily employs the emerging cult of the Bard to advertise and license a thorough indulgence in both. His play purports to be returning Shakespeare to his proper place, as the leading light of a morally and patriotically regenerate theatre, but it simultaneously subordinates the ghostly dignity of Scheemakers' monument to the flesh and blood charms of farce and song. Standing in front of Shakespeare's statue, Giffard's singers feign to extol the superiority of Shakespeare's art while in fact displacing it by their own.

Slight as it is, *Harlequin Student*, 'and more particularly that Part of it in which the Monument of Shakespear is introduc'd', would be repeated subsequently in different but recognizable form, on several momentous occasions. In 1769, at the very culmination of Shakespeare's canonization, another group of singers and musicians would accompany the Bard's representative on earth as, in front of yet another copy of Scheemakers' statue, he extolled the superiority of Shakespeare's art while in fact displacing it by his own—reciting his *Ode upon dedicating a building, and erecting a statue, to Shakespeare, at Stratford upon Avon*. (Frontispiece.)

The Actor

It seems strangely apt that *Harlequin Student* saw the theatrical debut not only of Scheemakers' idol of Shakespeare, but of Shakespeare's most celebrated idolater, the man who would in effect rerun the play as a setting for his Jubilee Ode twenty-eight years later. When Giffard's Harlequin, Richard Yates, fell ill one night in March 1741, he was secretly replaced at short notice by a stage-struck apprentice vintner, who would remember the occasion a busy nine months later:

You perhaps would be glad to know what parts I have play'd, King Richd—Jack Smatter in Pamela—Clody fop's fortune—Lothario fair Penitent—Chamont Orphan—Ghost Hamlet.... As to playing a Harlequin 'tis quite false—Yates last Season was taken very ill & was not able

---

[54] On Prelleur, see *BDA* xii. 151–2: on Devoto, *BDA* iv. 351–4.

to begin the Entertainment so I put on the Dress & did 2 or three Scenes for him, but Nobody knew it but him & Giffard . . . believe me yr Sincere Brothr

D:Garrick[55]

Such was Garrick's extraordinary success in appropriating both Burlington's project and the reformation ambivalently proclaimed by *Harlequin Student* that it eventually became impossible to believe that he had not been involved in commissioning Schee-makers' statue as well as in upstaging it. The standard Victorian guide to the Westminster Abbey memorials confidently declares that 'Shakspeare's monument was erected in 1741, out of the receipts from two benefits, played for the purpose, at each of the Theatres Royal, and the additional contributions of eminent men, amongst whom the Earl of Burlington, Pope, and Garrick, took the lead.'[56] In fact, however, Garrick's career was dedicated not to promoting Scheemakers' statue as an embodiment of Shakespeare, but to replacing it as such, and in the process establishing Drury Lane Theatre rather than Westminster Abbey as the rightful home of Shakespeare's spirit.

The strategy by which this was carried out might best be de-scribed as the cultivation in the public imagination of an intimate connection (not to say a familial one) between Garrick and Shake-speare's ghost. As we have seen, the identification of Shakespeare with the ghost of Old Hamlet, already close to being a cliché, is frequently repeated during the Shakespearean revival of the 1730s, particularly in connection with the Abbey monument: but as a silent representation of this ghost the statue can only play the King Hamlet of the first scene, mutely waiting for the Prince. It was this role which Garrick, making his brilliant debut at precisely the right moment, set out to fill, casting himself on stage as the greatest Hamlet since Betterton, and offstage as precisely the Hamlet for whom Shakespeare's royal ghost had been waiting.

That Garrick was regarded by his contemporaries as, above all, the definitive Hamlet is extensively demonstrated by the extant

---

[55] *The Letters of David Garrick*, ed. David M. Little and George M. Kahrl (3 vols., Cambridge, Mass., 1963), i. 34 (29 Dec. 1741). See also George Winchester Stone, Jr, and George M. Kahrl, *David Garrick: A Critical Biography* (Carbondale, Ill., 1979), 23–4.

[56] George Lewis Smyth, *Biographical Illustrations of Westminster Abbey* (London, 1843), 21.

accounts of his performance in this part (outweighing in number, detail, and enthusiasm even those of his Richard III, Macbeth, and Lear):[57] Fielding's Partridge in *Tom Jones*, most famously, identifies him so thoroughly with this role that he is hardly able to perceive his acting at all ('why I could act as well as he myself. I am sure if I had seen a ghost, I should have looked in the very same manner, and done just as he did').[58] That claiming and retaining the part of the Prince was of special importance to him is perhaps suggested by the care he lavished on preparing his interpretation. He followed his brilliant debut as Richard by accepting the role of the Ghost rather than immediately attempting Hamlet, and experimented with his performance of the latter at the Smock Alley theatre in Dublin before his Drury Lane première in this role in November 1742;[59] in later years he even enhanced the most famous of the 'points' in his interpretation (his start backward into the supporting arms of Horatio and Marcellus on 'Angels and ministers of grace defend us!'—1. 4. 20) by the use of a hydraulic wig able literally to make 'each particular hair to stand on end | Like quills upon the fretful porcupine' (1. 5. 19–20).[60] Garrick's self-presentation as Hamlet extended into offstage areas of his activities: he enjoyed a protracted relationship with his first Ophelia, Peg Woffington, before throwing her over abruptly in 1746;[61] and, writing to Powell (his deputy as Drury Lane's leading man) during a temporary exile on the Continent in 1764, we find him giving some familiar advice: 'guard against *the Splitting the Ears of the Groundlings, who are capable of Nothing but dumb Shew & noise*—. . . *be not too tame neither . . .*'[62]

---

[57] See Stone and Kahrl, *David Garrick* 515–72. The most vivid accounts of Garrick's Hamlet are probably those by Arthur Murphy (*The Life of David Garrick* (2 vols.; London, 1801), i. 46–7) and Georg Christian Lichtenberg (in *Lichtenberg's Visits to England, As Described in His Letters and Diaries*, ed. and trans. Margaret L. Mare and W. H. Quarrell, (Oxford, 1938)).

[58] *Tom Jones*, bk. XVI, ch. 5: Fielding, *Works*, vi. 332–6. See Brooks-Davies, *Fielding, Dickens*.

[59] See George Winchester Stone, Jr., 'Garrick's Handling of Shakespeare's Plays and his Influence upon the Changed Attitude of Shakespeare Criticism during the Eighteenth Century', Ph.D. thesis (Harvard, 1938), 115; Kalman A. Burnim, *David Garrick, Director* (Pittsburgh, 1961), 152–73.

[60] On Garrick's wig, see Joseph Roach, 'Garrick, the Ghost and the Machine', *Theatre Journal*, 34 (1982), 431–40, and Leigh Woods, *Garrick Claims the Stage: Acting as Social Emblem in Eighteenth-Century England* (Westport, Conn., 1984), 122.

[61] See Stone and Kahrl, *David Garrick*, 54–8.

[62] 12 Dec. 1764; Garrick, *Letters*, ii. 436.

The significance of this piece of casting for Garrick's relation-ship to Shakespeare was not lost on contemporary commentators. In an anonymous poem in the *London Magazine* of June 1750, for example, Shakespeare's ghost urges Garrick to replace the adapted texts of his plays still in the repertory with their originals, recog-nizing Garrick as his rightful avenger:

To thee, my great restorer, must belong
The task to vindicate my injur'd song,
To place each character in proper light,
To speak my words and do my meaning right...[63]

Going one better than those who merely praise Garrick for his pronunciation of Shakespeare's words, the poet is endowing him with unmediated access to Shakespeare's 'meaning' (not just that of the words—'their' would have scanned as readily as the second 'my' in the last line quoted above)—a point reiterated a couplet later, where Garrick utters not just Shakespeare's original words but his actual ideas: 'My genuine thoughts when by thy voice exprest, | Shall still be deemed the greatest and the best.'[64] As Hamlet to Shakespeare's ghost, simultaneously the father's heir and his living representative, Garrick is not only possessed by this spirit (giving Shakespeare life, speaking his words) but is in pos-session of it (able to declare what Shakespeare means), a point further suggested at this poem's conclusion: 'So by each other's aid we both shall live, | I, fame to thee, thou, life to me, shalt give.'[65] In that Garrick's own histrionic celebrity was furthering Shakespeare's popularity in the theatre, and Shakespeare was pro-viding Garrick's living, 'fame' and 'life' are interchangeable in this formulation, which in its swift succession of 'we', 'I', 'thee', 'thou', 'me' blurs the separation between Shakespeare's identity and Garrick's. The distinction is further confounded in the next poem to be published in this tradition, *A Poetic Epistle from Shakespear in Elysium to Mr. Garrick at Drury-Lane Theatre* (1752),[66] which

---

[63] *London Magazine* (June 1750), 278–9.

[64] Cf. Henry Howard's *A Visionary Interview at the Shrine of Shakespeare* (London, 1758), which reproaches the actor's critics for 'snarling' 'when *Garrick* speaks his *Shakespeare*'s mind'.

[65] Cf., of course, Sonnet 18; 'So long as men can breathe or eyes can see, | So long lives this, and this gives life to thee.'

[66] In the early 1750s, Shakespeare and Garrick seem to have been enjoying a regular and intimate correspondence, to judge not only from this epistle but a passage in *The Inspector in the Shades. A New Dialogue in the Manner of Lucan*

enthusiastically confirms the success with which Garrick has by now usurped the place of the Abbey monument as the definitive embodiment of the Bard. In his letter, Shakespeare complains that Scheemakers' statue is essentially irrelevant:

> What can avail the sculptor's curious art,
> Embodying rich the animated stone,
> Though high exalted in the sacred dome,
> Where all our venerable sages sleep,
> Where monarchs, with their poets, lie inurn'd?
>   (3–4)

However, he goes on to declare in triumph that this imperfect representation has now been gloriously replaced:

> THOU art my living monument; in THEE
> I see the best inscription that my soul
> Could ever wish: perish, vain pageantry, despis'd!
> SHAKESPEARE revives! in GARRICK breathes again!
>   (6)

Superior to any mausoleum, the actor, embodying Shakespeare better than does the published Shakespearean corpus, is also superior to any library: 'To relish *Shakespear*, read him o'er and o'er | See *Garrick* play him, and he'll charm you more,' recommends another anonymous admirer the following year.[67] Still another nameless fan declares in a later poem addressed to the actor that 'One meaning glance of eyes, like thine, can show | What lab'ring Critics boast in vain to know.'[68] Garrick has successfully established himself as an actor who does not just play Shakespeare's roles but plays Shakespeare, not so much a faithful interpreter as a legitimate reincarnation ('Sure Shakespeare's soul to Garrick took its flight', exclaims one admirer, 'Hail, Son of Shakespeare . . . !').[69] Returning once more in an anonymous poem of 1758, Garrick's spiritual father is suitably jubilant:

(London, 1752): 'SHAKESPEAR. You said you had a Letter to me from Mr. *Garrick*, I am always glad to hear from that Gentleman; for I own myself much indebted to him. Let me see *(reads)* "*Dear* Billy. . . ."' (15–16).

[67] *Gentleman's Magazine*, 23 (June 1753), 287.

[68] 'To Mr. GARRICK, On the Report of his leaving the Stage', *Universal Magazine* (1775), 93–4.

[69] 'To DAVID GARRICK, Esq; By a LADY', *Lloyd's Evening Post* (20–2 Sept. 1769).

'Again the hero's breast I fire,
'Again the tender sigh inspire,
'Each side, again, with laughter shake,
'And teach the villain heart to quake;
'All this (my son) again I do;
'I—no (my son)—'tis I and you.'[70]

At this the Bard offers to share his laurel wreath with the actor, a trophy Garrick disclaims while perfectly agreeing that his body indeed houses Shakespeare's soul:

'What! half thy wreath? wit's mighty cheif! [sic]
'O grant! (he cries) one single leaf:
'That far o'erpays his humble merit,
'Who's but the organ of thy spirit'.[71]

Given that the ghost invoked in the *London Magazine*'s poem of 1750 had returned specifically to demand that Garrick avenge him on his theatrical adaptors, it is particularly ironic that Garrick should have deliberately used his position as the Bard's own Hamlet to legitimize a series of further adaptations of the plays, a strategy admirably represented by one of the official souvenir engravings issued with Garrick's consent at the time of the Jubilee in 1769 (Plate 4). Executed by Isaac Taylor, and known as *Garrick with Shakespearean Characters, Commemorating the Jubilee at Stratford-upon-Avon, 1769*, it derives from the Thomas Gainsborough portrait of Garrick commissioned at the time of the Jubilee by the Stratford Corporation, in which the actor leans proprietorially on a bust of Shakespeare in a rural park:[72] however, the bust in Taylor's engraving has acquired a scroll on which is graven the motto supplied by a subscript to the whole picture: '*o'er step not the modesty of Nature*'. This detail, and the repositioning of Garrick's figure in relation to it, transforms Gainsborough's image of Garrick as Shakespeare's friend into an

---

[70] *Gentleman's Magazine* (Nov. 1758), 539.
[71] Ibid. The dispute is settled by the intervention of Phoebus Apollo, who grants his own immortal wreath to Shakespeare and insists that Shakespeare give the whole of his mortal one to Garrick. At the poem's conclusion the actor almost plays Christ to Shakespeare's God the Father:

'Each matchless, each the palm shall bear;
'In heav'n the bard; on earth the play'r.'

[72] The original of this painting was destroyed by fire in 1946, but an engraving by Valentine Greene survives: see e.g. Stochholm, *Garrick's Folly*, 10.

4. 'Garrick with Shakespearean Characters, Commemorating the Jubilee at Stratford-upon-Avon, 1769'. *Isaac Taylor*. Captioned '*o'er step not the modesty of Nature.* | Ham.' (Reproduced by courtesy of the Trustees of the British Museum.)

image of Garrick as Shakespeare's corrective editor. Indicating the scroll with one hand (a gesture borrowed from the Abbey monument?), the actor is using the inscription as the text of a sermon addressed not to his Drury Lane employees but to an attentive crowd of Shakespearean characters. Garrick, speaking for the ghostly author, is Prince, Shakespeare's characters merely the Players, for whom Garrick thus attains the authority to set down and insert as many speeches of some dozen or sixteen lines as he pleases. At the Jubilee itself, Garrick's very badge as Steward further reinforced the idea of Garrick as Hamlet, Shakespeare as Ghost, and further demonstrated its function in licensing Garrick's rewritings: it consisted of a medallion (carved from the wood of a mulberry tree allegedly planted by Shakespeare himself), bearing on one side a profile of the playwright and on the other the legend 'We [sic] Shall Not Look Upon His Like Again.' Just as he did on stage in the closet scene, Garrick was wearing an image of the Ghost to confirm himself in the role of righteous executor: the quotation on its obverse, however, uses this authority (in the very act of claiming it) to license the alteration and appropriation of Shakespeare's words.

As authorial usurper, using Shakespeare's own spectral authority to empower the revision of his plays, Garrick's most active years were those between 1754 and 1756, when *Catharine and Petruchio*, *Florizel and Perdita*, *The Tempest, An Opera*, and minor revisions to Tate's *The History of King Lear* followed each other in quick succession, and it was at this time that his work was subjected to particularly stinging attack. Appropriately, it takes the form of a rewriting of Garrick's own chosen scenario for representing himself as the most Shakespearean of Shakespeareans. Railing against Garrick's treatment of, in particular, *The Winter's Tale*, Theophilus Cibber (the son of the elder actor/adaptor Colley Cibber, whose King Richard had been usurped by Garrick) simply recasts his hated rival as Claudius:

No longer endure this insolent Innovation, on the works of your dear Countryman (your Nation's Glory) by the unmerciful Hand of this mongrel Pigmy of *Parnassus*: '*The insulted Bard complains that ye are slow, and Shakespear's Ghost walks unreveng'd amongst us.*'[73]

---

[73] Theophilus Cibber, *Two Dissertations on Theatrical Subjects* (London, 1756), 'First Dissertation', 37.

The most developed and revealing versions of the 'Garrick as Hamlet rewriting Shakespeare' plot, however, are two playlets, one satirical and one laudatory, composed as comments on Garrick's final and most daring act of authorial *lèse-majesté*, his adaptation of *Hamlet* itself, premièred on 18 December 1772. On 10 January 1773 he announced what he had done in a letter to Sir William Young, in one breathless, unpunctuated sentence which reads like the confession of a criminal still exhilarated by the outrage he has committed: 'I have ventured to produce Hamlet with alterations it was the most imprudent thing that ever I did in my life but I had sworn I would not leave the Stage until I had rescued that noble play from all the rubbish of the 5th act.'[74] In its rescued form, the play is spared the voyage to England, the Gravediggers, Ophelia's funeral, Osric, and the fencing bout, so that Garrick/Hamlet can rush into its abbreviated catastrophe (which Laertes survives, taking over the kingdom in place of Fortinbras) at the end of Act 4.[75] Most reviewers were highly enthusiastic, but Garrick's friend and rival Arthur Murphy had misgivings: hence his *Hamlet, with Alterations: A Tragedy in Three Acts*, which was circulated in manuscript among Garrick's colleagues.[76]

Murphy's critique of Garrick's adaptation takes the form of a skit on most of the first act of *Hamlet*, with Garrick's prompter, Hopkins, as Barnardo; his stage-manager, Johnson, as Francisco; his brother and assistant, George, as Horatio; and Garrick as both Prince Hamlet and, as in Cibber's pasquinade, King Claudius:

> Garrick, *solus.*
> Though yet of Shakespear our great poet's name
> The memory be green, and that it us befitted
> To bear his Jubilee to Avon's banks;

---

[74] Garrick, *Letters*, ii. 845.

[75] See George Winchester Stone, Jr., 'Garrick's Long Lost Alteration of *Hamlet*', *PMLA* 49 (1934), 890–921; Garrick, *Plays*, iv.

[76] The piece remained unpublished until after Murphy's death (1805); it appears in Jesse Foot, *The Life of Arthur Murphy, Esq.* (London, 1811), 256–74. Foot states in his prefatory remarks (253–5) that he has chosen to print it as a rebuke to those actor-managers who continue to adapt Shakespeare, an obvious allusion to the work of John Philip Kemble. Subsequent references to Murphy relate to this edition.

Yet so far hath discretion fought with nature,
That we think now to alter all his plays.

(Murphy, 263)

Shakespeare, needless to say, plays King Hamlet's ghost, a role
which Murphy, confirming the underlying structure of two crucial
pieces of Shakespearean iconography, identifies with both Scheemakers' statue and Garrick's Jubilee medallion:

[GEORGE.]   I've Shakespeare seen
Both in the Abbey, and that curious carving
In mulberry, which dangled at your breast;
These hands are not more like.

(265)

In Murphy's version of Act 1 Scene iv, Shakespeare berates Garrick
as Hamlet/Claudius for his treasonous revisions, successfully
forcing him to repent:

[GHOST.] ... Thus was I, ev'n by thy unhallow'd hand,
Of *both my grave-diggers* at once dispatch'd,
Cut off in the luxuriance of my wit,
Unstudied, undigested, and bemawl'd:
No critic ask'd,—but brought upon the stage
With all your imperfections on my head!
GARRICK. O, horrible! O, horrible! most horrible!

(272–3)

However, once the spectre has departed, Garrick briefly resumes
his first Shakespearean role, (Colley Cibber's) Richard III—''Tis
gone, and now I am myself again' (273)—and the sketch concludes with him brazenly informing George:

This Ghost is pleas'd with this my alteration,
And now he bids me alter all his Plays.
His plays are out of joint;—O *cursed spite!*
That ever I was born to set them right!

(274)

According to Murphy's biographer, Garrick's associates were
genuinely anxious lest this squib should succeed in alienating the
Shakespeare-loving public from 'Drury's Monarch'[77] and it is thus
not surprising that a pro-Garrick counter-playlet should have been

[77] Foot, *Arthur Murphy*, 273.

published (in the *Universal Magazine* during Garrick's farewell season in 1776). What is more surprising is that the panegyric, deliberately or not, has a great deal in common with the satire. Credited to 'X' (in fact composed by Garrick's protégé Richard Cumberland),[78] 'SHAKESPEARE *and* GARRICK, *a New* DIALOGUE, *occasioned by the* ALTERATIONS *lately made in the Tragedy of* HAMLET, *as acted at the Theatre Royal in* Drury Lane' finds Garrick engaged in a Pirandellian dialogue with the Gravediggers.

[SCENE *the* THEATRE]
[*Mr.* GARRICK *in the Character of*
Hamlet, and the two Grave-Diggers.]

FIRST GRAVE-DIGGER. SINCE you have thrust us out of your Play, Sir, be so good to say where you would have us dispose of our tools, and what we should put our hands to next.

2D GRAVE-DIGGER. Ay, and what we should do with the ready made grave.—There it is—I know you don't like to have property lie dead, and I'm afraid no man living will take it off your hands.

GARR. Truly, Gentlemen, that is a consideration; 'tis a pity men's labour should be lost: Suppose you step into it yourselves—

1ST GR.D. In good faith I have work'd so long for the dead, that I am scarce company for the living.

2D DITTO. Twenty and five years have I knockt Yorick's scull about this floor, and never thought any other scull would take up the quarrel: Under favour, why did you leave us out of your Play?

GARR. Because the age does not like to be reminded of mortality: 'tis an unseemly sight, and very disgustful to a well-bred company.

1ST GR.D. It won't be amiss, however, to keep the grave open; 'twill stand in place of a Theatrical Fund, and be a lasting provision for Actors retiring from the Stage.

(*Universal Magazine*, Feb. 1776, 101–2)

'Since you have thrust us out of your play...': addressed to Garrick as Hamlet (and with the actor capitalized but not the

---

[78] A manuscript copy of this playlet, attributed to Cumberland in Garrick's handwriting, is preserved among the Garrick manuscripts in the Folger Shakespeare Library. Very slightly longer than the *Universal Magazine* version (by a few jokes about other contemporary actors), it bears the title 'An Impromptu {by way of epilogue} [these words struck out] after the play of Hamlet.' It is reprinted in *The Plays of Richard Cumberland*, ed. Roberta S. Borkat (6 vols.; New York, 1982), 2. Borkat erroneously states that the play has never before been published. Borkat assumes that the 'Impromptu' was composed soon after the première of Garrick's adaptation, but the fact that it did not appear in the *Universal Magazine* until 1776 might suggest a later dating.

Prince), the 'you' and 'your' hover ambiguously between treating the actor as the character he has assumed (whimsically highlighting the clash of interests between the dramatic character and the adaptor who has tampered with the play in which he appears) and actually crediting Garrick himself with having appropriated, reauthored, *Hamlet*. How much irony does Cumberland really intend? As the dialogue develops it seems to promise a critique of Garrick's alteration along the lines of Murphy's (the last remark quoted above seems distinctly cruel, considering how close Garrick was to his own exhausted withdrawal from the stage), but when the phantom arrives it proves to be the most tame and acquiescent version of the old mole in the cellarage yet, and the playlet collapses uneasily into a rhyming eulogy so ripe with submerged Freudian accounts of the relationship between Garrick and the Bard that no reader can be surprised at its anonymity.

[GARR.] ...—But hark, what noise is this underground! mercy be good unto us—Who is this?
                   [*The Spirit of Shakespear arises*]
Angels and Ministers of Grace!—
SHAKESPEAR.   Proceed;
  And let my organs spiritually feed
  From those harmonious lips, whose quick'ning breath
  So oft hath chear'd me in the arms of death;
  And now by potency of magic sound
  Calls up my spirit from the deep profound:
  Speak to thy Shakespear—
GARRICK.   Hail, much honour'd name!
  Friend of my life and father of my fame:
  If whilst I draw each weed, that idly creeps
  Around the tomb, where thy lov'd Hamlet sleeps,
  Incautiously I have forgot to spare
  Some flower, which thy full hand had scatter'd there,
  Impute it not—
SHAKESPEAR.   Freely correct my Page:
  I wrote to please a rude unpolish'd age;
  Thou, happy man, art fated to display
  Thy dazling talents in a brighter day;
  Let me partake this night's applause with thee,
  And thou shalt share immortal fame with me.

The ghost who in the *London Magazine* poem twenty years earlier commanded Garrick to vindicate his injured song ('...save me from a dire impending fate, | Nor yield me up to Cibber and to Tate'),[79] and in Murphy's hands abandoned Garrick 'To the just vengeance critics will inflict',[80] now pleads with what seems like masochism to have his plays 'corrected.' In 'Garrick's' image of the playwright scattering flowers around Hamlet's tomb, Shakespeare merges disturbingly into the two unfortunate women in his protagonist's life, both the herb-dispensing Ophelia (rejected by Hamlet) and the mourning Gertrude who strews her grave (reviled and lectured by Hamlet, and ultimately killed off in his stead by poison). Giving himself pleadingly over to Garrick ('Speak to *thy* Shakespear!'), this enfeebled shade of the playwright most revealingly expresses his dependence on the actor in a bizarre image that, concurring with Cibber and Murphy, identifies Garrick with Claudius in the orchard—'let my organs spiritually feed | From those harmonious lips...' Garrick's voice in Shakespeare's ear gives him life, but it is also a poison that kills him, placing Garrick in the usurping role of authority for his text.

Garrick's great need to present himself so elaborately as Shakespeare's most zealous evangelist, adaptor or not, can in part be attributed to his social ambitions: his claim to embody the respectable Shakespeare promoted in the 1730s as the decent alternative to Harlequin forms part of a wider claim, and an extraordinarily successful one, on behalf of the theatre in general. In the long term, his greatest professional achievements may have been not aesthetic but social, in his promotion of acting to the status of a reputable vocation. As a contemporary account puts it:

Few while living have arrived at such eminence in their professions as Mr. Garrick, and indeed it may be said that while the art has advanced him he has no less advanced the art. What before now was considered by our laws as a trade taken up by vagrants, is now considered, through his great merits, as a profession tending to promote decency and inspire virtue.[81]

[79] *London Magazine* (June 1750), 279.

[80] Foot, *Arthur Murphy*, 273.

[81] *London Chronicle* (3 Jan. 1769). Cf. Leigh Woods, *Garrick Claims the Stage*, 23: 'The middle class in eighteenth-century England was fortunate to have had an actor, and a great one at that, as one of its most prominent representatives. The excellence of Garrick's acting, and its particular stress on sympathy, sentiment and sensibility, gradually came to stand for the worth and dignity of an entire social movement.'

The distance between the social position of a Betterton, Booth, or Quin in the first quarter of the century and Garrick at the start of the last is far greater, as this passage may suggest, than that between the latter and Irving's knighthood or Olivier's peerage,[82] and traversing it required Garrick to be enormously careful with his public image, from his strategic jilting of the *louche* Peg Woffington onwards.[83] This respectable persona was a major influence on his choice of roles, requiring him in modern comedy either to avoid Restoration rakes or to censor them (from his pruning of *The Provok'd Wife* in 1747 to his defusing of *The Country Wife* into *The Country Girl* in 1766), and to associate himself instead with the blameless paragons of sentimental comedy, even if he actually hated them. Evidence that he knew just what he was doing, and was gritting his teeth for some of the time, is provided by the account of his part in William Whitehead's *The School for Lovers* he sent to his brother Peter:

[I] don't appear in the Play till the beginning of the 2d when Sr John Dorilant (that's the Name) makes his Entrance—and a fine, polite, Sentimental, *Windling* Son of a Bitch it is—a great favourite of the Ladies, & much admir'd by the Clergy, & the Aldermen & Common Council of the City of London—Humbug for Nine Nights.[84]

Promoting decency and inspiring virtue, a great favourite of the ladies and much admired by the clergy, Garrick was rising in the world by posing as the very personification of the values attributed by the likes of George Lillo and James Miller to the Shakespeare Ladies' Club.[85] Garrick, indeed, never forgot the role the Ladies'

---

[82] Garrick was himself rumoured to have been offered a baronetcy after his retirement: see Stone and Kahrl, *David Garrick*, 443. Garrick certainly functioned as an important role-model for Britain's only thespian peer to date: Olivier, like Garrick, enjoyed one of his greatest successes in a part-Cibber version of *Richard III* (the film version even credits Garrick, misleadingly, with having carried out some of the alterations adopted by Olivier), and Olivier's self-identification with Hamlet, like Garrick's, extended beyond the grave, his chosen epitaph being 'Goodnight, sweet Prince'. On Garrick's funeral, see below.

[83] Cf. Stone and Kahrl, *David Garrick*, 57–8: 'He involved himself in no social scandal. His decision to forgo the life-style offered him by Peg Woffington and her lovers was all to the advantage of the English theatre.'

[84] 19 Feb. 1762; Garrick, *Letters*, i. 354–5. Signing off at the end of this letter, Garrick briefly adopts the role in which he has cast Shakespeare; 'I shall quit you in the words of Hamlet | *Remember Me!*'

[85] Cf. Richardson's approbatory comment on Garrick and his relationship to Shakespeare in the postscript to *Clarissa* (1748): '[Garrick] deservedly engages the

Club had played in claiming Shakespeare for polite society and thereby fostering the Shakespeare boom of which his unprecedented success as Richard had been an expression (as his Jubilee speech, quoted above, demonstrates), and his self-presentation as a social being is cluttered with domestic Shakespearean props, descendants of the scent bottle, by which his home life is seen to be permeated by the virtuous spiritual presence of their Bard—the bookplate bearing a head of Shakespeare, the chair made of the wood of the true mulberry, *et al.*[86] The playwright beginning to receive the highest praises yet heaped on a writer and the player achieving membership of the highest social niches yet occupied by a performer certify each other's value: the likenesses of Shakespeare and copies of his plays that are such conspicuous details of almost all the pictures (including the intimate portraits with his wife) which depict Garrick in his own character both confer and acquire the right social and intellectual tone.[87]

A good example of this mutual embedding in the upper gentry is provided by the autobiography involved in Garrick's revival of *Much Ado About Nothing*, in which he cast himself in the untried role of Benedick for his eagerly awaited first performances on returning from his honeymoon in November 1748. The in-joke between the manager and his public is evident: but what was its main purport? Was Garrick's widely discussed conversion at 31 from bachelorhood to bourgeois marriage thus being co-opted as publicity for Shakespeare's play, ratifying the claims made for its

public favour in all he undertakes, and . . . owes so much, and is gratefully sensible that he does, to that great master of the human passions'; Samuel Richardson, *Clarissa, or The History of a Young Lady* [1748], ed. Angus Ross (Harmondsworth, 1985), 1497.

[86] On the mulberry-wood chair, designed for Garrick by Hogarth, see Michael Snodin (ed.), *Rococo: Art and Design in Hogarth's England* (London, 1984), 67–8. See also Kalman Burnim, 'Looking on His Like Again: Garrick and the Visual Arts', in Shirley Strum Kenny (ed.), *The British Theatre and the Other Arts, 1660–1800* (London, 1986).

[87] On the links between Garrick's self-presentation as Shakespeare's truest disciple and his careful bid for social status, see Stephen Orgel's discussion of Zoffany's *Garrick and Mrs. Pritchard in Macbeth* in 'The Authentic Shakespeare', 20: 'The substitution of the elegant attire of high society for the costumes of the stage makes a clear and very new assertion that has nothing to do with *Macbeth*: that actors and actresses are gentlemen and ladies. This must be relevant to Garrick's claim to be presenting authentic texts, authorized by Shakespeare himself: the claim of authenticity is here extended to the persons of the actors and their physical surroundings.'

timeless truth to human nature and topically reinforcing its jokes, or was the play co-opted as a means of broadcasting Garrick's new social status? Was Shakespeare rendered more decent by this belated public participation in the Garricks' wedding, or was their marriage rendered more respectable by association with the bard of Truth, Virtue, and Humanity? In looking at the interrelations between Shakespeare's art, Garrick's art, and the new strain of Protestant nationalism both were coming to represent, it is hard to decide whether the playwright is being used to canonize the ideology, the ideology to canonize the performer, or the performer to canonize the playwright; but that they thrived on one another is indisputable. The mutually reinforcing trinity of Shakespeare, Garrick, and middle-class virtue is shown to further advantage by one of the official press releases widely printed in the month leading up to the Jubilee: consisting simply of consecutive potted histories of the man from Stratford and the man from Lichfield it accidentally (?) emerges as a Plutarchan exercise in parallel biography, showing how apprentices with talent and perseverance can always make good in the end if they find their proper profession.[88]

Fittingly, the greatest single symbol of Garrick's having made good is a likeness of the upwardly mobile playwright on whom both his own wealth and his own social status were founded, and it is equally fitting that this symbol represents another bid to upstage the Westminster Abbey monument as Shakespeare's finest embodiment. Already wealthy beyond the wildest dreams of any preceding actor, Garrick celebrated the arrival of the theatrical profession into the patronage-dispensing classes in style: he bought a villa on the Thames at Hampton in 1755, and soon set about commissioning an architect and a sculptor, just as Lord Burlington had but without the claim to public-spirited disinterest, to design a figure of Shakespeare. Where Burlington and his Patriot colleagues had erected a statue to the glory of Shakespeare in a national temple, Garrick would erect a temple to the glory of Shakespeare on his own private estate; and taking over the canonization of Shakespeare literally in person, he would place within it a statue probably most accurately described as a likeness of Garrick as Shakespeare. In 1757 he chose Louis-Francois Roubiliac as the sculptor, and during the theatrical season of 1757/8 his departures from rehearsals to supervise the commission became a frequent topic of conversation among his colleagues. The story soon got about that Garrick was not merely giving Roubiliac exhaustively detailed instructions as to the posture of the figure but was actually posing for it, and a close inspection of the statue does nothing to refute this account. The king of English literature is replaced even in effigy by the pre-eminent middle-class impostor.[89]

Completed in 1758, Roubiliac's Shakespeare—a translation of Scheemakers' national icon into capricious, individualized terms—metamorphoses the portentous scroll at which the Abbey figure points, and the ponderous volumes on which it rests a glum elbow, into an immense, Bard-sized blank page of infinite possibility, over which the writer leans; with an unconscious lifting of the left forefinger to the chin he is swiftly turning his head away, in a spontaneous movement of inspiration which is almost Shandean in quality (see Plate 5). It is a movement which is also highly characteristic of Garrick's own art, which excelled in the enaction of rapid passages of thought, the registering of sudden impulses of shock or delight through the whole agile body: one might compare the engraving of his Benedick published by Wenman in 1778,[90] in which, on the line 'Ha! the Prince and Monsieur Love. I will hide me in the arbour,' the actor starts up, lifting one index finger against his nose. There is a rococo note of *outré* technical virtuosity about the whole statue, as Roubiliac's nearly peach-coloured marble meretriciously simulates, with self-conscious ostentation, a dazzling range of incidental unstatuesque textures: drooping parchment, quill pen, the elaborate drapery of the moving cloak, the knee-frills of the breeches, the delicate lace of the cuffs, the crumpled shirt exposed by the casually gaping waistcoat, and, most showy of all, the soft leather of the right slipper, folded under the poet's heel at the back right-hand side through his neglect of a shoehorn.

[89] This view is supported by Roger Hinks, 'Le Bicentenaire de Louis-Francois Roubiliac', *Etudes anglaises*, 15 (1962), 1–14; see also Piper, *The Image of the Poet*, 83–6. Garrick bequeathed the statue to the British Museum, where it now stands in the King's Library: it is one of the very first items mentioned in his will, second only to his villa itself and the land surrounding it. See *Universal Magazine* (Feb. 1779), 63; Davies, *Memoirs of the Life of David Garrick*, ii. 372–87. On Roubiliac's statue, see also Whinney, *Sculpture in Britain*, 226.

[90] 'Published by J. Wenman 1 July 1778', Harvard Theatre Collection (hereafter HTC), 'Garrick in Roles,' 23.

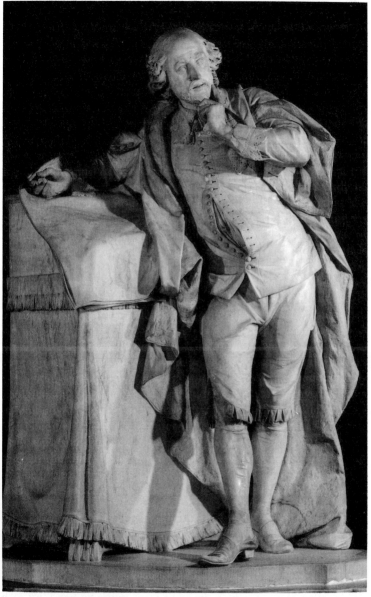

5. Statue of Shakespeare, 1758, commissioned by David Garrick for his Temple of Shakespeare at Hampton, and bequeathed to the British Museum in 1779. *Louis-Francois Roubiliac*. (Reproduced by courtesy of the Trustees of the British Museum.)

Garrick's Shakespeare as sculpted by Roubiliac, in short, exudes the discreet charm of the bourgeoisie. Compared to the statue it adapts, Roubiliac's is self-evidently the intimate portrait of a prosperous domestic man engaged in the profession at which he excels, and this, of course, fits to perfection the story of Garrick acting the role of the playwright while Roubiliac sketched and chiselled. Once more the actor is taking on the spirit not just of a Shakespearean character but of Shakespeare himself, and once more an anonymous flatterer takes the point perfectly. In some lines 'dropt in Mr. GARRICK's Temple of *Shakespear, at Hampton*', printed in the *London Magazine* soon after the statue's completion, Garrick 'Invokes the animated stone, | To make the poet's mind his own'—a project in which he is completely successful— Shakespeare's voice declares that:

'Unnotic'd long thy *Shakespear* lay,
'To dullness and to time a prey;
'But lo! I rise, I breathe, I live
'In you, my representative![91]

Garrick's Shakespeare statue is constructed not in the image of Britain's heroic past, but in exactly the image Garrick wishes to project for himself: a man of property, wealthy through his own professional expertise, undoubtedly inspired but completely respectable. Its presentation, in comparison to Scheemakers' monument, of a Shakespeare simultaneously domesticated and identified with Garrick (and thereby reclaimed for Thespis) is confirmed by a contemporary artefact it probably inspired, a figurine manufactured at this time by the Longton Hall porcelain works. The company had been producing porcelain figurines of the Abbey statue for some time, but around 1758 they refashioned this familiar boudoir Shakespeare into a likeness of Garrick.[92] Full of movement like Roubiliac's statue, and recognizable as a hybrid between Roubiliac's figure and that of the Abbey monument, this statuette converts the pose of Shakespeare's free arm (in the Abbey pointing severely at the scroll) into an expansive rhetorical gesture, and replaces Scheemakers' leatherbound Complete Works with a single, open play, on which the actor leans with one hand, his face

[91] *London Magazine* (Nov. 1758), 539.
[92] See R. J. Charleston (ed.), *English Porcelain, 1745–1850* (London, 1965), 75, pl. 25*b*.

turned away as he declaims tentatively from it, evidently learning his lines. The image of Shakespeare gravely drawing attention to his classic works has been replaced by an image of Garrick professionally internalizing them. Once more, the actor has successfully upstaged the statue.

As an embodiment of Shakespeare, however, Garrick had one major disadvantage when competing with Scheemakers' statue— mortality; and narratives about mortals who defy statues have a way of ending with the statue getting its own back. Ultimately Scheemakers' Shakespeare would in its turn upstage Garrick, and permanently at that: 'he was Interred in Westminster Abbey', records *David Garrick: The Original Drawings and Manuscript Notes Made of the Ceremony of his Lying In State and Subsequent Interment in Westminster Abbey 1779*,[93] 'about 2 feet from the monument of Shakespear'. Sheridan's elegy, *Verses to the Memory of Garrick*, brings out the *Don Giovanni* resonances of the occasion with particular emphasis, remembering

The general Voice, the Meed of mournful Verse,
The splendid Sorrows that adorned his Hearse,
The Throng that mourn'd as their dead Favourite pass'd,
The grac'd Respect that claim'd him to the last,
While SHAKESPEAR's Image from its hallow'd Base,
Seem'd to prescribe the Grave, and point the Place.[94]

Garrick's own memorial, a superbly histrionic piece by Webber, with Garrick leaping up to part what appear to be the curtains of his deathbed to take a final bow, was not installed until 1797;

---

[93] HTC.
[94] Richard Brinsley Sheridan, *Verses to the Memory of Garrick* (London, 1779). On *Hamlet* and *Don Giovanni*, see Garber, *Shakespeare's Ghost Writers*, 139–44. Cf. Samuel Jackson Pratt's *The Shadows of Shakespeare: A Monody, in irregular verse, Occasioned by the Death of Mr. Garrick*, in which, after a parade of Shakespearean characters (lastly 'his own HAMLET') have paid their respects at Garrick's tomb,

While wrapt in wonder of these various shews
The sovereign shade of SHAKESPEARE awful rose,
    His many-colour'd wand he wav'd,
    And soon the mournful train again were grav'd.
(Now was His genius even more divine,)
And all *alone* he stood before *his* GARRICK's shrine.
    Rest, rest, perturbed spirits, then, he said,
    To *me* belongs th'inestimable dead . . .
        Samuel Jackson Pratt, *Miscellanies* (4 vols.;
        London, 1785), ii. 25)

predictably it incorporates a likeness of Shakespeare, this time a profile on a sun-like disc revealed at the top of the proscenium by Garrick's drawing of the curtains.[95] It is undeniably appropriate, however, that for nearly twenty years, Shakespeare's statue—precisely the Abbey tomb which he himself, according to Jonson's poem in the Folio, didn't need—should have served as the actor's headstone. A spirit lacking a voice and a grave lacking a body, Shakespeare's image had been provided with both in David Garrick.

The mid-eighteenth century—from the commissioning of the Abbey monument to the Stratford Jubilee to this thoroughly Shakespearean funeral—marks both Shakespeare's official canonization as an august British Worthy and his widespread acceptance (particularly through Garrick's extraordinarily successful self-representation as his truly begotten son) as a writer of unimpeachable respectability. From the 1730s onwards, treatments of Shakespeare's texts, both on and off the stage, are profoundly conditioned by their author's newly achieved status as national poet and his simultaneous representation as a patron of bourgeois morality. It is with these interconnected developments, particularly the inextricable relations they confirm between the Shakespeare cult, contemporary conceptions of the family, and contemporary conceptions of nationhood, that my next and final chapter will be concerned.

---

[95] This design was chosen in preference to a monument designed by John Bacon, in which Garrick upstages Shakespeare for one last time: in Bacon's design Garrick and Shakespeare are before a pedestal on which stands an angelic figure of Immortality, holding out a crown. Shakespeare, looking amicably into Garrick's face, one friendly arm around his shoulders, gestures towards this figure, indicating that the crown is for Garrick: Garrick makes a histrionic gesture of reluctance, his bright eyes none the less fixed on the crown. Shakespeare, formerly figured as Caesar's royal ghost, has been relegated to the role of Mark Antony, Garrick promoted to the imperial diadem. See John Bacon, *Drawing: design for a memorial to David Garrick* (*c*.1780; HTC, pf MS Thr. 95).

5

Nationalizing the Corpus

THE promotion of Shakespeare as both symbol and exemplar of British national identity, which began in earnest with the Patriots in the 1730s and reached its climax at Garrick's Jubilee in 1769, had some profound and paradoxical consequences for contemporary treatments of his texts. The plays, now established as the productions and property of the national poet, acquired a new sanctity (which is one reason why so few successful adaptations were produced after the middle of the eighteenth century),[1] but at the same time they came to seem almost beside the point, so extensively did Shakespeare's authority now exceed the texts from which it supposedly derived. Less than an author in the 1660s, Shakespeare was by the 1760s something more than an author: both he and his characters, invested with significances no longer containable within the framework of the Complete Plays, began to escape from the Folio to appear in poems, novels, anthologies of quotations, pageants. Although Shakespeare's dramas, many still in their Restoration variants, now accounted for one in six of all plays produced in London, and various hitherto unacceptable plays were still being successfully altered for revival, the practice of adaptation itself was beginning to seem at odds with the nationalist appropriation of Shakespeare occurring in other media: moreover, the very nature of this period's adaptations, with their emphasis on identifying Shakespeare with a strictly domestic and therefore private propriety, helped to render the public performance of his works increasingly irrelevant to his status in British culture. Just as Scheemakers' effigy of Shakespeare as national

---

[1] The only major actor–manager after Garrick to prepare his own acting versions of Shakespeare by any means other than cutting or transposing Shakespeare's own words, John Philip Kemble, only rarely added any material not derived from adaptations already in the repertory. On the intellectual background to the passing of adaptation, see esp. Marsden, 'The Re-Imagined Text', 196 ff., where she argues that the minute textual criticism pursued by editors from Theobald onwards, more and more preoccupied with the letter of the text, precisely reverses earlier adaptors' assumptions about the nature of Shakespeare's meaning.

poet often superseded the contemporary likenesses which we, heirs to Malone, would regard as more authentic,[2] so the very idea of Shakespeare as national poet began to upstage the actual details of his dramatic output. At the Stratford Jubilee, the great national festival which confirmed his transcendent status, not a single line of his now transcended works needed to be performed. The Shakespeare of the mid-eighteenth century is imagined and re-written as an author at once domestic, national, and moral, and in all of these aspects, which spectacularly converge on the Jubilee, he is rapidly escaping from the stage altogether.

Domestic Affairs

For theatrical adaptors during this last phase of the usefulness or necessity of the practice, the consequences of Shakespeare's eleva-tion were twofold. On the one hand it required those playwrights who capitalized on Shakespeare's increased prestige by reviving previously unpopular plays 'with alterations' to present themselves none the less as engaged in reverently presenting the 'true' Shake-speare (as we have seen in the case of Garrick's personal publicity, obliged to claim Shakespeare's own ghostly authority for the changes imposed on his plays). Adaptation thus became in general a more covert practice; it is less frequently advertised by inverted commas in acting editions, for example, from whose title pages the names of the adaptors often vanish—Garrick, indeed, never openly admitted to the authorship of his unsuccessful operatic version of *A Midsummer Night's Dream*, publishing it only anonymously (as *The Fairies*, 1755).[3] On the other hand, Shake-speare's enhanced status provided new incentives for modifying his texts, however discreetly such rewriting had to be performed: the more securely Shakespeare was enshrined as a figure of national authority, the greater were the potential legitimating rewards of appropriating that authority by adaptation. Now that their author

---

[2] On Malone and 18th-cent. attitudes to the authority of different likenesses of Shakespeare, see De Grazia, *Shakespeare Verbatim*, 78–86.

[3] Cf. Garrick's nervous prologue: 'I dare not say WHO wrote it—I could tell ye, | To soften matters—Signor Shakespearelli' (Garrick, *Plays*, iii. 155–6). This adap-tation omits all the rude mechanicals (including Bottom). Cf. the equally anony-mous version by George Colman, *A Fairy Tale* (London, 1763).

had been monumentalized as one of Britain's heroic forefathers, amending Shakespeare's plays became part of the vital nationalist project of rewriting the national past in order to validate the aspirations of the present. Conscripted as a national hero or prophet, Shakespeare was now tactfully rewritten as one: from the 1730s onwards, to redeem the 'essential' Shakespeare at times embarrassingly obscured by the archaic or immoral lapses of his uncorrected texts was to participate in the wider process of showing that Britain had always been the chosen home of mercantile virtue.[4] While the plays successfully added to the Shakespearean repertory during the constitutional crises of the late seventeenth and early eighteenth century had predominantly been pathos-oriented adaptations of tragedies of state, the mid-eighteenth century saw a growing interest in the comedies. It is no accident that between the 1740s and the 1760s—a period of rapid mercantile and imperial expansion—the new alterations of Shakespeare which prosper, such as Garrick's *Florizel and Perdita* (*The Winter's Tale*), *Catharine and Petruchio* (*The Taming of the Shrew*), and *Cymbeline*, present a domestic Shakespeare who is at the same time eminently patriotic, identified at once with virtuous family life, vigorous trade, and British glory.

One side-effect of these developments is that contemporary writers about the theatre divide between those who believe that Shakespeare's plays have been triumphantly rescued by adaptation, and those who believe that they have been triumphantly rescued from it. While those who acknowledge the continuing use of adapted texts defend the practice as necessary and appropriate for an age more refined than that in which Shakespeare wrote, commentators who believe that adaptation has at last fallen into obsolescence and disuse, such as Thomas Seward, prefer to represent the eighteenth century as having achieved enlightenment from the more aristocratic bad taste of the Restoration:

---

[4] Cf. Gerald Newman, *The Rise of English Nationalism: A Cultural History, 1740–1830* (New York, 1987), on the 1750s: 'Consider the lesson taught by ethnic revivals in our own day, in which every assertion of ethnic pride is accompanied by exaggerated claims as to the inventiveness of the ethnic forebears, and by the erection of heroic "role models" to look up to. Was not this happening in England at this very moment...? The country's real ancestors may never have served her so well as the newly exhumed and cosmeticized Saxons and Shakespeare and Milton and all the other mythical paragons of English Sincerity did' (151–2).

The *Taste* and *Fashion* of Poetry varies in every Age, and tho' our old Dramatic Writers are as preferable to the Modern as *Vandike* and *Rubens* to our Modern Painters, yet most Eyes must be accustomed to their *Manner* before they can discern their *Excellencies*. Thus the very best Plays of *Shakespear* were forced to be dressed *fashionably* by the *Poetic Taylors* of the late Ages before they could be admitted upon the Stage, and a very few years since his *Comedies* in general were under the highest Contempt. Few very few durst speak of them with any sort of Regard, till the many excellent *Criticisms* upon that Author made People study him, and some excellent *Actors* revived these Comedies, which compleatly open'd Mens Eyes.[5]

Seward's assertion in 1750 that eighteenth-century playgoers were at last demanding and enjoying unmediated access to Shakespearean comedy *per se* is rather qualified by the subsequent fortunes of, for example, *The Winter's Tale*, which although revived in unaltered form at both Goodman's Fields and Covent Garden in the 1740/1 season (during the heyday of the Shakespeare Ladies' Club) would be seen most frequently between 1754 and 1800 as either Macnamara Morgan's *The Sheep-Shearing: or, Florizel and Perdita* (1754), Garrick's *Florizel and Perdita: A Dramatic Pastoral* (1756), or George Colman's *The Sheep-Shearing: A Dramatic Pastoral* (1777),[6] as well as undergoing still further metamorphosis in an unacted 1756 adaptation by Charles Marsh, *The Winter's Tale, a play alter'd from Shakespear*.[7] None the less, this belief that the dark days of adaptation were over was a widespread one, and one which Garrick in particular did all he could to encourage, characteristically advertising his 1744 production of *Macbeth*, for example, as a revival of the play 'As written by Shakespeare', despite his provision of additional material which includes a protracted dying speech for Macbeth.[8] Perfectly aware of his own strategy, Garrick is prepared even to taunt his audience with their inability to tell unaltered Shakespeare from his own adulterations. His prologue to the double bill of *Florizel and Perdita* and *Catharine and Petruchio* performed in January 1756, after playfully redefining the Theatre Royal as a cheerfully commercial

---

[5] Thomas Seward (ed.) *The Works of Francis Beaumont and John Fletcher* (10 vols.; London, 1750), i. 'Preface', pp. xv–xvi.

[6] See Hogan, ii. 674–89.

[7] Charles Marsh, *The Winter's Tale, a play alter'd from Shakespear* (London, 1756).

[8] See Orgel, 'The Authentic Shakespeare', 14–15.

public space (with Shakespeare serving as the sign under which the audience's pleasure and Garrick's profit are both guaranteed), mischievously celebrates his own success as an imitator of Shakespeare's style:

This night, for want of better simile,
Let this our theatre a tavern be:
The poets vintners, and the waiters we.

. . . .

To draw in customers our bills are spread; [*Shewing a playbill.*]
You cannot miss the sign, 'tis Shakespear's Head.

. . . .

   A vintner once acquired both praise and gain,
And sold much Perry for the best Champaign.
Some rakes the precious stuff did so allure,
They drank whole nights—what's that—when wine is pure?

. . . .

'Sir William, what say you?'—'The best, believe me
—'In this—Eh, Jack!—the Devil can't deceive me.'
Thus the wise critic too mistakes his wine,
Cries out with lifted hands, ''Tis great!—divine!'
Then jogs his neighbour as the wonders strike him;
'This Shakespear! Shakespear!—Oh, there's nothing like him!'

In this night's various and enchanted cup
Some little Perry's mixed for filling up.
The five long acts from which these three are taken,
Stretch'd out to sixteen years, lay by, forsaken.
Lest then this precious liquor run to waste,
'Tis now confined and bottled for your taste.

(Garrick, Plays, iii. 224–5)[9]

Knowing very well that in offering these sentimentalized versions of *The Winter's Tale* and *The Taming of the Shrew* he is offering his audience precisely the Shakespeare they wish to recognize as their own (bottling Leontes, and Petruchio, for their taste), Garrick here impudently challenges his auditors to distinguish the original Shakespeare from his own modern 'Perry', evidently perfectly confident that they will not be able to single out enough to fault his concluding assertion that:

---

[9] Garrick, *Plays*, iii. 224–5. On this prologue, see also Ch. 3, above.

'Tis my chief wish, my claim, my only plan,
To lose no drop of that immortal man!
                    (Ibid.)

   The two adaptations prefaced by this remarkable prologue in
fact provide characteristic examples of the ways in which Shakespeare was unobtrusively rewritten to endorse mid-eighteenth century views of both the family and the state. In *Florizel and Perdita*
and *Catharine and Petruchio*, a series of apparently minor alterations carried out in the interests of abbreviation and verbal propriety mute, respectively, the Renaissance royalism of *The Winter's
Tale* and the outright feudal masculinism of *The Taming of the
Shrew* in favour of guardedly egalitarian, and specifically private,
contemporary versions of sympathy and domestic virtue: the plays
become, in every sense, family entertainment for the 1750s.
   Garrick's version of *The Winter's Tale*, despite his claim that it
is part of his own special and unique campaign to preserve his
ghostly father's vital fluids, is in effect a priggish, corrective revision of Macnamara Morgan's bawdier adaptation, *The Sheep-
Shearing*, which had been in the repertory at Covent Garden since
1754. Morgan's adaptation—a short afterpiece—completely ex-
cises the first, second, third, and fifth acts of Shakespeare's romance,
leaving as the principal characters only the young lovers, the
Clown, Pollixenes [*sic*], Camillo, Autolicus [*sic*], and, ingeniously
spared the attentions of the bear to superintend the royal court-
ship under an alias, 'ANTIGONUS, a *Sicilian* Lord disguised as an
Old Shepherd, under the name of ALCON'.[10] The prologue lists the
chief ingredients of the play in accurate order of predominance
when it promises 'The clown's coarse jests, the fortunes of a maid,
| Whom nature's simple elegance array'd . . .' (Morgan, 1), although
the most striking 'coarse jest' added to *The Winter's Tale* in
Morgan's play is uttered not by a clown but by the King himself
when, admiring Perdita at the sheep-shearing feast, he appends a
comment of surprising frankness to an aside to Camillo:

This is the prettiest low-born lass, that ever
Ran on the green swerd; nothing she does, or seems,
But smacks of something greater than herself,
Too noble for this place.—Had *Florizel*

---

[10] Macnamara Morgan, *The Sheep-Shearing: or, Florizel and Perdita. A Pastoral Comedy* (London, 1762), 'Dramatis Personae', 2.

But thought of bedding without wedding her,
I well cou'd like his liking.

(13)

Florizel and Perdita, dominated by a pious and penitent Leontes (played by Garrick himself), is having none of this, needless to say: in fact it is so sensitive to verbal indelicacy that Perdita's lines to Florizel at the close of her flower-distributing speech—

No, like a banke, for Loue to lye, and play on:
Not like a Coarse: or if: not to be buried,
But quicke, and in mine armes. Come, take your flours...

(F1, 310)

(lines cheerfully retained by Morgan)—are not only made strictly private (specified in Garrick's script as '*apart to* Florizel') but are discreetly emended to:

No, like a bank for love to lie and play on;
Not like a corse. Come, come, take your flowers.

(Garrick, *Plays*, iii. 238)

Garrick's version, like Morgan's, cuts the first three acts of the play and confines the action to Polixenes' kingdom, but by having Leontes cast, Pericles-like, on the shores of Bohemia in a shipwreck at its opening (to witness the sheep-shearing feast unrecognized), he is able to preserve the family reunions of the fifth act, the statue scene being conducted by an *emigrée* Paulina. The stress in *Florizel and Perdita* is on Leontes' experience of the pastoral world's redemptive innocence, an innocence zealously protected by Garrick's prudish editing and made the centre of the sheep-shearing scene in the song he provides for Perdita:

Come, come, my good shepherds, our flocks we must shear;
In your holy-day suits, with your lasses appear.
The happiest of folk are the guiltless and free,
And who are so guiltless, so happy as we?

   .   .   .   .

By mode and caprice are the city dames led,
But we as the children of nature are bred;
By her hand alone are we painted and dressed;
For the roses will bloom when there's peace in the breast.

(239)

The action of the play depicts Leontes' psychological progress, on finding himself in the midst of this Dresden Arcadia, from self-absorbed remorse and despair to a rehabilitated, benign involvement in the world, an involvement both signified and rewarded by the concluding restoration of his family. This spiritual transformation, as in any good contemporary novel, is effected primarily by sympathy: Leontes is roused from his guilty introversion by the sensibility-touching spectacle of Florizel and Perdita's repudiation at the hands of Polixenes, and he takes over Camillo's role in the original as the friend and advocate of this caste-defying couple, taking them to Polixenes' court and interceding for them at the risk of his own life. The insistent moral of the entire piece is ably summed-up by Paulina, as she listens to an account of this event: 'O, the force, the charm of returning virtue!' (255). More striking than this added remark, however, and more revealing of the ideology to which *The Winter's Tale* is here assimilated, are the lines Garrick adds to the statue scene itself, which sacrifice the enigmatic tentativeness of the original in favour of a full-scale celebration of the sanctified nuclear family. Leontes' royalty is here explicitly subordinated to his role in the domestic sphere—he and Hermione, as far as Garrick is concerned, are first and foremost private beings, a long-separated husband and wife rather than a long-heirless king and queen.

LEONTES. Support me, gods!
    If this be more than visionary bliss,
    My reason cannot hold! My wife! My queen!
    But speak to me, and turn me wild with transport.
    I cannot hold me longer from those arms;
    She's warm! she lives!
    ·   ·   ·   ·   ·   ·   ·
    Her beating heart meets mine, and fluttering owns
    Its long-lost half. The tears that choke her voice
    Are hot and moist—it is Hermione! [*Embrace.*]
    ·   ·   ·   ·   ·   ·   ·   ·

HERMIONE. Before this swelling flood o'er-bear our reason,
    Let purer thoughts, unmix'd with earth's alloy,
    Flame up to heav'n, and for its mercy shown,
    Bow we our knees together.
LEONTES. Oh! if penitence
    Have pow'r to cleanse the foul sin-spotted soul,
    Leontes' tears have washed away his guilt.

> If thanks unfeign'd be all that you require,
> Most bounteous gods, for happiness like mine,
> Read in my heart, your mercy's not in vain.
> HERMIONE. This firstling duty paid, let transport loose,
> My lord, my king,—there's distance in those names,
> My husband!
> LEONTES. O my Hermione!—have I deserved
> That tender name?
> HERMIONE. No more; be all that's past
> Forgot in this enfolding, and forgiven.
> LEONTES. Thou matchless saint!—Thou paragon of virtue!
>   (263–4)

This scene becomes an even more pious specimen of *comedie larmoyante* in an unidentified contemporary promptbook preserved in the Harvard Theatre Collection,[11] in which an extra passage is inserted into Hermione's speech before 'This firstling duty paid':

Hermione kneels and speaks
O heavenly powers, hear and receive his prayer!
Let my long sufferings strengthen his petition.
Oh, grant that these my tears, my heart swoll'n tears,
Which flow, fast and unfeign'd from love and duty,
May wash his sins away, that he may shew
As white and guiltless in thy all-seeing eye
As to his true, long-lost Hermione! [*rises*]
                                              (HTC 401: 65)

Elsewhere, this promptbook continues Garrick's campaign to purify the play's language with still greater rigour. Autolycus no longer condemns himself as 'A fellow, sir, that I have known to go about with trol-my-dames' but 'A fellow, sir, that haunts wakes & fairs' (Garrick, *Plays*, iii. 234: HTC 401: 18); Dorcas's indelicate 'marry, but some garlic to mend her kissing with' is cut (240: cf. HTC 401: 24), and Florizel's

>   since my desires
> Run not before mine honor nor my lusts
> Burn hotter than my faith

is emended to a more restrained, if less metrical, boast of self-restraint:

---

[11] Catalogued as HTC 401. The promptbook is made in a copy of the first edition (1758).

> since my affections
Run not before mine honor, nor my desires
Burn hotter than my faith.
>   (Garrick, *Plays*, iii. 236; HTC 401: 19)

The social orientation of this promptbook, and indeed of Garrick's adaptation in general, is made especially clear in a similar emendation, where a passing remark endorsing the feudal system (the letter of which only is preserved by Garrick) is changed to suggest that Bohemia is in fact a society whose class system is based on income rather than rank, so that Florizel's desire/affection for the poor but honest Perdita (perhaps like the reclaimed Mr B's for Pamela) can represent an aspiration rather than an appetite. Leontes, commiserating with the disinherited Florizel, expresses his regret not that

> Your choice is not so rich in worth as beauty,
That you might well enjoy her

but that

> Your choice is not so rich in wealth as beauty,
That you might well atchieve her.
>   (Garrick, *Plays*, iii. 249; HTC 401: 39)

Florizel and Perdita successfully repackages what is one of the most thoroughly monarchist of Shakespeare's plays, with its plot of royal heredity triumphing over rustic environment, for a society now increasingly committed to the belief that rank does not necessarily equate with worth, and that even the inequalities between rich and poor can be transcended by those citizens who share the infinitely rewardable virtues of self-control, polite speech, love, and duty. It is appropriate that this adaptation, in which bourgeois values covertly subvert royal, should in the 1780s have come to figure as it did in moral criticism of the monarchy, when the Prince of Wales (the future George IV) and his mistress, the actress Mrs Robinson (well known for her performances as 'the prettiest low-born lass, that ever | Ran on the green swerd') were derisively nicknamed 'Florizel and Perdita': just as in Garrick's alterations to *The Sheep-Shearing*, 'bedding without wedding' was no longer acceptable, even for princes of the realm.[12]

---

[12] On this long-running scandal, see esp. *A poetical epistle from Florizel to Perdita: with Perdita's answer. And a preliminary discourse upon the education of princes* (London, 1781); also Bate, *Shakespearean Constitutions*, 75.

Similar modifications in the direction of propriety and affective individualism can be seen in the second adaptation on this double bill, *Catharine and Petruchio*—Garrick's greatly shortened version of *The Taming of the Shrew*—which had first appeared nearly two years earlier in March of 1754.[13] Here Garrick's emphasis is primarily on palliating Shakespeare's embarrassingly frank presentation of power relations between the sexes, suggesting that the transactions negotiated between the title characters have more to do with spontaneous affection and goodwill than any reader of *The Taming of the Shrew* would ever have suspected. In this version, Kate has already internalized some of her 'natural' subordination to Petruchio before they even speak together, acknowledging his exemplary virility even as she decides to behave shrewishly towards him, so that her resistance to his wooing is transformed into a mere perverse whim rather than a genuine attempt to remain single and independent. Her first speech in the play, as she arrives at Baptista's command to meet Petruchio, is an aside:

Reduced to this, or none, the maid's last prayer,
Sent to be wooed like bear unto the stake?
Trim wooing like to be! And he the bear,
For I shall bait him—yet the man's a man.
                    (Garrick, *Plays*, iii. 196–7)

Rather than having to be forced to go through the wedding ceremony, this acquiescent Kate actively chooses to marry Petruchio (if only to avenge herself on both him and the already married Bianca), as she confides to the audience in another two interpolations carefully designed to excuse the open violence of the Shakespearean passages they reinterpret:

[*aside*]. A plague upon his impudence! I'm vexed;
I'll marry my revenge, but I will tame him.
                    (199)

In the short soliloquy which glosses and expands this remark, Kate is even revealed to be already contemplating the possibility of absolute submission as an alternative should her bid for marital supremacy fail:

[13] For the 18th-cent. stage history of this popular adaptation, destined to remain in the repertory until the 1880s, see Hogan, ii. 613–36.

Why, yes: sister Bianca now shall see
The poor abandoned Cath'rine, as she calls me,
Can hold her head as high, and be as proud,
And make her husband stoop unto her lure,
As she, or e'er a wife in Padua.
As double as my portion be my scorn;
Look to your seat, Petruchio, or I throw you.
Cath'rine shall tame this haggard; or, if she fails,
Shall tie her tongue up and pare down her nails.

                                        (200)

With Kate thus prepared to assume the prescribed wifely role already, albeit as a last resort, the tactics Petruchio adopts after the wedding are in danger of looking even more sadistic than they do in Shakespeare's original: Garrick accordingly matches this latently tame Kate with a Petruchio who is secretly a hero of sensibility. A paragon of generosity to his social inferiors, Petruchio, it is revealed, only pretends to mistreat his household: after he has led a famished Kate offstage (having violently rejected their supper), the servant Peter exclaims in amazement: 'I did not think so good and kind a master could have put on so resolute a bearing' (212). Petruchio's concealed affinities with Sir Charles Grandison are revealed more fully and more crucially at the play's conclusion when, after Kate has recited only nineteen lines of her recantation speech (forty-three lines long in the original), he announces that his marital tyranny too has been a mere pretence:

Kiss me, my Kate; and since thou art become
So prudent, kind and dutiful a wife,
Petruchio here shall doff the lordly husband;
An honest mask, which I throw off with pleasure.
Far hence all rudeness, wilfulness and noise,
And be our future lives one gentle stream
Of mutual love, compliance and regard.

                                        (219–20)

Catharine and Petruchio thus offers an unusually bland and insidious version of *The Taming of the Shrew*, but the absolute physical and legal power of husband over wife on which this apparent idyll of unforced mutuality is still based remains extraordinarily visible, if only by accident, despite these attempts to pass the play off as a sentimental comedy. In shortening *The*

Taming of the Shrew into a three-act afterpiece, Garrick telescopes its time-scheme into three days: Petruchio meets Catharine on the first day (Act I), marries her, takes her to his country house, and sends her to (sleepless) bed without dining on the second (Act II), and on the third (Act III) humiliates the tailor and haberdasher, and forces Kate to call the sun the moon, before Baptista, Hortensio, and Bianca arrive (on a curiously arbitrary visit) and are amazed to hear Catharine's submission speech. In the process of abbreviation, the journey back to Padua, the truce between Kate and Petruchio (after their meeting with Vincentio and the ensuing altercation at Lucentio's house), and, more importantly, the feast at Baptista's house after which the competitive obedience-testing of Bianca, the Widow, and Kate is undertaken, have all disappeared completely. Thus, at the conclusion of *Catharine and Petruchio*, Garrick's Kate declares her husband to be her lord, her life, her keeper, her head, her sovereign, and one that cares for her when she has had no food for twenty-four hours and no rest for longer, and less than five minutes after seeing a tailor beaten up by her husband's servants for attempting to provide her with a gown. The companionate marriage *Catharine and Petruchio* celebrates proves, despite Garrick's cosmetic alterations, to be based as squarely as ever on the husband's absolute dominion over the wife: in fact, the play closes with some of Kate's recantation speech being taken from her for use as an epilogue, reallocated to the more authoritative male voice. Leading his wife downstage as an exhibit, Petruchio begins his and Kate's new gentle stream of mutual love, compliance, and regard by summing up the play's moral for the audience:

[*Goes forward with* Catharine *in his hand.*]
Such duty as the subject owes the prince,
Even such a woman oweth to her husband.
And when she's froward, peevish, sullen, sour,
What is she but a foul contending rebel
And graceless traitor to her loving lord?
How shameful 'tis when women are so simple
To offer war where they should kneel for peace;
Or seek for rule, supremacy, and sway,
Where bound to love, to honor and obey.
        [*Finis.*]

(220)

Just as *Florizel and Perdita* discreetly updates *The Winter's Tale*, so *Catharine and Petruchio* quietly transforms *The Taming of the Shrew* into a faithful expression of contemporary domestic ideology, contradictions and all. Even if Petruchio has become an Enlightenment citizen, Kate remains a subject. The feudal system which has been virtually erased from the public world of Bohemia remains in place, despite Petruchio's sentimental disclaimers, in the private realm of the merchants of Padua.

Foreign Affairs

To make Shakespeare an exemplar of middle-class domestic virtue, as do these two adaptations, was simultaneously to make him the foe of mid-century Britain's favourite personifications of aristocratic vice, the French—however vigorously nationalist writers were now prepared to execrate the practice of adaptation altogether. William Guthrie, for example, writing in 1747, shares Seward's delusion that the days of rewriting Shakespeare are over, but expresses this view in more militant terms which place Shakespeare's genius both socially (treating his works as innately anti-feudal) and internationally:

Where is the Briton so much a Frenchman to prefer the highest stretch of modern improvement to the meanest spark of Shakespear's genius. Yet to our eternal amazement it is true, that for above half a century the poets and the patrons of poetry, in England, abandoned the sterling merit of Shakespear for the tinsel ornaments of the French academy. Let us observe, however, to the honour of our country, that neither the practice of her poets, nor the example of her patrons, could extinguish in the minds of the people, the love of their darling writer. His scenes were still admired, his passion was ever felt; his powerful nature knocked at the breast; fashion could not stifle affection; the British spirit at length prevailed; wits with their patrons were forced to give way to genius; and the plays of Shakespear are now as much crowded as, perhaps, they were in the days of their author.[14]

The essential Shakespeare is here defined against both Britain's economic rivals the French and the allegedly Frenchified aristo-

[14] William Guthrie, *An Essay upon English Tragedy* (London, 1747), 10. On the importance of such anti-French sentiments to the 18th-cent. formulation of English national identity, see Newman, *The Rise of English Nationalism*, esp. 123–8.

crats at the apex of Britain's own resented and outmoded clientage system (the 'patrons' who are here sharply contrasted against the right-thinking 'people' and blamed for the perversely Francophile rewritings produced under the Stuarts).[15] To reject adapted versions of Shakespeare is, in this view, to participate in the victorious reassertion of 'the British spirit'. For many, Shakespeare's unfettered, irregular art was now a symbol at once of such domestic well-being (guaranteed against aristocratic tyranny by the Bill of Rights) and of international independence (guaranteed against French autocracy by the British Navy), its status as such only confirmed by the neo-classical objections voiced across the Channel by the likes of Voltaire. 'It does not in the least abate my Veneration for this Poet', declared Peter Whalley in 1748,

> that the *French Connoisseurs* have fixed on him the imputation of Ignorance and Barbarism. It would agree, I believe, as little with their Tempers to be freed from a Sovereign Authority in the Empire of Wit and Letters as in their civil Government.[16]

Fully sharing this perspective, Theophilus Cibber's *Two Dissertations on Theatrical Subjects* (1756) takes up Guthrie's patriotic wrath against adaptation to attack both *Florizel and Perdita* and *Catharine and Petruchio* on the grounds that they constitute acts of French Catholic treachery against British liberty. In this publication, Garrick, repeatedly stigmatized as a half-French 'mongrel' and as a 'Pontiff-like' dictator,[17] is for once disowned by Shakespeare's ghost, who, gazing sorrowfully at the applauding audiences of Garrick's revisions, suffers

---

[15] On the interconnections between rising nationalism, middle-class identity, and literature, see esp. Benedict Anderson, *Imagined Communities: Reflections on the Rise and Spread of Nationalism* (London, 1983), 74 ff.

[16] Peter Whalley, *An Enquiry into the Learning of Shakespeare* (London, 1748), 16–17. Cf. Arthur Murphy's observation in the *Gray's Inn Journal*, 173 (9 Mar. 1754) that 'the dramatic poetry of this country is like our constitution, built upon the bold basis of liberty', or *Avon, a Poem, in three Parts* (Birmingham, 1758), whose author, John Huckell, moves swiftly from his celebration of Shakespeare's unconfined imagination to discuss, 'in the person of Britannia's genius', as one reviewer describes it, 'the great Revolution in 1688, with such an approbation of it, as evinces his love of the rational Constitution of his Country' (*Monthly Review*, 19 (1758), 272–3).

[17] Theophilus Cibber, *Two Dissertations on Theatrical Subjects*, 'An Epistle from Mr. Theophilus Cibber to David Garrick, Esquire' (first published independently a year earlier), 17, 18.

Patriot-Anguish, sighing over your implicit Belief, and Passive Obedience; your non-resistance to this Profanation of his Memory . . .[18]

Cibber (perhaps hypocritically, given his own earlier activities as an adaptor) goes on to harangue his readers in still more virulent terms:

Resent the Injuries offer'd to this Poet. 'Tis expected from ye, Gentlemen, in Vindication of your Taste;—as in a political, and patriot Sense, 'tis your Duty to resist any audacious Attempt on your Liberties, or the Insolence of a *French* Invasion on your Country:—No wonder *Shakespear's* name is insulted by Foreigners, while he is thus tamely suffer'd to be thus maltreated at Home.
                    (Theophilus Cibber, 'The First Dissertation', 40–1).

With such partisans as Guthrie, Whalley, and Cibber championing the Bard's cause, it is not surprising that the political group keenest to adopt Shakespeare as a figurehead during the 1750s (in this respect, as in others, the successors to the Patriots and the Ladies' Club) should have been the Anti-Gallican Society. This long-lived mercantile pressure group—to whom Cibber's tract is dedicated—was founded in the late 1740s 'to extend the commerce of England . . . and oppose the insidious Arts of the French Nation':[19] a typical expression of its ideology is provided by a print (amazingly, by a French artist, Louis Philippe Boitard) dedicated in 1759 'to the Laudable Associations of Anti-Gallicans, and the generous promotors of the British Arts and Manufactories', namely *The Imports of Great Britain from France*.[20] This satire on aristocratic taste depicts the quay at Billingsgate piled high with French cheeses, wines, and other luxury consumer goods and crowded with miscellaneous French 'parasites' issuing from a packet-boat: a priest, dancing masters, dancers, actors, and 'At a distance, landing, swarms of milliners, tailors, mantua-makers, frisers, tutoresses for boarding-schools, disguis'd jesuits, quacks, valets de chambres

---

[18] Id., 'The First Dissertation', 37. According to Cibber, Garrick has adapted *The Winter's Tale* by throwing it to his cat (for whom he expects Garrick to arrange a benefit night accordingly), and the result, a mere 'Droll', represents a throwback to the days of Bartholomew Fair: similarly *Catharine and Petruchio*, another atavistically low entertainment, is merely '*The Taming of the Shrew*, made a Farce of' (32–6).

[19] Quoted in Linda Colley, 'The English Rococo: Historical Background', in Snodin (ed.), *Rococo*, 16. See also 48, 49, 176.

[20] Reproduced in Snodin (ed.), *Rococo*, 49.

&c.&c.&c.' The presence of dancers and actors in this catalogue is not fortuitous, and suggests how important a locus the theatre was at this time for the definition and assertion of national identity.[21] It was indeed the importation of French actors which first induced Shakespeare to enroll himself as an Anti-Gallican spokesman, in a 1749 poem by Mark Akenside. *The Remonstrance of Shakespeare, supposed to have been spoken at the Theatre-Royal while the French Comedians were acting by Subscription, 1749* depicts the spectre of the Bard once more looking back in anger to the manlier, Spain-bashing days of 1588:

I saw this England break the shameful bands
Forg'd for the souls of men by sacred hands,
I saw each groaning realm her aid implore,
Her sons the heroes of each warlike shore,
Her naval standard (the dire Spaniards bane)
Obey'd thro' all the circuit of the main;
Then too great Commerce for a late-found world
Around your coast her eager sails unfurl'd;
New hopes new passions thence the bosom fir'd,
New plans new arts the genius thence inspir'd,
Thence ev'ry science which private fortune knows
In stronger life with bolder spirit rose.[22]

Writing just after the War of Austrian Succession (1742–8), Akenside, with extraordinary bitterness, reidentifies the arch-enemy of Britain's destined imperial glory as France, whom Shakespeare, apparently acting under direct instructions from God, urges the British to reject, expel, distrust, and fight:

O blest at home with justly envy'd laws!
O long the chiefs of Europe's gen'ral cause!
Whom Heav'n hath chosen at each dang'rous hour
To check the inroads of barbarick Pow'r,

---

[21] On nationalism and the 18th-cent. theatre in general, and Theophilus Cibber and the Anti-Gallicans in particular, see esp. Kathleen Wilson, 'Empire of Virtue'.
[22] *The Poetical Works of Mark Akenside* (2 vols.; Edinburgh, 1781), i. 73. On this poem, see Harriet Devine Jump, 'Mark Akenside and the Poetry of Current Events, 1738–1770', D.Phil. thesis (Oxford, 1987), 140–55. The international cultural event to which this poem objects, the visit of Jean-Louis Monnet's troupe to the Little Theatre in the Haymarket, ended, like Garrick's later ill-fated Chinese Festival (see below), in violent anti-French rioting, some organized by the Anti-Gallicans. See Sybil Rosenfeld, *Foreign Theatrical Companies in Great Britain in the Seventeenth and Eighteenth Centuries* (London, 1955), 24–8.

The rights of trampled nations to reclaim,
And guard the social world from bonds and shame,
Oh! let not Luxury's fantastic charms
Thus give the lie to your heroick arms,
Nor for the ornaments of life embrace
Dishonest lessons from that vaunting race
Whom Fate's dread laws, (for in eternal Fate
Despotick Rule was heir to Freedom's hate)
Whom in each warlike each commercial part,
In civil counsel and in pleasing art,
The Judge of earth predestin'd for your foes,
And made it fame and virtue to oppose.

(75−6)

According to the Anti-Gallicans, Britain is being betrayed by its
Francophile aristocracy into effeminacy and luxury: the state ought
to be acting in the interests not of corrupt, decadent landowners,
but of Britain's virile, neo-Elizabethan capitalists; it should be
using its military strength to wrest colonial markets from the
encroaching French. Invoking Shakespeare as the fetishized exemplar of an exclusively British 'Nature', a sacred ancestor summoned
to represent all that they wish their nation to become, it is hardly
surprising that Anti-Gallican writers should be so hostile to those,
like Garrick, who still dared to tamper with his works. It was
indeed the Anti-Gallicans themselves who were responsible for the
worst crisis of Garrick's theatrical career, the Chinese Festival
Riots of 8−18 November 1755, when mobs incensed against the
temporary engagement of another unfortunate French troupe at
Drury Lane came close to demolishing the theatre.[23] Inevitably
one anti-Gallican drew Shakespeare into the fray. In *The Visitation; or, an Interview between the Ghost of Shakespear and
D--v--d G--rr--ck, Esq* (1755), the Bard is pictured, very
much in Akenside's manner, haranguing Garrick about this incident, proudly referring to the rioters as '*my Sons* by me inspir'd'
(8) and criticizing Garrick not only for employing 'servile Slaves
from *France*' (8) but for staging dances and pantomimes at all. In

---

[23] When Garrick appeared before the curtain on 15 Nov. to offer a compromise
—promising that the French dancers would appear only every alternate night for
the remainder of their visit—some audience members hissed and shouted
'Monsieur', and on the worst night of the rioting, 18 Nov., after which all further
performances by the troupe were cancelled, a gang broke the windows of his house
in Southampton Street. See Stone and Kahrl, *David Garrick*, 134−8.

response to Garrick's defence that he has been compelled to do so by the Continental tastes of the aristocracy, Shakespeare inveighs against the unpatriotic degeneracy of the modern upper classes, but finally forgives Garrick on condition that the manager sets about reforming the repertory by mounting a Shakespearean propaganda campaign against France:

'To give you Pardon, I encline,
'If you'll revive a Work of mine;
'You need not fear it will miscarry,'
'What Play d'ye mean, Sir'—'My *fifth Harry*'
                                        (12)[24]

The Anti-Gallican campaign to redefine the British, in the name of Shakespeare, as the only temporarily degenerate heirs to the commercial and imperial glories of Elizabeth (in the pursuit of colonial war against France), reached especial intensity at the time of the Seven Years' War (1756–63), and from this time onwards Garrick took considerable pains to ensure that even his most drastic adaptations were identified with the national cause. His abbreviated musical version of *The Tempest*, premièred on 11 February 1756, anxiously asserts its national credentials from its bills onwards, which describe it as 'a new English Opera, based on Shakespeare's play'.[25] Foisting this otherwise suspiciously foreign

---

[24] *Henry V* had been restored to the repertory, replacing Hill's version, at the time of the Ladies' Club, in 1738. Garrick had revived it at Drury Lane in 1748, playing the Chorus (see *The London Stage*, iv. 1, 68), but it was far more frequently performed at Covent Garden, where it was revived in every season during the Seven Years' War.

It is worth stressing here that the identification of the French as an ever-present threat to British culture, and the invocation of the National Poet as the type of native purity, are by no means confined at this time to hack poets or the perpetrators of theatrical riots. In the same year, after all, Garrick's former schoolteacher Dr Johnson provided literary nationalism with its definitive statement—'The chief glory of every people arises from its authors'—and went on to lament that the English language was deviating from its Elizabethan apogee 'towards a *Gallick* structure and phraseology, from which it ought to be our endeavour to recal it', suggesting that the English might yet prevent themselves from coming to 'babble a dialect of *France*' by emulating their Renaissance forebears, notably by taking 'the diction of common life, from *Shakespeare*'. Samuel Johnson, *A Dictionary of the English Language* (2 vols.; (London, 1755), i. 'Preface', C1^r, C2^v). Cf. Newman, *The Rise of English Nationalism* 112–13. Johnson's bid to preserve the Englishness of the language is indeed comprehensively underwritten by the use of Shakespearian quotations to illustrate the meanings of its words.

[25] See *The London Stage*, iv: 526. On Garrick's various revivals of *The Tempest*, see George Winchester Stone, Jr., 'Shakespeare's *Tempest* at Drury Lane during Garrick's Management', *Shakespeare Quarterly*, 7 (1936), 1–7.

musical genre on the Bard, the play is prefaced by a dialogue between an at first sceptical chauvinist, Wormwood, and Garrick's spokesman, Heartly, which mobilizes this musical Prospero against the French:

WORMWOOD. English music or any music enervates the body, weakens the mind, and lessens the courage—

HEARTLY. Quite the contrary.... Let us suppose an invasion!

WORMWOOD. Ha, ha, ha!—an invasion. Music and an invasion! They are well coupled, truly!

HEARTLY. Patience, sir, I say, let us suppose ten thousand French landed.

WORMWOOD. ... What then?

HEARTLY. Why, then I say, let but 'Britons strike home!' or God save the King' be sounded in the ears of five thousand brave Englishmen ... and they'll drive every Monsieur into the sea and make 'em food for sprats and mackrell.

WORMWOOD. Huzza! and so they will! 'Egad, you're in the right. I'll say no more. Britons strike home. You have warmed me and pleased me; you have converted me ...

(Garrick, *Plays*, iii. 272–3)

Any lingering doubts about the patriotic credentials of Garrick's Shakespeare are laid firmly to rest by his next Shakespearean entertainment. As Jonathan Bate has pointed out,[26] the festive *Harlequin's Invasion: A Christmas Gambol* (1759) celebrates the 'Year of Victories', 1759 (Quiberon Bay, Quebec, Minden), by an Anti-Gallican revision of *Harlequin Student*. The play depicts, via its vindication of the Bard against pantomime, the triumph of the English (here figured as the inhabitants of 'Dramatica's Realm') over the insidious arts of the French nation: it closes not only with the usual appearance, in effigy, of Shakespeare as national poet— a copy of Scheemakers' statue which, summoned by Mercury, successfully banishes the dramatic imports of Great Britain from France from the stage—but with the performance of Garrick's best-known original composition, the most successful patriotic song of its era, *Heart of Oak*.[27]

Garrick's next adaptation, *Cymbeline* (1761), may be less stri-

[26] Bate, *Shakespearean Constitution*, 27–8.

[27] On the allegedly decisive success of this song, see *London Magazine*, 38 (1769), 580: 'Mr. Garrick's Hearts of Oak warmed our seamen with the love of glory, made them look upon the French as beings utterly contemptible, and persuaded them that they were all voluntiers, when perhaps, half the crew of many ships had been pressed.'

dent than *Harlequin's Invasion* but it is no less revealing about the recruitment of Shakespeare in the promulgation of a new account of Britain's place in world affairs. Like Garrick's version of *The Winter's Tale*, it bears certain important resemblances to an earlier adaptation performed at Covent Garden, in this case the *Cymbeline* produced early in 1759 by William Hawkins, then Professor of Poetry at Oxford. Hawkins's own commitment to a Shakespearean version of British glory is amply displayed in his *Praelectiones Poeticae*, the first-ever series of lectures on Shakespeare given at an English university, delivered between 1751 and 1756 and published in 1758. In *Praelectiones Poeticae*, Shakespeare is made into an honorary Roman, 'Shakesperius' (even the quotations from his plays are translated into Latin in the text, with the original English supplied in footnotes), and precisely which city the professor imagines to be the centre of the new empire over which this Praetorian Bard presides is made resoundingly clear by his peroration, where, in the name of Shakesperius, Hawkins prophesies unlimited victory and prosperity to his auditors:

Quod quidem vobis optare, atque ominari non modo gratum animum, ac beneficiorum memorem, verum etiam honestum quemque ac patriae amantissimum; non modo *Academicum*, verum etiam *Anglicanum*.— Floreat itaque OXONIUM, Academiarum semper Regina, *Britanniae* ornamentum, Orbis Christiani decus, Mundi lumen!

[To wish and foresee this for you is fitting not only for a grateful heart, remembering your generosity, but also for every heart which is honourable and most loves the fatherland; not just the *Academic* heart, but the *English* one. Therefore may OXFORD flourish, the eternal Queen of Universities, the ornament of Britain, glory of the Christian World, light of the Universe!][28]

Hawkins's *Cymbeline*, produced, like *Harlequin's Invasion*, in the Year of Victories, similarly both classicizes Shakespeare and claims him for the imperial cause. In his preface to the printed edition of the play, Hawkins states that he was attracted to *Cymbeline*, despite its being 'one of the most irregular productions of *Shakespeare*,' because there is 'something . . . truly *British* in the subject

---

[28] William Hawkins, *Praelectiones Poeticae* (London, 1758), 366. On this text, see J. W. Binns, 'Some Lectures on Shakespeare in Eighteenth-Century Oxford: The *Praelectiones poeticae* of William Hawkins', in Bernhard Fabian and Kurt Tetzeli von Rosador (eds.), *Shakespeare: Text, Language, Criticism. Essays in Honour of Marvin Spevack* (Hildesheim, 1987), 19–33.

of it,' and in order to stress this truly British something he has both altered the play 'to reduce it, as near as possible, to the regular standard of the *drama* . . . almost upon the plan of *Aristotle* himself' and varied 'certain incidents and circumstances' to give 'a *new cast* to the whole *drama*'.[29] This 'new cast' is previewed in Hawkins's prologue, which promises an instructive tale of domestic virtue and martial prowess:

Our scenes awake not now the am'rous flame,
Nor teach soft swains to woo the tender dame;
Content, for bright example's sake, to shew
A wife distress'd, and innocence in woe.—
For what remains, the poet bids you see,
From an old tale, what Britons ought to be;
And in these restless days of war's alarms,
Not melts the soul to love, but fires the blood to arms.

Your great forefathers scorn'd the foreign chain,
Rome might invade, and Caesars rage in vain—
Those glorious patterns with bold hearts pursue,
To king, to country, and to honour true!

('Prologue', ix–x)

Hawkins's *Cymbeline* amply lives up to these promises, not only making much of the sentimental possibilities of the marriage plot by amplifying the reconciliation scene between Imogen and Post-humus in the manner of the statue scene in *Florizel and Perdita* (83–6), but completely revising Shakespeare's account of the war between Britain and Rome. In Hawkins's version, the evil Cloten has secretly defected to the Romans, and has deliberately commissioned Iachimo, confusingly renamed 'Pisanio', to belie Imogen, so that his general loathsomeness is associated not with the militant nationalism he voices in the original but with foreign treachery, which is thus also the ultimate cause of Posthumus' jealousy (10–15; Pisanio dies in the battle at the hands of Palador, repenting and confessing his misdeeds rather in the manner of Durfey's Shattilion). The close of Hawkins's play celebrates not Britain's return to sanity as a law-abiding province of Rome, with an enlightened Cymbeline consenting to pay tribute to Augustus after

[29] William Hawkins, *Cymbeline. A Tragedy, Altered from Shakespeare* (London [1759]), 'Preface', pp. v–vi.

all, but the complete victory of Britain over the Romans, the new ascendancy of one race of empire-builders over their teachers. Instead of releasing all his prisoners, pardoning everyone concerned, and pronouncing the Folio's pacific

Set on there: Neuer was a Warre did cease
(Ere bloodie hands were wash'd) with such a Peace
(F1, 907)

Hawkins's Cymbeline closes the play with the power-hungry and avaricious

—Caesar shall pay
Large ransom for the lives we have in hold,
And sue to us for terms—ne'er war did cease,
With fairer prospect of a glorious peace.
(92)

First performed two years later, Garrick's far less drastic alteration of the same play (in which he played Posthumus, which was to become one of his most popular roles) is among his most conservatively adapted acting texts of Shakespeare, but it none the less follows Hawkins in this crucial respect, suppressing Cymbeline's decision to pay tribute to the Romans. At the close of his play, Garrick's Cymbeline may seem to be the same peace-loving monarch as Shakespeare's—

Set on there. Never was a war did cease,
Ere bloody hands were washed, with such a peace.
(Garrick, *Plays*, iv. 169)

—but, like Hawkins's, he is ratifying not the Pax Romana, but the Pax Britannica.[30] Adaptation here covertly ensures that the national poet remains in sympathy with popular views of his nation's destiny.

---

[30] Francis Gentleman, who recognizes that Garrick's version acts better than Hawkins's but prefers the earlier adaptation as a reading text, is clearly in sympathy with these nationalistic alterations to the play, and suggests another: in his opinion, Cloten's patriotic lines—'There be many *Caesars*, | Ere such another *Julius*. Britain's a world | By itself, and we will nothing pay | For wearing our own noses'—should be reallocated to Cymbeline. See Gentleman, *The Dramatic Censor*, ii. 95; *Bell's Edition of Shakespeare's Plays*, ii. 270.

Exit the Playwright

Anti-Gallican purists notwithstanding, there were still contemporary commentators ready to admire such rewritings. According to the *Monthly Review*, for example, Hawkins's play represented Shakespeare adaptation at its best: 'Among the many alterations of Shakespeare's plays that have been offered to the public, we do not know of any more deserving encouragement than this of Cymbeline.'[31] Similarly, there were plenty of critics willing to regard Garrick as Shakespeare's saviour rather than a treasonous saboteur. A poem published '*By a* LADY' at the time of the Jubilee, addressed 'To the AUTHOR of some late paultry Attacks upon Mr. GARRICK', praises the actor as not only Shakespeare's Son but his Redeemer:

His taste refin'd, secures immortal fame,
And every muse shall celebrate his name;
At length convinc'd, ev'n envy's self shall own,
Great Shakespear's soul shone forth in him alone.
'Twas Garrick's, all his beauties to explore,
And trace the springs of his poetic lore.
Garrick to merit first gave all its due,
And brought his hidden treasures forth to view;
Lopp'd his luxuriances, his thoughts refin'd,
And held him up a mirror to mankind;
Where every mortal may his features scan,
And view each passion that's innate to man.[32]

Cast once more as Hamlet lecturing the Players (as in Taylor's engraving), Garrick is here credited with holding Shakespeare as a mirror up to Nature—but not without judiciously polishing him first, thereby proving himself both a truly enlightened judge (able to recognize and reveal 'merit' in whatever guise) and an honorary merchant venturer, questing successfully for 'hidden treasures'. This refining of Shakespeare's works, however, even when carried out by such a man of the theatre as Garrick, was in practice

---

[31] *Monthly Review*, 20 (1759), 462.
[32] *Lloyd's Evening Post* (6 Sept. 1769). Cf. *General Evening Post*, 17 Dec. 1772, which declares that Garrick's 'corrections' have 'given some of our celebrated poet's chief pieces a certainty of maintaining their ground in the catalogue of exhibiting plays, which without an assistance of such a nature had probably slept in oblivion, notwithstanding the exalted reputation of their author'. On the impact of Garrick's adaptations on contemporary Shakespeare criticism, see esp. Stone, 'Garrick's Handling of Shakespeare's Plays'.

contributing its share towards Shakespeare's increasing removal from the stage, a process adumbrated by Francis Gentleman in his contributions to the first-ever complete acting edition of Shakespeare, published towards the close of Garrick's career by John Bell in 1773–4. Bell's edition, as Gentleman's introduction and notes make clear, is an acting edition with a difference, marking a complete reversal in the relations between the theatre and the press. According to Gentleman, the campaign imagined by Addison in his 'Trunk-maker' essay to force the stage to uphold the standards of the coffee-house has by now triumphantly achieved its objectives, or even gone beyond them. Such has been the progress of manners and literature since Shakespeare's day, Gentleman argues, that it has been the duty of contemporary adaptors such as Garrick (to whom the edition is dedicated) retrospectively to project their own civilized standards onto Shakespeare's works, the virtues of which are now fully visible for the first time. Seconding him warmly, the *Monthly Review* notes that this edition presents

Shakespeare as *altered* and accommodated to the taste of an age more refined than that in which the Author lived and wrote,—more capable of tasting his beauties, and less apt to relish or even *tolerate* his defects. Those beauties, it must, to the honour of the stage, be allowed, are judiciously retained in the plays of this great poet, as acted at either theatre; and the deformities are, for the most part, with equal choice and discernment, expunged:

The rhiming clowns that gladded Shakespear's age,
No more with Crambo entertain the stage,
&c.[33]

This edition in effect celebrates the domestication of literature's last truly public sphere—the theatre—and with it the final salvation of Shakespeare from his own vulgar dramaturgy. According to Gentleman's prefatory 'Advertisement', his plays have now been made safe not only for men of delicate literary discernment but even for those definitively private beings, women and children:

it has been our peculiar endeavour to render what we call the essence of SHAKESPEARE, more instructive and intelligible; especially to the ladies and to youth; glaring indecencies being removed.

(i. 9)[34]

---

[33] *Monthly Review*, 50 (1774), 144.
[34] Given the increasing tendency to regard any tampering with the National Poet, no matter how virtuously inclined, as treasonous, it is not surprising that

Such now mercifully expunged 'deformities' are primarily symptoms of Shakespeare's unfortunate desire to please his popular theatrical audience. Citing that socially indecorous 'rhiming clown' Lear's Fool as a glaring example, Gentleman declares that Shakespeare

> frequently trifles, is now and then obscure, and sometimes, to gratify a vitiated age, indelicate . . . he no doubt, on many occasions, wrote wildly, merely to gratify the public . . . and it is matter of great question with us, whether the fool, in *King Lear*, was not a more general favourite, than the old monarch himself.
>
> (5–6)

In the current enlightened age, however, the stage, rid of these socially and aesthetically incoherent intrusions, has been successfully colonized as an appendix to the study: the acting texts of Shakespeare in use at the Theatres Royal now offer better examples of good literary taste than do more scholarly library editions. The most extraordinary 'evident use' which will accrue from the publication of Bell's edition, however, is that now

> those who take books to the THEATRE, will not be so puzzled themselves to accompany the speaker; nor so apt to condemn the performers for being imperfect, when they pass over what is designedly omitted.
>
> (7)

The experiences of reading Shakespeare and of seeing his plays performed—experiences divorced so emphatically in the days of Granville and Pope—are here reunited at last, but only because the private, self-contained activity of critical reading has completely subsumed the atavistic, communal, and socially miscegenating experience of play-going. Instead of reading the script to recapture the performance (as with previous playhouse texts, published 'As they were Acted'), one can now safely use the performance as an incidental gloss on the reading, if one bothers to look up at all. Garrick's brilliantly successful marketing of Shakespeare to eighteenth-century theatre-goers as an exemplar of bourgeois morality, commended repeatedly throughout Gentleman's notes to

other commentators are less enthusiastic about Bell's edition: William Kenrick, for example, refers sneeringly to 'The appearance . . . of a mutilated *play-house* copy, under the auspices of the MANAGERS, from whose affected veneration for Shakespeare better things might have been expected'; William Kenrick, *Introduction to the School of Shakespeare* (London, 1774), p. v.

Bell's edition, is here revealed as ultimately prejudicial to the theatre's own remaining cultural authority: by producing acting texts fit for domestic perusal Garrick, however successfully he may have reclaimed the Bard for the stage in his own lifetime, was unwittingly helping to turn the plays of 'this great poet' into closet drama.

In different ways, Shakespeare was by the time of this publication already diversifying into more private media, and would continue to do so. Bell's desire to present a Shakespeare made fit and instructive for ladies and youth is recognizably the same impulse which over the coming decades would produce not only the Bowdlers' *Family Shakespeare* (intended solely to be read in the home), but an equally sanitized incarnation of Shakespeare's plays which even rescues them from being drama at all—the Lambs' *Tales from Shakespear*.[35] It is in fact a comparatively short step for Shakespeare's plays, once certified as fit for decent home consumption, to be thus assimilated to the tradition of didactic domestic fiction: indeed, the Complete Plays had already been set within a history of the novel by Charlotte Lennox in 1753, with the publication of her *Shakespear Illustrated: or the Novels and Histories, On Which the Plays of Shakespear are Founded, Collected and Translated from the Original Authors*.[36] The connection between this generic domestication and the cleansing of Shakespeare from his associations with low theatricality subsequently celebrated by Bell's edition is confirmed by a memorable text published in 1755, *Memoirs of the Shakespear's-Head in Covent-Garden: By the Ghost of Shakespear*. In this first novel to include Shakespeare as a character, as in contemporary adaptations, Shakespeare, through being purged of his own Elizabethan vulgarity, is resurrected as a moralist to censure the transgressions of Georgian London. At its opening, the narrator, drowsing in the eponymous tavern, is surprised by the appearance of 'a Figure in every part resembling that we see drawn for *Shakespear*', and, inevitably identifying this spectre with the appropriate Shake-

---

[35] [Henrietta and Thomas Bowdler] (eds.), *The Family Shakespeare* (London, 1807): Charles [and Mary] Lamb, *Tales from Shakespear. Designed for the use of young persons* (2 vols.; London, 1807).

[36] On this pioneering work of feminist Shakespeare criticism, see Margaret Doody, 'Shakespeare's Novels: Charlotte Lennox Illustrated', *Studies in the Novel*, 19 (Autumn 1987), 296–310.

spearean character, asks it, 'What would thy gracious Figure?'[37]
Shakespeare replies that for a certain term his soul has been 'fix'd
the Guardian of this *Bacchanalian Temple*, a Post alloted to punish
me for the Errors of my youthful Conduct'. The 'errors' which
have occasioned this Tiresias-like purgatory, in so far as they are
ever described, seem to consist primarily in the embarrassingly
'low Scene of Life' in which Shakespeare shamefacedly admits to
having participated as a young man.

> You have been informed by those who have written my Life, that in my
> years of Nonage and Folly, I was oblig'd to fly to *London* for trespassing
> in a Park, not far from where I lived; and it has been lately revealed to the
> World, that my Distresses in *London*, consequential to my Elopement,
> reduc'd me to the Necessity of holding the Horses of Persons of Quality,
> as was then the Custom; from which Occupation my Diligence rais'd me
> to the Theatre; of which I have since been stil'd the Father.
>
> (5–6)

The degrading experience of horse-minding, however, apparently
did nothing to prepare Shakespeare for the 'heart-corroding Cares,
that have gnaw'd [his] Soul' in the course of its posthumous
punishment as unwilling spectator of the lowest of London's low-
life. As in Westminster Abbey, this Shakespeare (who rose to the
top of his profession by 'Diligence', like any good eighteenth-
century apprentice) is imagined not only as Old Hamlet but as
Prospero: he wields a magic 'Wand' (9), by which the narrator is
made invisible, thus permitted to witness the scandalous episodes
in the inn's various rooms which form the bulk of the novel's
narrative content. On each of these sub-plots, Shakespeare provides a disgusted, censorious commentary: transferred to the novel,
the Bard, rescued not only from the Elizabethan but from the
Georgian theatre, is co-opted to police the public space of the
tavern in the name of private virtue. Abstracted from his own
texts in early eighteenth-century prologues in order to claim and
supervise their revival on the stage, Shakespeare, in the mid-
century, takes on an existence quite independent of the live theatre,
from the demeaning associations of which he can be redeemed to
begin a new, moralistic career in eighteenth-century fiction.

The kind of extra-theatrical afterlife achieved by Shakespeare as

---

[37] *Memoirs of the Shakespear's-Head in Covent-Garden. By the Ghost of
Shakespear* (2 vols.; London, 1755), i. 4.

Old Hamlet in *Memoirs of the Shakespear's-Head* is bestowed on other members of the same play's cast in three rather better-known mid-century novels which successfully deploy the Shakespeare thus abducted from the theatre in the interests of nationalism at the same time as those of domestic virtue. The eponymous hero of Richardson's *Sir Charles Grandison* (1753–4), mourning his father at the story's opening, is in many respects a scrupulous, moral Hamlet rescued from the tragic stage for the instruction of novel-readers: he forgives and reclaims his sexually corrupt uncle, for example, instead of punishing him, and it is specifically in the role of the Prince that he conquers the heart of the Italian Catholic Clementina, with whom he reads *Hamlet* so eloquently that she turns into a she-tragic, domestic Ophelia.[38] The most famous comic fantasias on *Hamlet* in eighteenth-century fiction, those of Laurence Sterne (whose career-long self-casting as Yorick parallels Garrick's as Hamlet), similarly exploit the play in both domestic and international contexts, invoking Shakespeare on behalf of both domestic benignity and the prestige of English culture in Europe. The celebrated glimpse of the Oedipal primal scene which opens *Tristram Shandy* (1759–67) is a comically redeemed closet scene, safely confined not just within the novel but within its protagonist's harmlessly soliloquizing consciousness; in the novel's tangential sequel, *A Sentimental Journey* (1768), its presiding holy fool, Parson Yorick, wanders invulnerably across Europe, his claim to embody one of Shakespeare's characters sufficiently impressing the Count de B—— (an admirer of 'the great Shakespear') to procure a passport through France, despite the state of war in existence at the time of the journey in question.[39]

The obliqueness and pervasiveness with which Sterne re-uses this Shakespearian material is as symptomatic of his historical

---

[38] Richardson, *Sir Charles Grandison*, iii. 155. Dazzling all Europe with his impeccable English manners, Grandison patriotically declares that Shakespeare is 'one of the greatest genius's of any country or age,' and 'the age in which Shakespeare flourished, might be called, The age of English Learning, as well as of English Bravery' (vi. 245). Hamlet's tragic procrastination is retained as the mainspring of this novel's plot (or lack of it), metamorphosed into Sir Charles's seemingly endless prevarication as to whether he will marry Clementina or Harriet Byron.

[39] Laurence Sterne, *A Sentimental Journey Through France and Italy* [1768] ed. Graham Petrie (Harmondsworth, 1967), 89, 106–12. On Sterne and Shakespeare, see esp. Peter Conrad, *Shandyism: The Character of Romantic Irony* (Oxford, 1978).

position as it is of his own carefully cultivated eccentricity. The more exalted Shakespeare's authority becomes, the more thoroughly it is diffused, and the less visibly it is connected with his actual achievements as a playwright. Not only do Shakespeare and his characters begin to migrate independently into the novel during the 1750s and 1760s, but his characters give rise to new plays entirely (such as William Kenrick's *Falstaff's Wedding*, 1766), and his plays are dispersed into quotable fragments (in the tradition of Gildon's *Shakespeariana*, the most illustrious follower of which is William Dodd's endlessly reprinted *The Beauties of Shakespear*, 1752),[40] or distilled into sermons (as in Elizabeth Griffith's *The Morality of Shakespeare's Drama Illustrated*, 1775).[41] Once Shakespeare's works have been comprehensively nationalized (whether through their illustrative propping of the language throughout Johnson's *Dictionary*, or through the activities of both Garrick and his Anti-Gallican adversaries), allusions and appropriations such as those of Sterne can be as indirect as they like. By the 1760s Shakespeare is so firmly established as the morally uplifting master of English letters that his reputation no longer seems to depend on his specific achievements as a dramatist: a ubiquitous presence in British culture, his fame is so synonymous with the highest claims of contemporary nationalism that simply to be British is to inherit him, without needing to read or see his actual plays at all.

Enter the Bard

This paradox is made nowhere more visible than at the culmination of Shakespeare's canonization, the Stratford Jubilee of 1769, at which, as every modern commentator has pointed out, not a single Shakespeare play was performed, or even directly quoted: in

[40] On such publications, see De Grazia, *Shakespeare Verbatim*, 202–4.

[41] Griffith's belief that the value of Shakespeare's works resides above all in a moral system deducible from them is of course shared by Dr Johnson, for whom this is one of the most important reasons for editing them: see Samuel Johnson (ed.), *The Plays of William Shakespeare* (8 vols., London, 1765), i. 'Preface'. On Johnson's edition and its rationale, see esp. G. F. Parker, *Johnson's Shakespeare* (Oxford, 1989): on the widespread determination to find a common morality in the great authors of the national past, see Newman, *The Rise of English Nationalism*, 127–8.

the event, even the proposed Grand Procession of Shakespeare's Characters (a further example of their escape from their respective plays) had to be cancelled because of torrential rain. The events of Garrick's polite carnival have been chronicled elsewhere (most expertly in Christian Deelman's *The Great Shakespeare Jubilee*),[42] but both they and the contemporary texts which record and dramatize them amply repay further inspection because they display so vividly the domestic, national, and moral concerns which converge on the Shakespeare cult the festival definitively initiates.

To hold a Shakespearean festival without including any Shakespearean performances might seem like staging *Hamlet* without the Prince, but this expression could hardly be applied to the Jubilee, given that it was dominated by a Steward, Garrick, whose very badge of office declared him to be Shakespeare's own chosen Hamlet (see Chapter 4). One ostensible purpose of the whole event was to celebrate Garrick's presentation to the town of a likeness of his spiritual father as Old Hamlet—yet another copy of the Scheemakers monument[43]—and its climax, Garrick's recitation, in front of this effigy, of his *Ode upon dedicating a building, and erecting a statue, to Shakespeare, at Stratford upon Avon* once more juxtaposed the eloquent Prince as spokesman to the mute King, 'his features expressive of the filial veneration glowing in his bosom', as one enthusiastic commentator recognized.[44] This *coup de théâtre*, staged in the temporary Jubilee Rotunda (built near the site of the present-day Memorial Theatre), reran the structure of *Harlequin Student* and *Harlequin's Invasion* almost precisely, once again pitting the national poet against the Continental dramatic genres it none the less slyly appropriated. Before the *Ode* began, an actor Garrick had planted in the audience, Thomas King, rose to his feet in order to complain, in the character of a languid aristocratic fop corrupted by the Grand Tour, that

[42] Christian Deelman, *The Great Shakespeare Jubilee* (London, 1964); see also Stochholm, *Garrick's Folly*; Martha W. England, *Garrick's Jubilee* (Ohio, 1964).

[43] The presentation of the statue, along with Gainsborough's portrait of Garrick with a bust of Shakespeare, was to mark the opening of the new Town Hall: although the painting was later destroyed by fire, the statue is still displayed in a niche half way up the building's west front.

[44] *Anti-Midas: a jubilee preservative from unclassical, ignorant, false and invidious criticism* (London, 1769), 20. Cf. Robert Edge Pine's choice of this scene as the definitive moment of Garrick's career for his posthumous, idealized portrait *Garrick delivering the ode to Shakspeare at the jubilee, surrounded by Shakspearean characters* (1784), (see Frontispiece).

Shakespeare was a low and over-rated English provincial whose plays demanded levels of emotional and intellectual engagement incompatible with good breeding.[45] Like Jupiter arriving to banish Harlequin and his pantomimic playmates in *Harlequin Student* or Mercury appearing to expel Harlequin and the French fleet in *Harlequin's Invasion*, Garrick then proceeded to quell this anti-Shakespearean anti-masque by invoking the Scheemakers monument to enact the Bard's triumph through the performance of his Ode—a poem which, for all Garrick's supposed rejection of opera, is largely cast in recitative, with full orchestral accompaniment (composed by Thomas Arne) and extensive choral passages (sung by the assembled Drury Lane company).[46]

The *Ode* itself, considering that it represents the Jubilee's most important substitute for Shakespeare's own words, has a remarkably indirect opening, and one which tellingly foregrounds patriotism rather than literary appreciation (in so far as the two, in this instance, are remotely separable). Shakespeare (whose 'lov'd, rever'd, immortal name' is ingeniously withheld until the poem's thirty-first line, where it appears three times, in capitals, with exclamation marks) is selected after the rhetorical questions with which the poem begins to fill what is apparently a pre-existing vacancy for a national deity:

To what blest genius of the isle,
Shall Gratitude her tribute pay,
    Decree the festive day,
Erect the statue, and devote the pile?

[45] See *Town and Country Magazine*, 1 (Sept. 1769), 475; *St. James Chronicle* (9–12 Sept. 1769); *Universal Magazine*, 45 (Sept. 1769), 158–9.

[46] This rhetorical trick was recognized as one more restaging of Shakespeare's supposed antipathy to Harlequin by Henry Woodward, who avenged Garrick's subsequent Drury Lane representation of his Stratford doings (in his afterpiece *The Jubilee*) by producing his own *Harlequin's Jubilee* at Covent Garden in Jan. 1770. 'The scene closes', reports an amused reviewer, 'with the descent of the statue of the late Mr Rich, under the name of Lun, which he always adopted when he performed the character of Harlequin; and in imitation of the adulation paid to Shakespear, at Drury-Lane, Harlequin, and the rest of the pantomime characters, from the different pieces produced by that genius, who walk in the procession, bow and pay him homage; after which they sing a chorus, in honour of his memory'; *Town and Country Magazine*, 2 (1770), 43. See also [Henry Woodward], *Songs, Chorusses, &c. which are introduced in the New Entertainment of Harlequin's Jubilee* (London, 1770), a minutely detailed parody of Garrick's own *Songs, Chorusses, &c. which are introduced in the New Entertainment of the Jubilee* (London, 1769).

Do not your sympathetic hearts accord,
　　To own the 'bosom's lord?'
'Tis he! 'tis he!—that demi-god!
Who Avon's flow'ry margin trod,
　　While sportive *Fancy* round him flew,
Where *Nature* led him by the hand,
　　Instructed him in all she knew,
And gave him absolute command!
　　　　'Tis he! 'tis he!
'The god of our idolatry!'
　　　　　　　(Garrick, *Ode*, 1)

Shakespeare is thus summoned to serve as Prospero (attended by sportive Fancy as Ariel) to the grateful enchanted island of Britain, his Nature-given 'absolute command' (an internalized descendant of Divine Right?) sanctioned, as in *Florizel and Perdita*, by that quintessentially mid-century cement of enlightened society, sympathy. Apart from incidental echoings of *Henry V*, *A Midsummer Night's Dream*, and *Romeo and Juliet* and more extended allusions to Prospero, Lear, and Falstaff, the remainder of the poem is equally preoccupied with the generalized hymning of Shakespeare as a transcendent national spirit (hailing him as the certificate of Britain's privileged access to Nature), and, as by now we might expect, the principal characteristic of Shakespeare's works it praises is their morality. Like Francis Gentleman surveying Bell's edition, Shakespeare gazes approvingly down on his plays' fitness for domestic perusal:

With no reproach, even now, thou view'st thy work,
To nature sacred as to truth,
Where no alluring mischiefs lurk,
To taint the mind of youth.
　　　　　　　(14–15)

Having thus once more guaranteed the Bard's qualifications to embody the national ideal, the poem can conclude with a restatement of its patriotic opening flourish, this time leaving Shakespeare in the familiar role of King Hamlet:

Can *British* gratitude delay,
To him the glory of this isle,
　　To give the festive day
The song, the statue, and devoted pile?

To him the first of poets, best of men?
'*We ne'er shall look upon his like again!*'
(15)

The Jubilee's invocation of this national spirit was in fact so vague that one contemporary wag was able to suggest that Shakespeare was utterly irrelevant to the entire proceedings, a mere pretext for a far more useful patriotic exercise. The *Middlesex Journal* jokingly represents Garrick's celebrations as a deliberate bid to further British manufactures and commerce by fomenting the Industrial Revolution, primarily a festival not of native literature but of native productivity (in every sense).

It has been generally believed, that the institution of the Stratford jubilee was only a matter of taste and amusement; but the more sagacious see a great political view carried on at the bottom of it: this is the population of that manufacturing part of the country, which will be effected by drawing great numbers of people from the neighbouring towns, to repose together on the verdant banks of the Avon. The season seems peculiarly favourable to this important view by its heat, should the same continue.[47]

Industrial or amusing, the Jubilee was undeniably national, catering amply to Anti-Gallican sensibilities, whether by the quashing of King's Frenchified fop at the Ode ceremony, or by the assertions of Shakespeare's native superiority to all foreign competitors liberally sprinkled among the Bardolatrous ballads performed in the streets by Garrick's actors:

Our SHAKESPEARE compar'd is to no man,
No French man, nor Grecian, nor Roman,
Their swans are all geese to the Avon's sweet swan,
And the man of all men was a Warwickshire man.

(Garrick, *Songs, Chorusses*, 4)[48]

---

[47] *Middlesex Journal* (10 Aug. 1769). The heat, of course, did not continue, but the labouring populations of Birmingham and Coventry seem to have expanded none the less: equally the Jubilee, in its promotion of the Shakespearean tourist industry, undeniably provided a lasting stimulus to the local economy of Stratford.

[48] The kind of emergent cultural nationalism which Garrick's poem voices, as we have seen, was more often deployed in the 18th cent. by oppositional groups such as the Anti-Gallicans than by more Establishment figures, and it is thus not altogether surprising that Garrick's great Shakespearean festival should have been associated in the minds of some contemporaries with the activities of that most maverick of contemporary demagogues, John Wilkes. (See e.g. *Lloyd's Evening Post*, 8 Sept. 1769). These contemporaries included Garrick himself, who combined

It is here, however, that one of the central contradictions inherent in Shakespeare's deification at the Stratford Jubilee becomes most apparent. Now for the first time being praised as the 'man of all men', directly inspired by Nature to voice the universal truths of humanity, and hymned throughout Garrick's proceedings as self-evidently the supreme writer in world literature, the timeless and transcendent Bard must none the less be claimed as specifically and uniquely English. Supposedly celebrating the limitless inclusiveness of Shakespeare's genius, the Jubilee is in fact premissed on the exclusion of mere prejudiced foreigners (or quasi-foreigners, such as King's caricatured aristocrat) from the festivities. This point is conspicuously underlined in Garrick's immensely popular afterpiece *The Jubilee*, first performed at Drury Lane within days of the festival itself, which offers a half-satirical, half-idealized version of the recent doings at Stratford for London consumption, right down to restoring the cancelled procession. (Its lasting popularity amply recouped the financial losses Garrick had sustained at the Jubilee itself.) The central running joke of this entertainment is its presentation of the Jubilee through the uncomprehending eyes of an utterly excluded character, one Captain O'Shoulder (designated in the script simply as 'Irishman'), who, unable even to pronounce 'the loved, rever'd, immortal name' of Shakespeare in the approved manner, never discovers what the celebrations he has come to witness are about. Instead he serves as the comic butt of all the event's hardships—compelled to sleep in a postchaise for want of adequate accommodation, badgered by mulberry salesmen, charged extortionate rates for food, and extensively rained on (despite the deluge which virtually drowned the real Jubilee, O'Shoulder is the only character in Garrick's play who gets wet)—

a puff for the Jubilee with a cryptic salute to Wilkes's most recent acquittal on libel charges in the *Public Advertiser* of 8 July 1769, and may have partly modelled his Stratford festivities on the jubilees celebrated in honour of 'Wilkes and Liberty' or 'Liberty, Property and No Excise' over the preceding decade. See Hugh Tait, 'Garrick, Shakespeare and Wilkes', *British Museum Journal*, 24 (1961), 100–07. On Garrick's friendship with Wilkes, see also Stone and Kahrl, *David Garrick*, 373–6: on Wilkes's jubilees, see John Brewer, Neil McKendrick, and J. H. Plumb, *The Birth of a Consumer Society: The Commercialization of Eighteenth-Century England* (Bloomington, Ind., 1982), 248–9, 275. One conservative reviewer of the *Ode*, indeed, objects anxiously to Garrick's invocation of Euphrosyne by 'a new title, not to be found in any books of celestial heraldry, either ancient or modern, I mean that of "Goddess of *Liberty*"'. Quoted in *Anti-Midas*, 29. For the offending passage, see Garrick, *Ode*, 7–8.

and he finally falls asleep just before the grand procession of Shakespeare's characters, thereby missing the central point of the whole affair. As far as Bardolatry is concerned, the Irish, just as much as the French or the Italians, are, in every sense, beyond the pale ('Ara! I'll go home and be nowhere,' mutters O'Shoulder, exiting).[49]

Perhaps more remarkably, this definition of the Shakespearean norm by exclusion similarly denies any rights in the Bard to Shakespeare's own townspeople. If at the top of the domestic social scale overrefined and overtravelled aristocrats (as caricatured by King) are outside Shakespeare's England, and the inhabitants of Britain's Celtic fringes (as represented by O'Shoulder) are equally disqualified from full membership, it seems from Garrick's play that national identity as figured by the national poet does not include Shakespeare's own rural province either. However heartily its songs hail Shakespeare as a Warwickshire Will, *The Jubilee* works for its London audience not only by congratulating them on being nationally eligible to participate in the Shakespeare cult (encouraging them to laugh at the ignorant or affected foreigners it excludes), but by congratulating them on being socially eligible, providing for their further amusement a whole gallery of stupid Warwickshire yokels. In the terms of Garrick's play, to be a native of Stratford is to be self-evidently beyond the notice or purview of polite letters, either hilariously ignorant of the Jubilee's purpose (like the old rustics of the opening scene, who, having heard of the gunpowder imported for Garrick's firework display, speak in terror of what they call the 'Jew bill' as 'a plot of the Jews and Papishes'), or comically inept in the Bard's praises (like Sukey, who assures her friend Nancy that 'I'm sure I cried for a whole night together after hearing his Romy and July at Birmingham, by the London gentlemen and ladies player people ... O, the sweet Creature, the dear Willy Shakespur ...'; Garrick, *Plays*, ii. 104–5, 122). Just as

---

[49] See Garrick, *Plays*, ii. 124–5. George Colman's *Man and Wife; or the Shakespeare Jubilee* (London, 1770), the Covent Garden spectacular which preceded Garrick's own exploitation of public interest in the Jubilee, is similarly premissed on the exclusion of the un-English from Shakespeare's universal accessibility: rerunning the Fenton–Ann Page plot from *The Merry Wives of Windsor* (with the Shakespeare-loving Colonel Frankly successfully exploiting the confusions of the occasion to elope with the virtuous Charlotte) it is esp. harsh on the opinionated Francophile fop Marcourt, the only character in the play who disparages Shakespeare.

the claiming of Shakespeare as a national icon requires the performed exclusion of foreigners from his festival, so the redemption
from vulgarity which it entails requires the performed exclusion of
the vulgar.[50] Despite canonizing Shakespeare in Stratford, the
Jubilee canonizes him for having utterly transcended it, becoming
the god of 'our' idolatry—not Warwickshire's—in the process: if
Shakespeare appears to be remotely understood in his own home
town, apparently, his status as a national prophet may be jeopar-
dized. In this respect the central event of the ceremonies, the
public donation to the town of Scheemakers' official likeness of
Shakespeare-as-national-poet, looks more like an erasure of the
local worthy whose funerary bust Garrick's gift supersedes than a
tribute to him, a replacement of mere 'Shakespur' by timeless and
placeless (if irreducibly English) Shakespeare.

In this respect, too, it is very much in keeping with the spirit of
the occasion that the Grand Procession of Shakespeare's Characters
should in the event have been withheld from Stratford altogether:
the song written to present the pageant, banishing the unlettered
from its vicinity, thereby became, in its Platonic London enact-
ment within *The Jubilee*, completely self-fulfilling:

Hence, ye profane! And only they,
Our pageant grace our pomp survey,
Whom love of sacred genius brings . . .
            (Garrick, *Plays*, ii. 119)

The triumphant canonization of Shakespeare, as performed by the
Jubilee, in short, is a strictly metropolitan triumph, the elevation
of the moral essence of Shakespeare (independent of his actual
texts) to stand for the national essence of Britain (independent of
its actual regions). Garrick's *The Jubilee*, wordlessly summarizing
the emblematic essentials of the Complete Plays and parading
Scheemakers' statue of Shakespeare-as-national-poet in their midst

---

[50] Cf. Carrington's *The Modern Receipt*, ch. 3, above. It is interesting to note in
this connection that the representations of O'Shoulder and of Nancy and Sukey in
The Jubilee derive from disowned pieces of Shakespearean low comedy: O'Shoulder,
drowsing through the show under delusions of grandeur, is an Irish Christopher
Sly (excised from *Catharine and Petruchio*), while Nancy and Sukey, buying the
Shakespeare myth as foolishly and as avidly as their originals buy Autolycus'
ballads, derive from Mopsa and Dorcas (toned down in *Florizel and Perdita*).
Excluding vulgarity from Shakespeare's plays and excluding the vulgar from
Shakespeare again go hand in hand.

(o'erstepping not the modesty of Nature, Shakespeare's characters are here reduced by Garrick to an inexplicable dumb show), is thus perhaps the ultimate Shakespeare adaptation, a popular Shakespearean entertainment determined to appropriate and extend the Bard's fame by condensing his dramatic achievements to the point of virtual non-existence. A century of the rewriting and repositioning of Shakespeare's plays within British culture here culminates in a festive entertainment marking, in spectacular fashion, their accession to an unprecedented symbolic value which renders their actual contents irrelevant, drowned out in the noise of national rejoicing.

> But see, in crowds, the gay, the fair,
> To the splendid scene repair,
> A scene as fine, as fine can be,
> To celebrate our Jubilee.

Every character, tragic and comic, join[s] *in the Chorus and go*[es] *back, during which the guns fire, bells ring, etc. etc. and the audience applaud*[s].
Bravo Jubilee!
Shakespeare forever!
The End.

(Garrick, *Plays*, ii. 126)

Conclusion

THE Stratford Jubilee not only marks a convenient end-point to the history of Shakespeare's accession to pre-eminence in English literary culture, but in a number of ways seems to encode and recapitulate that history. Perhaps the most important of its traces, for example, the published edition of Garrick's *Ode*, is supplemented by an appendix, 'Testimonies to the Genius and Merits of Shakespeare', which constitutes a chronological anthology of the texts which have defined and built the Shakespeare cult completed by Garrick's poem: among these 'undeniable Testimonies (both in prose and verse) of [Shakespeare's] unequalled original talents' are Jonson's commendatory poem from the First Folio and Dryden's prologue to *The Enchanted Island*, along with excerpts from prefaces by Rowe, Pope, Theobald, Hanmer, Dr Johnson, and Edward Capell, and passages drawn from the writings of Joseph Addison, William Dodd, Arthur Murphy, and others.[1] Assembled between two covers for the first time, these progressive steps towards fullblown Bardolatry add up to 'undeniable' evidence of supremacy—between them, Garrick suggests, these writers have authorized Shakespeare.

Elsewhere, too, Garrick's festival carries with it the pre-history of the national cult it initiates. The Grand Procession of Shakespeare's Characters (albeit of necessity deferred until the Jubilee's London incarnation) is visibly indebted to at least one of the adaptors who had made Shakespeare safe for Enlightenment politics during the Exclusion Crisis—the tableau representing *King Lear* depicts 'Edgar in the mad dress with a staff, King Lear, Kent, Cordelia', all together amidst 'Thunder and Lightning' (Garrick, *Plays*, ii. 120), a grouping only possible in the terms of Nahum Tate's version of the play, which was still in use. By now, however, the peak period of adaptation was long over: even Tate's additions to *Lear* were beginning to be replaced by restorations from the original, and one of Garrick's songs is able to celebrate Shakespeare's established supremacy not only to a former rival in both

---

[1] See Garrick, *Ode*, 'Advertisement', 19–35.

the Renaissance and Restoration repertories but to two of his most distinguished Restoration adaptors, and even to a modern playwright whose comedies his own had helped to supplant in the days of the Ladies' Club:

Old Ben, Thomas Otway, John Dryden,
And half a score more, we take pride in,
Of famous Will Congreve we boast too the skill,
But the Will of all Wills was a Warwickshire Will . . .
                                                        (108)

The Ladies' own contributions to Shakespeare's canonization were recorded in Garrick's oration (see above, Chapter 4), and indeed the work of Elizabeth Montagu, one blue-stockinged successor, takes pride of place in the printed introduction to the Ode, the 'Advertisement', where Garrick recommends that 'those who are not sufficiently established in their dramatic faith' should

peruse a work lately published, called, *An Essay on the Writings and Genius of* SHAKESPEARE, by which they will with much satisfaction be convinced, that *England* may justly boast the honour of producing the greatest dramatic poet in the world.[2]

Shakespeare's continuing appeal for contemporary women is further registered elsewhere in connection with the Jubilee, not only by the voluptuous enthusiasm for *Romeo and Juliet* exhibited by Sukey in *The Jubilee* ('I never let Mr Robin keep me company till I had been moved by that fine piece. Why he cuts Romeo into little stars as fine as fipence', Garrick, *Plays*, ii. 122) but in two remarkable letters written in 1769 by an eloquent heir of Shakespeare's Ladies:

I am not going to write a panegyric on this immortal bard, but I shall forever love and honour his memory, because he is the only poet (that I know of) who has delineated to perfection the character of a *female friend.* . . . Pray, pray, now, good lords of the creation, let us do justice to my favourite heroine: while David and Jonathan, Pylades and Orestes, Damon and Pythias, are so triumphantly held up on your side, let us at least erect one standard of friendship on own, and inscribe it with the names of Celia and Rosalind.

        .   .   .   .

---

[2] See Elizabeth Montagu, *An Essay on the Writings and Genius of Shakespeare* (London, 1769).

DAUGHTERS of Britannia's Isle,
  Of every age, and each degree,
Leave your native plains a while,
  And haste to Shakespeare's Jubilee.
        ·   ·   ·   ·   ·   ·

Ye virgins, pluck the freshest bays,
  Ye matrons, deck his honour'd bier,
Ye mothers, teach your sons his praise,
  Ye widows, drop the silent tear.
        ·   ·   ·   ·   ·   ·

But where, O Muse! can strains be found,
  T'express each virtue, charm, and grace,
With which benignant Shakespeare crown'd
  The female mind, the female face?

Let me restrain my grateful tongue,
  And the exhausted subject quit;
Let Celia's truth remain unsung,
  And Rosalinda's sprightly wit.[3]

In these respects, the Jubilee may appear simply to repeat long-established tropes in Shakespeare's praises—continuing the tradition and fulfilling the prophecies of Ben Jonson's elegy, supplemented with a few incidental accretions courtesy of the Countess of Shaftesbury—and it is undeniably true that certain structures already in place in 1623 which derived from the plays themselves are still shaping conceptions of Shakespeare in 1769 and beyond, however extensive and unanticipated the cultural changes and cultural work which intervene between the publication of the Folio and the staging of the Jubilee. Most importantly, the authorship of Shakespeare's plays (themselves concerned far more centrally than those of his contemporaries with dramatizing the patriarchal family) is still imagined primarily as itself a form of fatherhood, with Shakespeare himself regularly and pervasively identified with the most powerful fathers in his own *œuvre*—whether those who refuse to die (King Hamlet, Julius Caesar), or

---

[3] The correspondence from which these letters are drawn was published anonymously as *The Correspondents, an original novel; in a series of letters* (London, 1775). These observations on Shakespeare (found on pp. 27–8, 175–80) attracted considerable notice, excerpted in *Monthly Review*, 52 (1775), 430–7 and *Gentleman's Magazine*, 45 (1775), 394–5, respectively. Their author has been identified as Mrs Apphia Peach (widow of the Governor of Bombay), her correspondent as George, 1st Baron Lyttleton.

the magician Prospero, able to raise the dead.[4] However, the
specific changes in the status of this paternity negotiated over the
century between the Restoration and the Jubilee—with Shakespeare mutating from the obsolete father-king of *The Enchanted
Island* to the timeless national forefather commemorated in Westminster Abbey—produce by the middle of the eighteenth century
a completely new and unprecedented strain in Shakespearean panegyric, and one which has conditioned all subsequent responses to
Shakespeare's work and mythos. Surviving the fall of the Stuarts
(partly, as we have seen, through the efforts of adaptors who
found it expedient to offer his works as classics able to transcend
mere politics), Shakespeare, in the course of the reformulation of
British national identity which followed the Glorious Revolution,
came to serve as part of the acceptable face of the national past,
and ultimately, suitably moralized, became by the 1760s one of
the symbols of British national identity itself.[5] The fully developed
Bardolatry proclaimed at the Jubilee, declaring Shakespeare the
blest Genius of the Isle, expresses a remarkably enduring version
of cultural nationalism unimaginable in the time of Heminge and
Condell: despite its name's grandiloquent implications to the contrary, today's Royal Shakespeare Company, subsidized by the
state in the interests of maintaining a particular aspect of Britain's
cultural identity, occupies a position worlds away from that of
Shakespeare's own King's Men, a position much more recognizably
based on the cultural work carried out by Garrick and his contemporaries.[6] It is no accident that the adoration of Shakespeare's
'unequalled original talents' should have been adopted so whole-

---

[4] Cf. Garber, *Shakespeare's Ghost Writers*, 124–76.

[5] Cf. the more uninflectedly Marxist formulation of Francis Barker: 'the sign of
the literary greatness of Shakespeare has played a major part in remaking the late
feudal world in the image of the bourgeois settlement that grew up inside it, and
ultimately brought it down' *The Tremulous Private Body: Essays on Subjection*
(London, 1984), 17.

[6] On a purely literal level, the RSC's Stratford headquarters occupies virtually
the same site as Garrick's Jubilee rotunda. It is perhaps worth observing here that
Garrick's willingness to initiate the Shakespearean pilgrimage industry without
having any of Shakespeare's plays performed—the way in which Bardolatry, even
at the moment of its inception, is declared independent of Shakespeare's actual
art—persists to this day in the willingness of so many tourists to visit the key
shrines of Shakespeare's England (principally Anne Hathaway's Cottage and
Shakespeare's Birthplace) without displaying the slightest interest in attending the
theatre: the performance of Shakespeare's plays remains irrelevant to some of the
major functions of his cult.

heartedly within a few years of the Jubilee by the next European country to experience a literate middle-class national movement, Germany (and thereafter by so many other emergent nations— Poland, Hungary, Czechoslovakia).

The celebration of Shakespeare's transcendent originality enacted at the Jubilee thus prefigures the subsequent spread of his cult eastwards through Europe, and its spread westwards is equally determined by the particular phase of nationalist ideology which Garrick's festival registers. If Shakespeare is celebrated as more than an author at the Jubilee, it is at least in part because the Britain of which he is invested as literary deity is becoming more than a nation. Throughout the period of the Seven Years' War and its aftermath, as Britain acquired ever greater colonial dependencies in the East and the Americas, ever larger claims were made for the national poet's art, praised more and more insistently in terms of world exploration and conquest. William Havard's 1757 *Ode to the Memory of* SHAKESPEARE concludes, pointedly, by likening Shakespeare's daring imagination to Columbus, finding out 'Worlds unknown':[7] similarly, a famous passage in Garrick's Jubilee ode develops an analogy between Shakespeare and Alexander the Great (Garrick, *Ode*, 4). One unidentified contemporary poem, preserved in manuscript (with music attributed to William Boyce) in the Bodleian Library, is franker still in its equation of Shakespeare's untrammelled imaginative power with Britain's contemporary aspirations to world dominion. This particular *Ode to Shakespeare* concludes, like *Harlequin Student* (from which the first couplet quoted below is lifted), with a duet for Minerva and Mars:

While Britons bow at Shakespear's shrine
Britannia's sons are sons of mine.
Like him shou'd Britons scorn the Art
That binds in chains the human heart
Like him shou'd still be unconfin'd
And rule the World as he the mind.[8]

---

[7] The text is printed in the *London Chronicle, or Universal Evening Post* (9 Apr. 1757).

[8] *Ode to Shakespeare*, in Bodleian Library MS Mus d 14. It is interesting in this connection that *The Tempest* is illustrated in *The Jubilee*'s grand procession not only by Ariel, Prospero, and Miranda but by 'Caliban with a wooden bottle and 2 Sailors all drunk' (Garrick, *Plays*, ii. 116), just as the frontispiece to the play in Bell's edition (1774) depicts Stephano and Trinculo forcing Caliban to swear allegiance on the bottle—a primal scene of colonialism if ever there was one.

In more assertive vein yet, Maurice Morgann, writing a year after Garrick's retirement, celebrates Shakespeare as the patron spirit of a world empire on which the sun will never set, destined to achieve its rightful goal in the total extinction of the French. In a passage from *An Essay on the Dramatic Character of Falstaff* (a character whose physical resemblances to this period's newly adopted national stereotype, John Bull, are perhaps worthy of comment),[9] Morgann declares of 'this great *Magician*, this daring *practicer of arts inhibited*' that

Aristotle himself . . . would fall prostrate at his feet and acknowledge his supremacy. . . . When the hand of time shall have brushed off his present Editors and Commentators, and when the very name of *Voltaire*, and even the memory of the language in which he has written, shall be no more, the *Apalachian* mountains, the banks of the *Ohio*, and the plains of *Scioto* shall resound with the accents of this Barbarian: In his native tongue he shall roll the genuine passions of nature; nor shall the griefs of *Lear* be alleviated, or the charms and wit of *Rosalind* be abated by time. There is indeed nothing perishable about him.[10]

With Shakespeare thus serving as the sign not only of middle-class cultural nationalism but specifically of British imperialism in America, it is perhaps inevitable that the nation which was coming into being by taking over both, even as Morgann wrote this passage (published within a few months of the Declaration of Independence), should have taken such early steps towards appro-

---

[9] A mediating term between Falstaff and John Bull is supplied by the gluttonous Kitchen in Colman's *Man and Wife*, itself derived from *The Merry Wives of Windsor* (see above, ch. 5). Kitchen, derisively called 'John Bull' by the foppish Marcourt in the course of an argument about Shakespeare (Colman, *Man and Wife* 17), memorably eulogizes the Bard in terms of abundance and consumption: 'Shakespeare, Mr. Marcourt—Shakespeare is the Turtle of Literature. The lean on him may perhaps be worse than the lean of any other meat;—but there is a deal of green fat, which is the most delicious stuff in the world' (19).

[10] Maurice Morgann, *Shakespearian Criticism*, ed. Daniel A. Fineman (Oxford, 1972), 172, 170. This passage was widely reprinted in the national press: see e.g. the condensed extract published in *London Magazine*, 46 (1777), 313–14, as '*A new Character of the celebrated* Shakespeare'. Given the continuing opposition of Shakespeare to all things French which it exemplifies—traditionally placing Shakespeare as exemplar of British liberty against despotic French feudalism—it is hardly surprising that the British Shakespeare 'industry' should have been thrown into such a ferment in the years following the French Revolution, the familiar antithesis redefined, in the writings of Burke and Malone at least, to contrast Shakespeare as representative of British constitutional conservatism against the excessive liberty of revolutionary France. Cf. De Grazia, *Shakespeare Verbatim*, 6–8.

priating the Bard in the interests of its own national and imperial project. The United States' first ambassadors to England, Thomas Jefferson and John Adams, went so far as to retrace the Jubilee's pilgrimage to the banks of the Avon in 1786, specifically to declare Stratford utterly transcended.

There is nothing preserved of this great genius which is worth knowing; nothing which might inform us what education, what company, what accident turned his mind to the drama. His name is not even on his gravestone. An ill-sculptured head is set up by his wife, by the side of his grave in the church. But paintings and sculpture would be thrown away upon his fame. His wit, his fancy, his taste and judgment, his knowledge of nature, of life and character, are immortal.[11]

Adams's comments here suggest both that the English are no longer worthy to be the custodians of Shakespeare's fame (already implicit in his first few sentences are all the 'improvements' the American tourist industry has prompted in Stratford since, from the 'World of Shakespeare' waxworks display to the mock-Tudor Macdonald's on Waterside) and that the timeless truth to nature of the Bard's genius renders his original native context irrelevant anyway. Declared universal at the Jubilee, albeit in the service of English nationalism, Shakespeare is ripe for appropriations which deny that his relation not just to Stratford but to England itself is of any interest: disparaging Shakespeare's former Warwickshire home, Adams is preparing the ground for the removal of an Americanized Bard to the United States. A year later, indeed, the Philadelphian poet Peter Markoe would publish a poem which enacts an American Jubilee, rewriting Garrick's *Ode* to claim at its conclusion that only the free citizens of the United States are worthy to canonize the world-conquering, emigrating Shakespeare:

Ye Patriots! for the poet's honour'd brow
The festive wreath, the laurel crown prepare,
   Which only you can well bestow,
   And only he deserves to wear.
Monopolizing Britain! boast no more
His genius to your narrow bounds confin'd;
Shakspeare's bold spirit seeks our western shore,

[11] John Adams, *The Works of John Adams, Second President of the United States* [1851] (6 vols.; repr. New York, 1971), iii. 393: cited in Michael Bristol, *Shakespeare's America, America's Shakespeare* (New York, 1990), 53–4.

A gen'ral blessing for the world design'd,
And, emulous to form the rising age,
The noblest Bard demands the noblest Stage.[12]

In the hands of the American Shakespeare industry which this poem inaugurates, the connections established in the 1750s and 1760s between Bardolatry and imperialism have been faithfully maintained, especially since the United States' twentieth-century accession to the status of a major world power. An American history of Shakespeare's reputation, published by Louis Marder in preparation for the tercentenary celebrations of 1964—just as America's aspirations to extend its dominion beyond the globe (if not entirely beyond the Globe) were being put into motion—concludes, not unlike Morgann's paean, by hailing the Bard once more as the legitimizing spirit of Anglophone empire-building.

On this planet at least the reputation of Shakespeare is secure. When life is discovered elsewhere in the universe and some interplanetary traveler brings to this new world the fruits of our terrestrial culture, who can imagine anything but that among the first books carried to the curious strangers will be a Bible and the works of William Shakespeare.[13]

If the Shakespeare cult has thus survived, on both sides of the Atlantic, since the eighteenth century, in substantially recognizable form, it is presumably because some of the major assumptions on which our culture is still based—the patriarchal family, constitutionalism, economic individualism, nationalism, the supremacy of the printing press—have done so likewise, their predominance still ratified by the reproduction of Bardolatry within the national

---

[12] Peter Markoe, 'The Tragic Genius of SHAKSPEARE; AN ODE', in *Miscellaneous Poems* (Philadelphia, 1787), 27. The poem opens with rhetorical questions evidently imitated from Garrick's Jubilee ode. Perhaps inevitably, the Shakespearean tragedy for which it displays most enthusiasm is *Julius Caesar*, read, as in the post-1688 'Whig' acting version, as unambiguously on the side of Brutus against Caesar's would-be royal imperial tyranny.

Given that this American appropriation of an ethereal, universal Shakespeare requires the denial of any important relationship between the Bard and his historical home town, it is less surprising that early 19th-cent. American responses to Shakespeare should have been so dominated by conspiracy theories (such as those of Delia Bacon, and indeed of Colonel Hart, quoted above, 'Introd.') determined to go one stage further by denying any connection whatsoever between the Bard and Mr William Shakespeare of Stratford.

[13] Louis Marder, *His Exits and his Entrances: The Story of Shakespeare's Reputation* (Philadelphia, 1963), 362.

educational systems of Britain and America alike.[14] The fact that these particular and contingent factors are becoming ever more visible to contemporary criticism (notably in a number of recent studies of Shakespeare's reception, of which this book is itself an example)[15] may suggest, however, that this particular matrix is beginning to lose its hold; on the other hand, it may prove that today's more sceptical analyses of the Shakespeare industry will have no more effect on the perceived naturalness of the Bard's exalted status than did the eloquent protest launched by an anonymous writer to the *Public Advertiser* in the aftermath of the Jubilee itself:

SIR,

. . . It has been so long the Fashion, in this Country, to '*gulp down* every *Drop* of this *immortal Man*,' as Roscius has chosen to express himself in one of his Prologues, that even Shakespeare, with all his Merit, is become a public Nuisance in every Company. Every Puppy of an Apprentice and Trull of a Mantua-maker, without the least Judgment of poetical Beauties, is eternally belching out some Quotation from Shakespeare. The great vulgar imitate, in this Respect, the small, and as a *celebrated* Ode expresses it, nothing rings, from Morning to Noon, in your Ears, but *Shakespaire! Shakespaire! Shakespaire!* pronouncing the Name in the *Irish Way*. This general *Prejudice*, for it is impossible to call it *Taste*, has encouraged every *little Pretender* to Literary Fame, to endeavour to send down the *Stream* of Shakespeare, his own *dirty*, *crazy* Bark, by writing Criticisms, and ecchoing, in childish Commentaries, the public Applause. The press, as well as Conversation, labours under the Weight of a Subject, rendered unsufferably Dull by injudicious Repetition. After all this general (one perhaps might call it, universal) Applause, ninety [*sic*] Parts out of twenty of Shakespeare's Works might, without any Injury to Genius or Poetry, be thrown on Mr. Voltaire's *Fumier*, to manure the sterile Heads of many of the Poet's foolish Admirers and dull Commentators.

Your's, &c.

An IMPARTIAL READER.[16]

Today, even the claim to 'impartiality' on this subject—the possibility of distinguishing between any supposedly essential 'Merit' in

---

[14] On the contemporary survival of Bardolatry, esp. in the academy, see Howard Felperin, 'Bardolatry Then and Now', in Marsden (ed.), *The Appropriation of Shakespeare*.

[15] See also Robert Weimann, 'Shakespeare (De)Canonized: Conflicting Uses of "Authority" and "Representation"', *New Literary History*, 20 (1988), 65–81.

[16] *Public Advertiser* (31 Jan. 1777).

Shakespeare's plays and the 'general Prejudice' in their favour on which our culture has premissed itself for over two centuries—would be impossible to sustain: the fashion of gulping down every drop of Shakespeare (with or without any reservations about the cultural filtration mechanisms by which it has reached us) is too deeply ingrained in dull commentators and foolish admirers alike —not least the sender down the stream of Shakespeare of this latest 'dirty, crazy bark'.

Bibliography

Note: Eighteenth-century editions of Shakespeare are listed under the names of their editors.

A.B. (comp)., *Covent Garden Drollery* [1672], ed. Montague Summers (London, 1927).

ADAMS, JOSEPH QUINCY, *The Dramatic Records of Sir Henry Herbert, Master of the Revels, 1623–1673* (New Haven, Conn., 1917).

The Adventurer (London, 1753–4).

AKENSIDE, MARK, *The Poetical Works of Mark Akenside* (2 vols.; Edinburgh, 1781).

ANDERSON, BENEDICT, *Imagined Communities: Reflections on the Origin and Spread of Nationalism* (London, 1983).

Anti-Midas: A jubilee preservative from unclassical, ignorant, false and invidious criticism (London, 1769).

AVERY, EMMETT L., 'The Shakespeare Ladies Club', *Shakespeare Quarterly*, 7 (Spring, 1958), 153–8.

—— et al., *The London Stage, 1660–1800* (5 pts. in 11 vols.; Carbondale, Ill., 1960–8).

BABCOCK, ROBERT WITBECK, *The Genesis of Shakespeare Idolatry, 1766–1799* (Chapel Hill, NC, 1931).

BACON, JOHN, *Drawing: design for a memorial to David Garrick*, c.1780 (MS Harvard Theatre Collection; pf MS Thr. 95).

BARKER, FRANCIS, *The Tremulous Private Body: Essays on Subjection* (London, 1984).

BATE, JONATHAN, *Shakespearean Constitutions: Politics, Theatre, Criticism, 1730–1830* (Oxford, 1989).

BATZER, HAZEL M., 'Shakespeare's Influence on Thomas Otway's *Caius Marius*', *Revue de l'Université d'Ottawa*, 39 (Oct–Dec. 1969), 533–61.

[BAYLE, PIERRE, et al.], *A General Dictionary, Historical and Critical* (10 vols., London, 1734–41).

BEAUMONT, FRANCIS, and FLETCHER, JOHN, *Comedies and Tragedies* (London, 1647).

'BEDLOE, WILLIAM', *The Excommunicated Prince, or, The False Relique: Being the Popish Plot in a Play. As it was Acted by His Holiness's Servants. By Capt. Bedloe* (London, 1679).

BEHN, APHRA, *Works*, ed. Montague Summers (6 vols.; [1915]; New York, 1967).

BELL, JOHN (publ.), *Bell's Edition of Shakespeare's Plays, as they are now performed at the Theatres Royal in London; Regulated from the Prompt Books of each House by Permission; with Notes Critical and Illustrative; by the Authors of the Dramatic Censor* [ed. Francis Gentleman] (8 vols.; London, 1774).

BELSEY, CATHERINE, *The Subject of Tragedy: Identity and Difference in Renaissance Drama* (London, 1985).

BETTERTON, THOMAS, *King Henry IV, With the Humours of Sir John Falstaff* (London, 1700).

—— *The sequel of Henry the Fourth: With the Humours of Sir John Falstaffe, and Justice Shallow* (London [1723]).

BICKHAM, GEORGE, *The Beauties of Stow* (London, 1750).

BINNS, J. W., 'Some Lectures on Shakespeare in Eighteenth-Century Oxford: The *Praelectiones poeticae* of William Hawkins', in Bernhard Fabian and Kurt Tetzeli von Rosador (eds.), *Shakespeare: Text, Language, Criticism. Essays in Honour of Marvin Spevack* (Hildesheim, 1987), 19–33.

BOWDLER, THOMAS (ed.), *The Family Shakespeare* (London, 1807).

BOYD, ELIZABETH, *Don Sancho: or, The student's whim, a ballad opera of two acts, with Minerva's triumph, a masque* (London, 1739).

—— *The Female Page* (London, 1737).

—— *The Happy-Unfortunate* (London, 1732).

BOYLE, ROGER, 1ST EARL OF ORRERY, *The History of Henry the Fifth. And the Tragedy of Mustapha* (London, 1668).

BOYSE, SAMUEL, *The Triumphs of Nature, a Poem* [1742], in *The Works of the English Poets, from Chaucer to Cowper* (21 vols.; London, 1810), xiv, 534–8.

BREWER, JOHN, MCKENDRICK, NEIL, and PLUMB, J. H., *The Birth of a Consumer Society: The Commercialization of Eighteenth Century England* (Bloomington, Ind., 1982).

BRISTOL, MICHAEL, *Shakespeare's America, America's Shakespeare* (New York, 1990).

BROOKE-HUNT, VIOLET, *The Story of Westminster Abbey* (London, 1902).

BROOKS-DAVIES, DOUGLAS, *Fielding, Dickens, Gosse, Iris Murdoch and Oedipal Hamlet* (New York, 1989).

BROWN, FRANK C., *Elkanah Settle: His Life and Works* (Chicago, 1910).

BROWN, LAURA, 'The Defenceless Woman and the Development of English Tragedy', *Studies in English Literature 1500–1900*, 22 (1982), 429–43.

—— *English Dramatic Form, 1660–1760: An Essay in Generic History* (New Haven, Conn., 1981).

BROWNELL, MORRIS R., *Alexander Pope and the Arts of Georgian England* (Oxford, 1978).

BULLOCK, CHRISTOPHER, *The Cobler of Preston. And the Adventures of Half an Hour* (4th edn.; London, 1723).

BURLING, WILLIAM J., 'Summer Theatre in London, 1661–1694', *Theatre Notebook*, 47 (1988), 14–22.

BURNABY, WILLIAM, *Love Betray'd; or, The Agreeable Disappointment* (London, 1703).

BURNIM, KALMAN A., 'Looking on His Like Again: Garrick and the Visual Arts', in Shirley Strum Kenny (ed.), *The British Theatre and the Other Arts, 1660–1800* (London, 1986).

—— *David Garrick, Director* (Pittsburgh, 1961).

BUTT, JOHN, *Pope's Taste in Shakespeare* (London, 1936).

BYSSHE, EDWARD, *The Art of English Poetry* (London, 1702).

CAIRNS, EDWARD A., *A Critical Edition of Charles Gildon's Measure for Measure, or Beauty the Best Advocate* (New York, 1987).

CANFIELD, DOUGLAS, 'Royalism's Last Dramatic Stand: English Political Tragedy, 1679–89', *Studies in Philology*, 82 (1985), 234–63.

CAPELL, EDWARD (ed.), *Mr. William Shakespeare his Comedies, Histories, and Tragedies* (10 vols.; London, 1768).

CARE, HENRY, *The New Anti-Roman Pacquet; or, Memoirs of Popes and Popery since the Tenth Century* (London, 1680).

—— *The Popes Harbinger, By way of Diversion* (London, 1680).

—— *The Popish Courant, or, Some occasional Jaco-serious Reflections on Romish Fopperies* (London, 1678–83).

—— The *Weekly Pacquet of Advice from Rome: or, the History of Popery* (London, 1678–83).

[CARYLL, JOHN], *The English Princes, or, the Death of Richard the III* (London, 1667).

CASANAVE, DON SHELDON, 'Shakespeare's *The Tempest* in a Restoration Context: A study of Dryden's *The Enchanted Island*', Ph.D. thesis, University of Michigan, 1972.

CAVENDISH, MARGARET, *CCXI Sociable Letters, written by the Thrice Noble, Illustrious, and Excellent Princess, The Lady Marchioness of Newcastle* (London, 1664).

CHARKE, CHARLOTTE, *A Narrative of the Life of Mrs. Charlotte Charke, (youngest daughter of Colley Cibbler [sic], Esq.). Written by herself* (2nd edn., London, 1755).

CHARLESTON, R. J. (ed.), *English Porcelain, 1745–1850* (London, 1965).

CIBBER, COLLEY, *Papal Tyranny in the Reign of King John* (London, 1745).

CIBBER, COLLEY, *The Tragical History of King Richard III* [1700], repr. in Christopher Spencer (ed.), *Five Restoration Adaptations of Shakespeare* (Urbana, Ill., 1965).

CIBBER, THEOPHILUS, *An Historical Tragedy of the Civil Wars in the Reign of King Henry VI* (London [1723]).

—— *Romeo and Juliet, a Tragedy, Revis'd and Alter'd from Shakespear* (London, [1748]).

—— *Two Dissertations on Theatrical Subjects* (London, 1756).

CLARKE, GEORGE, 'Grecian Taste and Gothic Virtue: Lord Cobham's Gardening Programme and its Iconography', *Apollo*, 97 (1973), 566–71.

A Collection and Selection of English Prologues and Epilogues (4 vols., London 1779).

COLLEY, LINDA, 'The English Rococo: Historical Background', in Michael Snodin (ed.), *Rococo: Art and Design in Hogarth's England* (London, 1984), 9–17.

COLLIER, JEREMY, *A Short View of the Immorality and Profaneness of the English Stage* (London, 1698).

COLMAN, GEORGE, THE ELDER, *A Fairy Tale* (London, 1763).

—— *Man and Wife: or, The Shakespeare Jubilee* (London, 1770).

—— *The Sheep-Shearing: A Dramatic Pastoral* (London, 1777).

A Comparison Between the Two Stages (London, 1702).

CONGREVE, WILLIAM, *Amendments of Mr. Collier's False and Imperfect Citations* (London, 1698).

CONRAD, PETER, *Shandyism: The Character of Romantic Irony* (Oxford, 1978).

COOKE, THOMAS, *A Demonstration of the Will of God by the Light of Nature* (London, 1742).

—— *An Epistle to the Right Honourable the Countess of Shaftesbury, with a Prologue and Epilogue on Shakespeare and his Writings* (London, 1743).

—— *The Mournful Nuptials* (London, 1739).

The Correspondents, an original novel; in a series of letters (London, 1775).

Covent Garden Journal (London, 1752).

COWLEY, ABRAHAM, *Cutter of Coleman Street* [1663], ed. Darlene Johnson Gravett (New York, 1987).

COWPER, MARY, 'On the Revival of Shakespear's Plays by the Ladies in 1738', in *The Cowper Family Miscellany* (British Library: BM Add. MSS 28101), 93^v–94^v.

Craftsman (London, 1727–50).

Critical Review (London, 1756–90).

CROWNE, JOHN, *Henry the Sixth, The First Part. With the Murder of Humphrey Duke of Glocester* (London, 1681).

—— *The Misery of Civil-War* (London, 1680).

CUMBERLAND, RICHARD. *The Plays of Richard Cumberland*, ed. Roberta S. Borkat (6 vols.; New York, 1982).

Daily Advertiser (London, 1730–1809).

Daily Journal (London, 1720–37).

DAVENANT, SIR WILLIAM, *The Works of Sr William D'avenant Kt: Consisting of Those which were formerly Printed, and Those which he design'd for the Press: Now Published Out of the Authors Originall Copies* (London, 1673).

—— *Macbeth, a Tragedy: With all the alterations, amendments, additions and new songs* (London, 1674). (See also Christopher Spencer (ed.), *Davenant's Macbeth*).

—— *The Prologue to His Majesty at the First Play Presented at the Cockpit in Whitehall; Being Part of That Noble Entertainment Which Their Majesties Received Novemb. 19. from His Grace the Duke of Albemarle* (London, 1660).

—— *The Rivals* (London, 1668).

—— [ed.] *The Tragedy of Hamlet, Prince of Denmark. As it is now Acted at his Highness the Duke of York's Theatre. By William Shakespeare* (London, 1676).

DAVENANT, SIR WILLIAM, and DRYDEN, JOHN, *The Tempest, or the Enchanted Island* (London, 1670).

DAVENANT, SIR WILLIAM, and DRYDEN, JOHN, [and THOMAS SHADWELL], *The Tempest, or the Enchanted Island* (London, 1674).

'DAVENANT, SIR WILLIAM, and DRYDEN JOHN', *The tragedy of Julius Caesar: with the death of Brutus and Cassius. Written originaly by Shakespear, and since alter'd by Sir William Davenant and John Dryden, late Poets Laureat* (London, 1719).

David Garrick: The Original Drawings and Manuscript Notes Made of the Ceremony of his Lying In State and Subsequent Interment in Westminster Abbey 1779 (MS. Harvard Theatre Collection).

DAVIES, THOMAS, *Dramatic Miscellanies* (3 vols.; Dublin, 1784).

—— *Memoirs of the Life of David Garrick, Esq.* (2 vols.; London, 1780).

DAWSON, GILES, 'The Copyright of Shakespeare's Dramatic Works', in Charles T. Prouty (ed.), *Studies in Honor of A.H.R. Fairchild* (Columbia, Mo., 1956).

DEELMAN, CHRISTIAN, *The Great Shakespeare Jubilee* (London, 1964).

DE GRAZIA, MARGRETA, 'Shakespeare in Quotation Marks', in Jean Marsden (ed.), *The Appropriation of Shakespeare: Post-Renaissance Reconstructions of the Works and the Myth* (Hemel Hempstead, 1991), 57–71.

—— *Shakespeare Verbatim: The Reproduction of Authenticity and the 1790 Apparatus* (Oxford, 1991).

DENNIS, JOHN, *The Comical Gallant: or the Amours of Sir John Falstaffe* (London, 1702).

—— *The Critical Works of John Dennis*, ed. Edward Niles Hooker (2 vols.; Baltimore, 1939).

—— *The Invader of his Country, or the Fatal Resentment* (London, 1720).

—— *The Usefulness of the Stage, to the Happiness of Mankind, to Government, and to Religion. Occasioned by a late Book, written by Jeremy Collier, M.A.* (London, 1698).

DOBSON, MICHAEL, 'Authorizing Shakespeare: Adaptation and Canonization, 1660–1769', D.Phil. thesis (Oxford, 1989).

—— 'Accents yet Unknown: Canonization and the Claiming of *Julius Caesar*', in Jean Marsden (ed.), *The Appropriation of Shakespeare: Post-Renaissance Reconstructions of the Works and the Myth* (Hemel Hempstead, 1991).

—— (ed.), *Adaptations and Acting Versions, 1660–1980*, Unit 22 of the *Bibliotheca Shakespeariana* Microfiche Collection, general ed. Philip Brockbank (Oxford 1987; republished as *Shakespeariana*, Ann Arbor, Mich., 1990).

—— 'Remember | First to possess his books: the appropriation of *The Tempest*, 1700–1800', *Shakespeare Survey*, 43 (1991), 99–108.

DODD, WILLIAM (ed.), *The Beauties of Shakespeare, Regularly Selected* (London, 1752).

DODSLEY, ROBERT, *Beauty: or the Art of Charming* (London, 1735).

DOODY, MARGARET ANNE, 'Shakespeare's Novels: Charlotte Lennox Illustrated', *Studies in the Novel*, 19 (Autumn 1987), 296–310.

DOWNES, JOHN, *Roscius Anglicanus* [1708], ed. Judith Milhous and Robert D. Hume (London, 1987).

DRYDEN, JOHN, *Of Dramatic Poesie, an Essay* (London, 1668).

—— *Troilus and Cressida, or, Truth Found Too Late* (London, 1679).

DUFFETT, THOMAS, *Three Burlesque Plays of Thomas Duffett*, ed. R. E. Di Lorenzo (Iowa City, 1972).

DURFEY, THOMAS, *The Comical History of Don Quixote* (3 vols.; London, 1694–6).

—— *A Commonwealth of Women* (London, 1686).

—— *A Fond Husband; or, The Plotting Sisters* (London, 1677).

—— *The Fool Turned Critick* (London, 1678).

—— *The Injured Princess, or the Fatal Wager* (London, 1682).

—— *Love for Money; or, The Boarding School* (London, 1691).

—— *Madame Fickle; or, The Witty False One* (London, 1677)

—— *New Operas, with Comical Stories and Poems* (London, 1721).

—— *The Siege of Memphis; or, The Ambitious Queen* (London, 1676).

—— *Sir Barnaby Whigg; or, No Wit Like a Woman's* (London, 1681).

—— *Trick for Trick; or, The Debauched Hypocrite* (London, 1678).

EDWARDS, PHILIP, 'The Danger not the Death: The Art of John Fletcher', in John Russell Brown and Bernard Harris (eds.), *Jacobean Theatre*, Stratford-upon-Avon Studies, 1 (London, 1960), 159–77.

EMSLIE, MACDONALD, 'The Pepys–Morelli "To be, or not to be"', *Shakespeare Quarterly*, 6 (1955), 159–70.

ENGLAND, MARTHA W., *Garrick and Stratford* (New York, 1962).

—— *Garrick's Jubilee* (Columbus, Oh., 1964).

ETHEREGE, SIR GEORGE, *The Plays of Sir George Etherege*, ed. Michael Cordner (Cambridge, 1982).

EVELYN, JOHN, *The Diary of John Evelyn*, ed. E. S. de Beer (6 vols.; Oxford, 1955).

FARQUHAR, GEORGE, *Dramatic Works*, ed. Shirley Strum Kenny (2 vols.; Oxford, 1988).

FELPERIN, HOWARD, 'Bardolatry Then and Now', in Jean Marsden (ed.), *The Appropriation of Shakespeare: Post-Rennaissance Reconstructions of the Works and the Myth* (Hemel Hempstead, 1991).

The Female Faction: or the Gay Subscribers (London, 1729).

FIELDING, HENRY, *The Works of Henry Fielding, Esq; with the Life of the Author* (2nd edn., 8 vols.; London, 1762).

FILMER, SIR ROBERT, *Patriarcha and Other Political Works*, ed. Peter Laslett (Oxford, 1949).

FISH, STANLEY, *Is There A Text In This Class? The Authority of Interpretive Communities* (Cambridge, Mass., 1980).

FOOT, JESSE, *The Life of Arthur Murphy, Esq.* (London, 1811).

FOUCAULT, MICHEL, 'What is an Author?', in Josue Harari (ed.), *Textual Strategies* (Ithaca, NY, 1979).

FREEHAFER, JOHN, 'The Formation of the London Patent Companies in 1660', *Theatre Notebook*, 20 (1965), 6–30.

FREUD, SIGMUND, *Totem and Taboo: Resemblances Between the Psychic Lives of Savages and Neurotics*, trans. A. A. Brill (London, 1919).

FURNESS, H. H. (ed)., *Much Ado About Nothing*, New Variorum edn. (Philadelphia, 1899).

GARBER, MARJORIE, *Shakespeare's Ghost Writers: Literature as Uncanny Causality* (New York, 1987).

GARRICK, DAVID, *Florizel and Perdita. A Dramatic Pastoral* (London, 1758. Unidentified contemporary promptbook. Harvard Theatre Collection, HTC 401).

—— *The Letters of David Garrick*, ed. David M. Little and George M. Kahrl (3 vols.; Cambridge, Mass., 1963).

—— *An ode upon dedicating a building, and erecting a statue, to Shakespeare, at Stratford upon Avon* (London, 1769).

—— *The Plays of David Garrick*, ed. Harry William Pedicord and Fredrick Lois Bergmann (6 vols.; Carbondale, Ill., 1981).

—— *Songs, Chorusses, &c. which are introduced in the New Entertainment of the Jubilee* (London, 1769).

The General Evening Post (London, 1735–1822).

GENTLEMAN, FRANCIS, *The Dramatic Censor; or, Critical Companion* (2 vols.; London, 1770).

The Gentleman's Magazine (London, 1731–1833).

GERRARD, CHRISTINE, 'The Patriot Opposition to Sir Robert Walpole: A Study of the Politics and Poetry, 1725–42', D.Phil. thesis (Oxford, 1986).

[GIFFARD, HENRY], *Harlequin Student: or the Fall of Pantomime, with the Restoration of the Drama* (London, 1741).

GILDON, CHARLES, *The Complete Art of Poetry* (2 vols.; London, 1718).

—— *Measure for Measure, or Beauty the Best Advocate* (London, 1700).

GOLDGAR, BERTRAND, *Walpole and the Wits* (Lincoln, Nebr., 1976).

GRADY, HUGH, *The Modernist Shakespeare: Critical Texts in a Material World* (Oxford, 1991).

GRANVILLE, GEORGE (LORD LANSDOWNE), *The Genuine Works of George Granville, Lord Lansdowne* (3 vols.; London, 1736).

—— *The Jew of Venice* [1701], in Christopher Spencer, *Five Restoration Adaptations of Shakespeare* (Urbana, Ill., 1965).

GRANVILLE, MARY, *The Autobiography and Correspondence of Mary Granville, Mrs. Delany*, ed. Lady Llanover (3 vols.; London, 1861).

The Gray's Inn Journal (London, 1753–4).

GRIFFITH, ELIZABETH, *The Morality of Shakespeare's Dramas Illustrated* (London, 1775).

GUFFEY, GEORGE R., 'Politics, Weather and the Contemporary Reception of the Dryden–Davenant *Tempest*', *Restoration*, 8 (1984), 1–9.

GUTHRIE, WILLIAM, *An Essay upon English Tragedy. With Remarks upon the Abbe de Blanc's Observations on the English Stage* (London, 1747).

HANDASYDE, ELIZABETH, *Granville the Polite: The Life of George Granville Lord Lansdowne, 1666–1735* (Oxford, 1933).

HANMER, SIR THOMAS (ed.), *The Works of Shakespeare* (6 vols.; Oxford, 1744).

HARBAGE, ALFRED, *Cavalier Drama: An Historical and Critical Supplement to the Study of the Elizabethan and Restoration Stage* (New York, 1936).

HARRIS, TIM, *London Crowds in the Reign of Charles II: Politics and Propaganda from the Restoration until the Exclusion Crisis* (Cambridge, 1987).

HART, JOSEPH C., *The Romance of Yachting* (New York, 1848).

HAWKES, TERENCE, *That Shakespeherian Rag: Essays on a Critical Process* (London, 1986).

HAWKINS, WILLIAM, *Cymbeline. A Tragedy, Altered from Shakespeare* (London, 1759).

—— *Praelectiones Poeticae* (London, 1758).

HAYWOOD, ELIZA, *The Female Spectator* (5th edn., 4 vols.; London, 1755).

HENDERSON, PHILIP (ed.), *Shorter Novels: Seventeenth Century* (New York, 1930).

HIGHFILL, PHILIP H., BURNIM, KALMAN A., and LANGHANS, EDWARD A., *A Biographical Dictionary of Actors, Actresses, Musicians, Dancers, Managers & Other Stage Personnel in London, 1660–1800* (10 vols. to date; Carbondale, Ill., 1973–).

HILL, AARON, *King Henry the Fifth. Or The Conquest of France By the English. A Tragedy* (London, 1723).

HINKS, ROGER, 'Le Bicentenaire de Louis-Francois Roubiliac', *Etudes anglaises* 15 (1962), 1–15.

An Historical Description of Westminster-Abbey, Its Monuments and Curiosities (London, 1754).

HOBBES, THOMAS, *The English Works of Thomas Hobbes of Malmesbury*, ed. Sir William Molesworth (11 vols.; London, 1839–45), (repr. Aalen, Germany, 1962).

HOGAN, CHARLES BEECHER, *Shakespeare in the Theatre: 1701–1800* (2 vols.; Oxford, 1952–7).

HOGARTH, WILLIAM, *Engravings by Hogarth*, ed. Sean Shesgreen (New York, 1973).

HOHENDAHL, PETER UWE, *The Institution of Criticism* (Ithaca, NY, 1982).

HOLDERNESS, GRAHAM (ed.), *The Shakespeare Myth* (Manchester, 1988).

HOTSON, LESLIE, *The Commonwealth and Restoration Stage* (Cambridge, Mass., 1928).

HOWARD, HENRY, *A Visionary Interview at the Shrine of Shakespeare* (London, 1758).

HOWARD, JEAN F., and O'CONNOR, MARION (eds.), *Shakespeare Reproduced: The Text in History and Ideology* (New York, 1987).

HOWARD, SIR ROBERT, *The Committee*, in *Four New Plays* (London, 1665).

HUCKELL, JOHN, *Avon, A Poem in Three Parts* (Birmingham, 1758).

HUGHES, LEO, and SCOUTEN, ARTHUR H. (eds.), *Ten English Farces* (Austin, Tex., 1948).

HUME, ROBERT D., *The Development of English Drama in the Late Seventeenth Century* [1976] (Oxford, 1990).

—— *Dryden's Criticism* (Ithaca, NY, 1970).

HUME, ROBERT D., Securing a Repertory: Plays on the London Stage 1660–5', in Antony Coleman and Antony Hammond (eds.), *Poetry and Drama, 1570–1700: Essays in Honour of Harold F. Brooks* (London, 1981), 156–72.

The Inspector in the Shades. A New Dialogue in the Manner of Lucan (London, 1752).

ISAACS, JACOB, 'Shakespearian Scholarship', in Harley Granville-Barker and G. B. Harrison (eds.), *A Companion to Shakespeare Studies* (Cambridge, 1964), 305–24.

J.C. [JOHN CARRINGTON], *The Modern Receipt: or, A Cure for Love* (London, 1739).

J.D., *The Coronation of Queen Elizabeth, With the Restauration of the Protestant Religion: or the Downfal of the Pope* (London, 1680).

JOHNSON, CHARLES, *The Cobler of Preston* [1716], in Leo Hughes and Arthur H. Sconten (eds.), *Ten English Farces* (Austin, Tex., 1948), 143–69.

—— *Love in a Forest* (London, 1723).

JOHNSON, SAMUEL, *A Dictionary of the English Language* (2 vols.; London, 1755).

—— *Samuel Johnson: The Complete English Poems*, ed. David Fleeman (Harmondsworth, 1971).

—— (ed.), *The Plays of William Shakespeare* (8 vols.; London, 1765).

JONSON, BEN, *Workes* (London, 1616).

—— *Workes. The second volume* (London, 1641).

JOSÉ, NICHOLAS, *Ideas of the Restoration in English Literature, 1660–1671* (Cambridge, Mass., 1984).

JUMP, HARRIET DEVINE, 'Mark Akenside and the Poetry of Current Events, 1738–1770', D.Phil. thesis (Oxford, 1987).

KENRICK, WILLIAM, *Falstaff's Wedding* (London, 1766).

—— *Introduction to the School of Shakespeare* (London, 1774).

KENYON, JOHN, *The Popish Plot* [1972], (Harmondsworth, 1984).

KIRKMAN, FRANCIS (trs.), *The Loves and Adventures of Clerio & Lozia. A Romance* (London, 1652).

—— (ed.), *The Wits: or, Sport upon Sport* (2 pts. London, 1672–3).

KNOWLES, JACK, and ARMISTEAD, J. M., 'Thomas D'Urfey and Three Centuries of Critical Response', *Restoration*, 8: 2 (1984), 72–80.

KRAMNICK, ISAAC, *Bolingbroke and his Circle: The Politics of Nostalgia in the Age of Walpole* (Cambridge, Mass., 1968).

LACY, JOHN, *Sauny the Scott: or, The Taming of the Shrew* (London, 1698).

LAMB, CHARLES [and MARY], *Tales from Shakespear. Designed for the use of young persons* (2 vols.; London, 1807).

LAMPE, JOHN FREDERICK, *Pyramus and Thisbe: a mock opera* (London, 1745).

LANGBAINE, GERARD, *An Account of the English Dramatick Poets* (Oxford, 1691).

—— *Momus Triumphans: or, the Plagiaries of the English Stage* (London, 1688).

LAQUEUR, THOMAS, *Making Sex: Body and Gender from the Greeks to Freud* (Cambridge, Mass., 1990).

LEE, NATHANIEL, *The Works of Nathaniel Lee*, ed. Thomas B. Stroup and Arthur L. Cooke (2 vols.; New Brunswick, 1954–5).

LENNOX, CHARLOTTE, *Shakespear Illustrated: or the Novels and Histories, On Which the Plays of Shakespear are Founded, Collected and Translated from the Original Authors* (London, 1753).

LEVERIDGE, RICHARD, *Pyramus and Thisbe. A Comic Masque* (London, 1716).

LICHTENBERG, GEORG CHRISTIAN, *Lichtenberg's Visits to England, As Described in His Letters and Diaries*, tr. and ed. Margaret L. Mare and William H. Quarrell (Oxford, 1938).

LILLO, GEORGE, *The Plays of George Lillo*, ed. Trudy Drucker (2 vols.; New York, 1979).

Lloyd's Evening Post (London, 1757–1805).

LOCKE, JOHN, *Two Treatises of Government*, ed. Peter Laslett (2nd edn., Cambridge, 1967).

LOFTIS, JOHN, *The Politics of Drama in Augustan England* (Oxford, 1963).

London Chronicle, or Universal Evening Post (London, 1757–1823).

London Daily-Post and General Advertiser (London, 1736–86).

London Evening Post (London, 1727–1806).

London Magazine; or, Gentleman's Monthly Intelligencer (London, 1732–85).

McGUGAN, RUTH, *Nahum Tate and the Coriolanus Tradition in English Drama, With a Critical Edition of Tate's The Ingratitude of a Commonwealth* (New York, 1987).

MAGUIRE, NANCY KLEIN, 'Nahum Tate's *King Lear*: "The King's blest restoration"', in Jean Marsden (ed.), *The Appropriation of Shakespeare: Post-Rennaissance Reconstructions of the Works and the Myth* (Hemel Hempstead, 1991).

MARDER, LOUIS, *His Exits and His Entrances: The Story of Shakespeare's Reputation* (Philadelphia, 1963).

MARKOE, PETER, *Miscellaneous Poems* (Philadelphia, 1787).

MARSDEN, JEAN (ed.), *The Appropriation of Shakespeare: Post-Renaissance Reconstructions of the Works and the Myth* (Hemel Hempstead, 1991).

—— 'Pathos and Passivity: Thomas D'Urfey's Adaptation of Shakespeare's *Cymbeline*', *Restoration*, 14: 2 (1990), 71–81.

—— 'Rewritten Women: Shakespearean Heroines in the Restoration', in (ed.), *The Appropriation of Shakespeare*, 43–56.

—— 'The Re-Imagined Text: Shakespeare, Adaptation and Theory in the Eighteenth Century', Ph.D. thesis (Harvard, 1986).

MARSH, CHARLES, *The Winter's Tale, a play alter'd from Shakespear* (London, 1756).

MAUS, KATHARINE EISAMAN, 'Arcadia Lost: Politics and Revision in the Restoration *Tempest*', *Renaissance Drama*, NS 13 (1982), 189–209.

—— '"Playhouse Flesh and Blood": Sexual Ideology and the Restoration Actress', *English Literary History*, 46 (1979), 595–617.

Memoirs of the Shakespear's-Head in Covent-Garden. By the Ghost of Shakespear (2 vols.; London, 1755).

The Merry conceited Humors of Bottom the Weaver (London, 1661).

Middlesex Journal; or, Chronicle of Liberty (London, 1769–76).

MILLER, JAMES, *Of Politeness. An Epistle to the Right Honourable William Stanhope, Lord Harrington* (London, 1738).

The Universal Passion (London, 1737).

MILTON, JOHN, *The Complete Poems*, ed. B. A. Wright and Gordon Campbell (London, 1980).

MOLLOY, CHARLES, *The Half-Pay Officers* (London, 1720).

MONTAGU, ELIZABETH, An *Essay on the Writings and Genius of Shakespeare* (London, 1769).

Monthly Review (London, 1749–89).

MOORE, LEWIS D., 'For King and Country: John Dryden's *Troilus and Cressida*', *College Language Association Journal*, 26 (1982), 98–111.

MORGAN, MACNAMARA, *A Letter to Miss Nossiter Occasioned by her First Appearing on the Stage, in Which Is Contained Remarks on Her Playing the Character of Juliet* (London, 1753).

—— *The Sheep-Shearing: or, Florizel and Perdita. A Pastoral Comedy* (London, 1762).

MORGANN, MAURICE, *Shakespearian Criticism*, ed. Daniel A. Fineman (Oxford, 1972).

MURPHY, ARTHUR, *The Life of David Garrick* (2 vols.; London, 1801).

NEVILLE, HENRY, *The Isle of Pines, or, A Late Discovery of a Forth Island near Terra Australis, Incognita* [1688], in *Shorter Novels: Seventeenth Century*, ed. Philip Henderson (New York, 1930).

A New Miscellany for the Year 1739 (London, 1740).

NEWMAN, GERALD, *The Rise of English Nationalism: A Cultural History, 1740–1830* (New York, 1987).

N.H., *The Ladies Dictionary; being a general entertainment for the fair-sex* (London, 1694).

NOVY, MARIANNE (ed.), *Women's Re-Visions of Shakespeare* (Urbana, Ill., 1990).

OATES, TITUS, *A tragedy, called the Popish Plot, reviv'd* (London, 1696).

—— A True Narrative of the Horrid Plot and Conspiracy of the Popish Party Against the Life of His Sacred Majesty, The Government and the Protestant Religion (London, 1679).

Ode to Shakespeare. Bodleian Library MS Mus. d.14.

ODELL, GEORGE C. D., Shakespeare from Betterton to Irving (2 vols.; New York, 1920–1).

ODUARAN, AKPOFURE, 'The first "collected edition" of Shakespeare: A Study of Nicholas Rowe's edition of 1709', Ph.D. thesis (University of New Brunswick, 1985).

ORGEL, STEPHEN, 'The Authentic Shakespeare', Representations, 21 (Winter, 1988), 1–25.

—— 'Prospero's Wife', in Margaret Ferguson, Maureen Quilligan, and Nancy Vickers (eds.), Rewriting the Renaissance (Chicago, 1986), 50–64.

OTWAY, THOMAS, The Works of Thomas Otway: Plays, Poems and Love Letters, ed. J. C. Ghosh (2 vols.; Oxford, 1932).

—— The History and Fall of Caius Marius (London, 1680).

PARKER, G. F., Johnson's Shakespeare (Oxford, 1989).

PATEMAN, CAROLE, The Sexual Contract (Stanford, Calif. 1988).

PEPYS, SAMUEL, Diary, ed. Robert Latham and William Matthews (11 vols.; Berkeley, Calif., 1970–6).

PERRY, RUTH, The Celebrated Mary Astell (Chicago, 1986).

'PERSON OF QUALITY, A.', Cromwell's Conspiracy. A Tragy-Comedy, Relating to our latter Times. Beginning at the Death of King Charles the First, And ending with the happy Restauration of King Charles the Second (London, 1660).

PHILIPS, AMBROSE, Humfrey Duke of Gloucester, a Tragedy (London, 1723).

PIPER, DAVID, The Image of the Poet: British Poets and their Portraits (Oxford, 1982).

POEL, WILLIAM, The Stage-Versions of Romeo and Juliet (London, 1915).

Poeta Infamis: or, a Poet not worth Hanging (London, 1692).

A Poetical epistle from Florizel to Perdita: with Perdita's answer. And a preliminary discourse upon the education of princes (London, 1781).

A Poetical Epistle from Shakespear in Elysium to Mr Garrick at Drury-Lane Theatre (London, 1752).

POPE, ALEXANDER, The Twickenham Edition of the Poems of Alexander Pope, ed. John Butt, et al. (6 vols. in 7; London, 1954–61).

—— (ed.), The Works of Shakespeare, Collated and Corrected (6 vols.; London, 1723–25).

—— (ed.) [and George Sewell], The Works of Shakespeare, Collated and Corrected (7 vols.; London, 1725).

The Pope's Down-fall at Abergaveny (London, 1679).

POTTER, LOIS, *Secret Rites and Secret Writing: Royalist Literature, 1641–1660* (Cambridge, 1989).

POWELL, JOCELYN, *Restoration Theatre Production* (London, 1984).

PRATT, SAMUEL JACKSON, *Miscellanies* (4 vols.; London, 1785).

Public Advertiser (London, 1752–94).

RADDADI, MONGI, *Davenant's Adaptations of Shakespeare* (Uppsala, 1979).

RALPH, JAMES, *A Critical Review of the Public Buildings, Statues and Ornaments In, and about London and Westminster* (London, 1734).

RAVENSCROFT, EDWARD, *Titus Andronicus, or the Rape of Lavinia* (London, 1687).

RICHARDSON, SAMUEL, *The Apprentice's Vade Mecum; or, Young Man's Pocket Companion* (London, 1733).

—— *Clarissa, or The History of a Young Lady* [1748], ed. Angus Ross (Harmondsworth, 1985).

—— *Pamela, or, Virtue Rewarded* [1741–2], (4 vols.; Stratford-upon-Avon, 1929).

—— *Sir Charles Grandison* [1753–4], ed. Jocelyn Harris (Oxford, 1972; 3 pts. in 1, 1986).

RIPLEY, JOHN, *Julius Caesar on stage in England and America, 1599–1973* (Cambridge, 1980).

ROACH, J. R., 'Garrick, the Ghost, and the Machine', *Theatre Journal*, 34 (1982), 431–40.

ROCHESTER, JOHN WILMOT, EARL OF, *Complete Poems*, ed. David M. Vieth (New Haven, Conn., 1968).

Rome's Follies: or, the Amorous Fryers (London, 1681).

ROSE, MARK, 'The Author as Proprietor: *Donaldson* v. *Becket* and the Genealogy of Modern Authorship', *Representations*, 23 (1988).

ROSENFELD, SYBIL, *Foreign Theatrical Companies in Great Britain in the Seventeenth and Eighteenth Centuries* (London, 1955).

—— *The Theatre of the London Fairs in the Eighteenth Century* (Cambridge, 1960).

ROSENTHAL, LAURA J., '(Re)Writing *Lear*: Literary Property and Dramatic Authorship', in John Brewer and Susan Staves (eds.), *Early Modern Conceptions of Property* (London, forthcoming).

—— 'Shakespearean Adaptation and the Genealogy of Authorship', Ph.D. thesis (Northwestern University, 1990).

ROTHSTEIN, ERIC, and KAVENIK, FRANCES M., *The Designs of Carolean Comedy* (Carbondale, Ill., 1988).

ROWE, NICHOLAS, *The Tragedy of Jane Shore* [1714], ed. Harry William Pedicord (Lincoln, Nebr., 1975).

—— (ed.), *The Works of Mr. William Shakespear* (6 vols.; London, 1709).

—— (ed.), [and Charles Gildon], *The Works of Mr. William Shakespeare* (7 vols.; London, '1709' [1710]).

RYSKAB, CHARLES, *William Cowper of the Inner Temple, Esq.* (Cambridge, 1959).

St. James's Chronicle; or, British Evening Post (London, 1761–).

St. James's Magazine (London, 1762–4, 1774).

SAINT JOHN, HENRY, VISCOUNT BOLINGBROKE, *Letters, on the Spirit of Patriotism: on the Idea of a Patriot King: and on the State of Parties at the Accession of King George the First* (London, 1749).

SCHOENBAUM, SAMUEL, *Shakespeare's Lives* (Oxford, 1970).

—— *William Shakespeare: A Documentary Life* (Oxford, 1975).

SCOUTEN, ARTHUR H., 'The Increase in Popularity of Shakespeare's Plays in the Eighteenth Century: A *Caveat* for Interpreters of Stage History', *Shakespeare Quarterly*, 7 (1956), 189–202.

A Seasonable Rebuke to the Playhouse Rioters (London, 1741).

SEATON, ETHEL, *Literary Relations of England and Scandinavia in the Seventeenth Century* (Oxford, 1935).

SETTLE, ELKANAH, *The Female Prelate: being the history of the life and death of Pope Joan* (London, 1680).

—— *The Heir of Morocco; With the Death of Gayland* (London, 1682).

—— *The Fairy-Queen: an Opera* (London, 1692).

SEWARD, THOMAS (ed.), *The Works of Francis Beaumont and John Fletcher* (10 vols.; London, 1750).

SHADWELL, THOMAS, *The History of Timon of Athens, the Man-Hater* (London, 1678).

—— *The Lancashire Witches* (London, 1681).

SHAKESPEARE, WILLIAM. *The First Folio of Shakespeare: The Norton Facsimile*, ed. Charlton Hinman (New York, 1968).

—— *Comedies, Histories and Tragedies* [Second Folio] (London, 1632).

—— *Comedies, Histories and Tragedies* [Third Folio] (London, 1663–4).

—— *Comedies, Histories and Tragedies* [Fourth Folio], (London, 1685).

—— *The Complete Oxford Shakespeare*, Modern spelling edition (ed.) Stanley Wells and Gary Taylor (Oxford, 1986).

—— *Poems on several occasions. By William Shakespeare* (London, n.d. [1740?]).

SHEFFIELD, JOHN, *The Works of His Grace John Sheffield Duke of Buckingham* (2 vols.; London, 1723).

SHERIDAN, RICHARD BRINSLEY, *Verses to the Memory of Garrick* (London, 1779).

SHERIDAN, THOMAS, *Coriolanus: or the Roman Matron. A Tragedy. Taken from Shakespeare and Thomson* (London, 1755).

SIDNEY, HENRY, *Diary of the Times of Charles the Second by the*

Honourable Henry Sidney (2 vols.; London, 1843).

SMITH, HILDA L., *Reason's Disciples: Seventeenth-Century English Feminists* (Urbana, Ill., 1982).

SMITH, JOHN HARRINGTON, *The Gay Couple in Restoration Comedy* (Cambridge, Mass., 1948).

SMYTH, GEORGE LEWIS, *Biographical Illustrations of Westminster Abbey* (London, 1843).

SNODIN, MICHAEL (ed.), *Rococo: Art and Design in Hogarth's England.* Exhibition catalogue (London, 1984).

The Solemn Mock Procession of the Pope Cardinalls Jesuits Fryars &c: through the Citty of London November the 17th, 1680 (London, 1680).

SORELIUS, GUNNAR, *'The Giant Race Before the Flood:' Pre-Restoration Drama on the Stage and in the Criticism of the Restoration* (Uppsala, 1966).

—— 'The Rights of the Restoration Theatre Companies in the Older Drama', *Studia Neophilologica*, 37 (1965), 174–89.

SPEAIGHT, GEORGE, *The History of the English Puppet Theatre* (London, 1955).

The Spectator (1711–14), ed. Donald F. Bond (5 vols.; Oxford, 1965).

SPENCER, CHRISTOPHER (ed.), *Davenant's Macbeth from the Yale Manuscript* (New Haven, Conn., 1961).

—— (ed.), *Five Restoration Adaptations of Shakespeare* (Urbana, Ill., 1965).

—— 'A word for Tate's *King Lear*', *Studies in English Literature 1500–1900*, 3 (1963), 241–51.

SPENCER, HAZELTON, *Shakespeare Improved: The Restoration Versions in Quarto and on the Stage* (Cambridge, Mass., 1927).

SPRAGUE, ARTHUR COLBY, *Beaumont and Fletcher on the Restoration Stage* (Cambridge, Mass., 1926).

STALLYBRASS, PETER, and WHITE, ALLON, *The Politics and Poetics of Transgression* (Ithaca, NY, 1986).

STAVES, SUSAN, *Players' Scepters: Fictions of Authority in the Restoration* (Lincoln, Nebr., 1979).

STERNE, LAURENCE, *A Sentimental Journey Through France and Italy* [1768], ed. Graham Petrie (Harmondsworth, 1967).

—— *The Life and Opinions of Tristram Shandy* [1759–67], ed. Graham Petrie (Harmondsworth, 1967).

STEVENSON, JOHN ALLEN, *The British Novel, Defoe to Austen* (New York, 1991).

STOCHHOLM, JOHANNE M., *Garrick's Folly* (London, 1964).

STONE, GEORGE WINCHESTER, JR., 'Garrick's Handling of Shakespeare's Plays and his Influence upon the Changed Attitude of Shakespearian Criticism during the Eighteenth Century', Ph.D. thesis (Harvard, 1938).

—— 'Garrick's Long Lost Alteration of *Hamlet*', *PMLA* 49 (1934), 890–921.

—— 'Shakespeare's *Tempest* at Drury Lane during Garrick's Management', *Shakespeare Quarterly*, 7 (1936), 1–7.

—— and Kahrl, George M., *David Garrick: A Critical Biography* (Carbondale, Ill., 1979).

TAIT, HUGH, 'Garrick, Shakespeare and Wilkes', *British Museum Journal* 24 (1961), 100–7.

TATE, NAHUM, *The History of King Lear* (London, 1681).

—— *The History of King Lear*, ed. James Black (Lincoln, Nebr., 1975).

—— *The History of King Richard the Second* (London, 1681).

—— *The Ingratitude of a Common-Wealth: Or, the Fall of Caius Martius Coriolanus* (London, 1682).

—— *The Loyal General* (London, 1679).

The Tatler (London, 1709–11).

TAYLOR, ALINE MACKENZIE, *Next to Shakespeare: Otway's Venice Preserv'd and The Orphan, and their History on the London Stage* (Durham, NC, 1950).

TAYLOR, GARY, *Reinventing Shakespeare: A Cultural History from the Restoration to the Present* (New York, 1989).

TAYLOR, ISAAC, *Garrick with Shakespearean Characters, Commemorating the Jubilee at Stratford-upon-Avon, 1769* (engraving; London, 1769).

THEOBALD, LEWIS, *Double Falshood; Or, the Distrest Lovers* (London, 1728).

—— *The Mausoleum* (London, 1714).

—— *Shakespeare Restored* (London, 1726).

—— *The Tragedy of King Richard II* (London, 1720).

—— (ed.), *The Works of Shakespeare, Collated with the Oldest Copies, and Corrected, with Notes, Explanatory and Critical* (7 vols.; London, 1733).

Thesaurus Dramaticus (London, 1724).

TODD, JANET (ed.), *A Dictionary of British and American Women Writers* (London, 1985).

The Tory Poets, A Satyr (London, 1682).

Town and Country Magazine (London, 1769–).

The Tragick-Comedy of Titus Oates (London, 1685).

Universal Magazine (London, 1747–1814).

Universal Spectator (London, 1728–46).

VANBRUGH, SIR JOHN, *A Short Vindication of The Relapse and The Provoked Wife from Immorality and Profaneness* (London, 1698).

VICKERS, BRIAN, *Returning to Shakespeare* (London, 1989).

—— (ed.), *Shakespeare: The Critical Heritage, 1623–1800* (6 vols.; London, 1974–81).

The Visitation; or, an Interview between the Ghost of Shakespear and

D—v—d G—rr—k, Esq. (London, 1755).

WAITH, EUGENE M., *The Pattern of Tragicomedy in Beaumont and Fletcher*, Yale Studies in English, 120 (New Haven, Conn., 1952).

WALLACE, JOHN M., 'Otway's *Caius Marius* and the Exclusion Crisis', *Modern Philology*, 85 (May 1988), 363–72.

Weekly Register (London, 1731–).

WEIMANN, ROBERT, 'Shakespeare (De)Canonized: Conflicting Uses of "Authority" and "Representation"', *New Literary History*, 20 (1988), 65–81.

WELLS, STANLEY, 'A Shakespearean Droll?', *Theatre Notebook*, 15 (1961), 116–7.

WHALLEY, PETER, *An Enquiry into the Learning of Shakespeare* (London, 1748).

WHEELER, DAVID, 'Eighteenth-Century Adaptations of Shakespeare and the Example of John Dennis', *Shakespeare Quarterly*, 36 (1985), 438–49.

WHINNEY, MARGARET, *Sculpture in Britain, 1530 to 1830* [1964], revised by John Physick (London, 1988).

WIKANDER, MATTHEW H., '"The Duke My Father's Wrack": The Innocence of the Restoration *Tempest*', *Shakespeare Survey*, 43 (1991), 91–8.

—— 'The Spitted Infant: Scenic Emblem and Exclusionist Politics in Restoration Adaptations of Shakespeare', *Shakespeare Quarterly*, 37 (1986), 340–58.

WILLEMS, MICHELE, *La Genèse du mythe shakespearien* (Paris, 1979).

WILSON, JOHN HAROLD, *All the King's Ladies: Actresses of the Restoration* (Chicago, 1958).

—— 'Granville's "Stock-Jobbing Jew"', *Philological Quarterly*, 13 (1934), 1–15.

—— *The Influence of Beaumont and Fletcher on Restoration Drama* (Columbus, Oh., 1928).

WILSON, KATHLEEN, 'Empire of Virtue: The Imperial Project and Hanoverian Culture, *c.*1720–1785', in Lawrence Stone (ed.), *The British State and Empire in War and Peace* (London, forthcoming).

—— 'Empire, Trade and Popular Politics in Mid-Hanoverian Britain: The Case of Admiral Vernon', *Past and Present*, 121 (Nov. 1988), 73–109.

WILSON, MICHAEL I., *William Kent: Architect, Designer, Painter, Gardener, 1685–1748* (London, 1984).

WINN, JAMES, *John Dryden and his World* (New Haven, Conn., 1987).

WINSTANLEY, WILLIAM, *The Lives of the most Famous English Poets, or the Honour of Parnassus* (London, 1687).

Wit for Money, or, Poet Stutter (London, 1691).

Woods, Leigh, *Garrick Claims the Stage: Acting as Social Emblem in Eighteenth-Century England* (Westport, Conn., 1984).

[Woodward, Henry], *Songs, Chorusses, &c. which are introduced in the New Entertainment of Harlequin's Jubilee* (London, 1770).

Worsdale, James, *A Cure for a Scold. A Ballad Farce of Two Acts* (London [1735]).

Index